PICCADILLY
BOOK XI OF
THE PERFORMERS

Piccadilly is the eleventh novel in Claire Rayner's
sequence *The Performers*, in which she will follow
the fortunes of two families through succeeding
generations from the beginning of the nineteenth
century into the twentieth. The very different
professions of medicine and the theatre set the
background for this compelling family saga.
These are the paths chosen by Abel Lackland
and Lilith Lucas, the two London waifs who first
met in *Gower Street*, whose fortunes become
inextricably mingled – and whose children
continue the saga through the later volumes.
Readers who meet Abel and Lilith for the first
time will want to share their earlier experiences
in the other books.

Also in Arrow by Claire Rayner

THE RUNNING YEARS
FAMILY CHORUS

THE PERFORMERS

GOWER STREET
THE HAYMARKET
PADDINGTON GREEN
SOHO SQUARE
BEDFORD ROW
LONG ACRE
CHARING CROSS
THE STRAND
CHELSEA REACH
SHAFTESBURY AVENUE

Piccadilly

Book XI of

The Performers

Claire Rayner

ARROW BOOKS

Arrow Books Limited
62–65 Chandos Place, London WC2N 4NW

An imprint of Century Hutchinson Limited

London Melbourne Sydney Auckland
Johannesburg and agencies throughout
the world

First published in Great Britain by
George Weidenfeld & Nicolson Limited 1984
Arrow edition 1987

Printed and bound in Great Britain by
Anchor Brendon Limited, Tiptree, Essex

ISBN 0 09 941270 5

For Carole
A great member of the team – with affection

ACKNOWLEDGEMENTS

The author is grateful for the assistance given with research by the Library of the Royal Society of Medicine, London; Macarthy's Ltd, Surgical Instrument Manufacturers; the London Library; the London Museum; the Victoria and Albert Museum; Leichner Stage Make-up Ltd; Mr Joe Mitchenson, theatrical historian; Miss Geraldine Stephenson, choreographer and dance historian; Miss Rachael Low, film historian; the General Post Office Archives; the Public Records Office; the Archivist, British Rail; Mr Edmund Swinglehurst, archivist, Thomas Cook Ltd; the Curator, National Railway Museum, York; Historical Records Department, British Transport; Meteorological Records Office; Archives Department of *The Times*; Mr David Mancur, IPC Archives; Borough of Westminster Libraries; the Lodgekeeper, Albany, Piccadilly; the Archivist, Guildhall School of Music and Drama; Beth Hatefutsoth (Museum of the Diaspora), Tel Aviv; and other sources too numerous to mention.

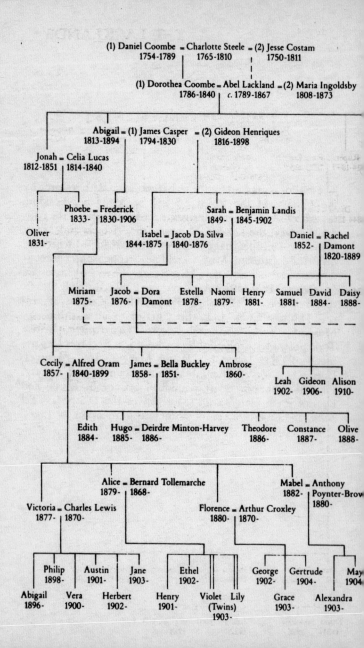

THE LACKLANDS

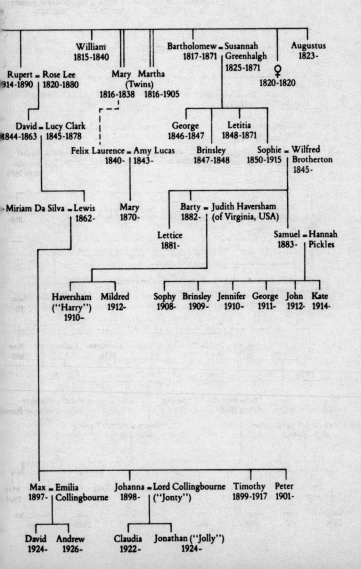

THE LUCASES

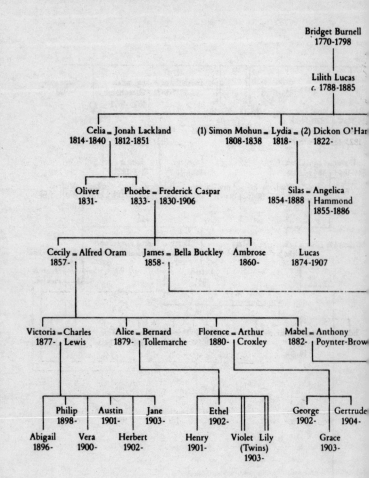

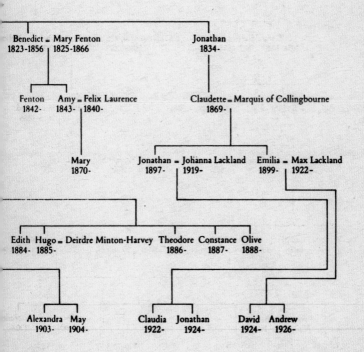

'My poor dear sainted mother,' announced Cecily in the ringing tones of the somewhat deaf, 'must be turning in her grave,' and she squinted up at the sun glinting through the leaves of the Japanese cherry tree under which she was sitting and then sighed gustily. 'So meagre a wedding reception! I doubt if there has been anything quite like this in the family since – well, I don't know when!'

'Hardly meagre, Gran'ma,' murmured Gertrude Croxley and patted her shoulder. 'Jacob has invited all of us, after all, even the children –' And she looked round the garden at the many excited children running and tumbling between the adults' feet and sighed too, but more with boredom than anything else. A modern young woman was Gertrude Croxley, who found her relatives boring in the extreme; to be so firmly in the bosom of her family irked her considerably. To be present at an event simply as one of Grandmamma's fifteen grandchildren and thirty-two great-grandchildren was hardly to feel oneself an important individual.

'And why should he not invite us all?' Cecily snapped. 'We *are* family, aren't we? Darling Mamma never failed to invite absolutely everybody to everything –' And she sniffed and wiped her eyes rather ostentatiously as Gertrude hastily patted her shoulder again. The last thing anyone would thank her for today was setting Gran'ma off on one of her tantrums; indeed she was getting more and more like awful old Great-grandmamma Phoebe with her displays of character, except that where old Phoebe had been imperious Cecily was merely peevish, and where Phoebe's rages had been awesome Cecily's were just tiresome.

'I'm sure he's very happy to have everyone here, Gran'ma,'

she said soothingly. 'Though of course you're right – it is rather an unusual wedding reception, but –'

'But then it's an unusual wedding, isn't it?' The voice behind them was high and a little drawling and Gertrude scowled even before she turned to see who was there; she cordially loathed her Tollemache cousins who gave themselves such airs that you'd think they were duchesses at the very least, and knew their voices only too well. 'I mean, who would *ever* have thought Cousin Jacob would let one of his precious crew marry someone who was not of the tribe? Who would have believed it of him?'

'But darling, needs must when the devil drives – and let's face it, Leah's hardly a blushing girl any more, is she? Thirty-two, I make her – that's old enough to make any father glad to take whatever comes along –' And Lily, Ethel's sister, gave a sly little sideways grin at Gertrude and smoothed her frock over her very noticeably pregnant shape as Gertrude flushed angrily, feeling the jibe at her own single state at the age of thirty.

'Hardly old,' she murmured. 'And at least she's found herself an attractive husband. So good-looking – such lovely curly hair.' And it was her turn to give Lily a malicious glance, for her husband was singularly plain, being rather short, almost totally bald and needing to wear the thickest of pebble glasses. 'And of course, a professional man –' And now it was Ethel's turn to flush, for her husband earned his living (albeit a rich one) dealing in scrap metal, hardly the most salubrious of trades. And again Gertrude patted her grandmother's shoulder and went drifting away across the garden, leaving them to say what they liked about her, and knowing perfectly well that they would seize on the opportunity. All of her cousins would, she told herself furiously. Spiteful cats, each and everyone of them, and she scowled again at the people standing around her on the lawn, glasses of champagne in their hands, and wished herself anywhere at all except the garden of the Landis house in Golders Green this hot June afternoon.

Gertrude Croxley wasn't the only unwilling guest reluctantly aware of the gossip going on all around her. Standing under the shade of a rose arbour as far away as she could get

2

from them all, Letty Lackland heard all the chatter and hated it as she leaned against the rough pole that supported the flowers and watched the hubbub around her. She made no attempt to dress her face in the sort of polite smiles considered de rigueur by everyone else, any more than she had made any attempt to dress correctly for the afternoon. She was wearing a severely cut suit in fine blue linen and a flat beret which clung casually to the side of her head while all the other women were in the long flowing pastel-coloured chiffon teagowns and wide-brimmed floppy straw hats much bedecked with flowers that all the fashion magazines had announced were the Proper Wear for Summer Weddings this year of grace 1934. But it was they and not she who suffered from the contrast, for her suit had been made by Schiaparelli, and her hair had been cut and marcelled by Anton at the Ritz so that she looked coolly elegant while they looked hot and fussy.

But she didn't feel cool. Deep inside her, resentment was simmering, and the harder she tried to push it down the hotter it got. Not that she blamed Harry; not that she blamed Leah either, come to that. How could it be anyone's fault that the pair of them had fallen so helplessly in love? If anyone deserved an accusatory finger pointed at them it was herself, for hadn't she been the stupid one who had arranged for them to meet? And now, looking down the garden to where the guests were beginning to cluster expectantly round the French windows that led from the drawing-room on to the small terrace, she pursed her lips and whistled the tune softly: 'I don't know why I did it, but it seemed like a good idea at the time –' and then grimaced at her own foolishness.

But it was true for all that; it *had* seemed like a good idea a year ago to give a party at which she could introduce her nephew, newly arrived from America, to all his more distant relations. She had filled her elegant chambers in Albany with them, holding open house for a full day so that he could be comfortable with them all, and what had happened? As soon as Jacob and Dora Landis had arrived with Leah in tow that had been that. From then on the two had been almost inseparable – 'and after all,' Letty had pointed out to him severely, 'that's not why your father sent you here. To finish

3

your medical education at your family's own hospital was the plan, not to make love to your cousin –'

'Hardly a cousin, Aunt Letty!' Harry had said and grinned at her with that broad disarming grin that was so very much a part of him. 'It's a relationship so remote it hardly counts – and I'm working very hard at Nellie's, you know! Leah inspires me, that's the thing. Dr Hemmingway says I'm the best registrar he's had since he joined the staff, and it's all because of Leah. Isn't she the most lovely creature you ever saw, Aunt Letty? Do be happy for us – we are for ourselves, but it'd be great if everyone else was too.'

'Yes, of course. She's lovely,' Letty had said and smiled at him, not able to resist his delight in himself and his state of mind. 'And of course I'm happy for you – though there is the age gap, you know, my dear old chap and –'

'Oh, to blazes with that!' Harry had said cheerfully and kissed her cheek before shrugging on his overcoat ready to leave Albany and start his brisk morning walk over to Covent Garden and Queen Eleanor's Hospital in Endell Street. 'It's only eight years, dammit – and if she doesn't mind, and I don't mind, who else can possibly object?'

'Her father,' Letty had murmured, but to empty air, for he had gone whistling down the stairs and away, leaving her to start her own busy day. 'Her father –'

And heavens, how her father had tried to stop the match! she thought now, watching the French windows as activity around them seemed to increase. He'd huffed and puffed and made all the difficulties he could, worrying over the age gap almost as much as he seemed to worry over the differences in religion.

'It's asking for trouble, Letty, you must see that!' he had said to her the first time he had come over to Albany to try to enlist her aid in stopping the match. 'It's always been a problem of course, being so closely related to – ah – gentiles. It's an unusual situation for a family like ours – like Dora and me and the children – but it's not our fault Grandmamma Abigail wasn't – well, anyway, what can we do? We try to keep a good Jewish home, we've reared the children to be observant; and now look at what happens. She goes and falls in love with a

4

boy who's half her age and –'

'Only eight years younger, Jacob, for pity's sake – no need to exaggerate –' Letty had said but he'd ignored that completely, just running on and on.

'– and what his own family must think, I can't imagine. What will your brother say about it? And the boy's mother? I understand that the Havershams are fine Virginia stock – they won't be any happier to have one of their family marrying out of their religion than we are –'

'My dear Jacob, I haven't the least idea what any of them will say. And I don't care much, because really, it's none of our business! These two are set on each other, and they're both of age and of independent means, so you might as well save your breath to cool your porridge for all you say will make any difference! I'm no happier about it than you are, though for different reasons, but I've more sense than to try to meddle. Do go home, my dear man, and settle for what you have – a good loving young man for your daughter. He *is* good, you know – he's an excellent doctor, I'm told, and suitably ambitious, and from what I know of his character he'll take good care of her. And you have your other two children to share religious affairs with you, after all. I hear that your son Gideon is to become a father soon? How delightful that must be for you all –'

And Jacob had gone home, but had come back time and again, unwilling to accept her advice at first; but then he had been forced to as Leah and Harry went serenely on their way adoring each other, and when his son Gideon had become the proud father of a fine son and there had been much excitement in the family (who celebrated the child's circumcision with all the ritual they could) he had at last come to terms with the situation. His beloved Leah was to marry a gentile younger than herself in a Register Office (since no reasonable decision could be made about whether the ceremony should take place in a church or a synagogue) and he would have to weep his tears of disappointment as best he could. And so would her mother, Dora, though for her, it seemed, it was less of a blow. Privately she had been more concerned about Leah's single state than about anything else; to have her oldest child settled

5

in marriage at last would more than compensate for the lack of a Jewish son-in-law.

Across the garden there was a sudden flurry of excitement and then they were there, standing in the doorway, the bride and groom, ready at last after their session with the photographer to talk to their guests. Letty watched them, amused, as the women fluttered round Leah – who was looking very suitable in ivory chiffon and the most floppy of wide-brimmed hats rather than the sort of veil and orange-blossom affair that would have looked excessive in a Register Office – and the men slapped Harry on the back and laughed and teased him.

Dear Harry, Letty thought as she moved away from the arbour and began to walk up the broad sloping lawn to the house. He's only lived with me a year and I'm going to miss him dreadfully, the wretched boy! I should have put him in a place of his own right from the start instead of bringing him to live at Albany with me, but it seemed the best thing at the time – and again the silly jigging tune came into her head. 'It seemed like a good idea at the time –'

But it *had* seemed a good idea, and so indeed it had turned out, if she were to be honest. His good-tempered company had been more than agreeable and she had found life a lot more pleasant since he had arrived from Richmond in Virginia, hard on the heels of his father's letter announcing his arrival. She had never really got on well with her brother Barty; indeed, they had parted on very bad terms when he'd gone off to live in America, and she hadn't seen him for years. She'd never met his wife, the rich Miss Judith Haversham of Arlington (and trust Barty to marry money, she'd thought sourly when she'd heard the news) but she must be a likeable lady, if her son was any measure; he must have taken more from her than his Christian name, she had decided within a week of the boy's arrival, for there was none of Barty's rigidity or meanness about him.

And I mustn't be mean either, she told herself firmly as at last she reached the outskirts of the cluster of people around the bridal pair. He's been good for me, helped me a great deal, and I must see him on his way as happily as I can, however lonely I'll be when he's gone – and she moved through the pathway the men had made for her as soon as they were aware of her presence and stood before him with her hands loosely clasped in front of her and smiled up at him.

'Well, Doctor Haversham Lackland? How does it feel to be a married man?'

'Fantastic, Aunt Letty, truly fantastic! As soon as I saw her I knew this'd have to happen, but a bit of me was afraid it never would. And now here we are, Dr and Mrs Lackland Junior! Isn't that something? Isn't it just something?' And he leaned down and hugged her till her ribs ached and she could hardly breathe.

'Fantastic is the word!' she managed when at last he let go. 'I wish you every joy, my dear boy. Have you heard from your parents?'

'Cable, this morning. They send their love and want to know when we can go visit them –' He laughed. 'I'd better not answer that, hmm? I mean, just look at her now!'

Letty turned her head to follow his gaze, which was decidedly starry-eyed, and saw Leah crouching down in the middle of a flower-bed, paying no attention at all to the way her frock trailed on the earth, to salvage one of the smaller Tollemache children who was lying there kicking its heels in the air and bawling furiously. Behind her stood two more small children and alongside her another was clutching her skirt and crying shrilly over and over again, 'Auntie Lee, play with me, Auntie Lee, play with me, Auntie Lee –'

'You see?' Harry said fondly, never taking his eyes from his new wife. 'She's besotted with them! All she talks about is babies, babies, babies, how many we'll have and what we'll call 'em and how we'll rear 'em! If I didn't know better I'd say she only married me for my fathering abilities! I'll never get her to Virginia until we've a quiverful –'

'She's certainly good with children,' Letty said as the bawling child, now held in Leah's arms as she crooned to it, at last stopped crying and the other children at her skirts laughed and chattered as she led them away to the marquee at the end of the garden where cakes and lemonade were being dispensed. 'But I'm sure she wants to be your wife as much as she wants to be a mother –'

'Of course she does!' Harry said and grinned down at her again. 'You've no need to worry, you know, Aunt Letty. We're going to be very happy indeed.'

'I'm sure you are,' she said and lifted her chin and kissed him and he reddened at that, for she was not one to offer many physical tokens of her feelings. A self-contained person, his Aunt Letty, Harry had always thought, and had privately wondered a good deal about her history. That so handsome and clever and successful a woman should be alone was amazing to him; had there never been any man in her life? But he had never asked her and never would, knowing it would be an impertinence, dearly though he had learned to love her. And even now, on his own wedding day, when a certain amount of leeway might be permitted him, he made no effort to breach the barrier that lay between them.

'Go and rescue her, all the same,' she said, and gave him a gentle push towards the marquee. 'Those children will exhaust her, and you've a long journey ahead of you. Or are you staying in London tonight?'

He grinned again. 'The Savoy. I don't know about Lee being exhausted – I am! Bless you, Aunt Letty, for everything. Without you I'd never have found her –' And he went loping across the lawn, leaving her to watch him make his way through the crowd and feeling more desolate than she would have thought possible.

She, who had lived alone for so long, to be miserable because her nephew was to set out on married life? Absurd! Even after dear old Uncle Oliver had died – and it didn't seem possible that had been fourteen years ago – she hadn't felt so bad. She'd grieved for him, of course, but he'd been so old and so tired and had died so peacefully and indeed happily that she could not feel more than a delicate sadness at his loss. But this loss bit more keenly, and she shook her head at herself in irritation.

And refused to think about the fact that one of the reasons she had taken to the boy so warmly was his appearance. He had a distinct look of the long-dead Luke O'Hare about him, with his broad shoulders and his thick hair, and he'd reminded

8

her all too sharply of the loneliness of her life. To have lost
Luke as she had, and then Theo – and as that thought came into
her head she had to grin. Of course she hadn't lost Theo! She'd
never had him, that was the truth of it; it had been just a stupid
crush, that was all, but at least it had ended in good friendship.
And soon he'd be in England again for a visit and that would
be something to look forward to –

She left without saying goodbye, not waiting till the bride
and groom had changed and left for their honeymoon as
wedding guests were supposed to do. She'd write a thank-you
note to Jacob and Dora tomorrow, she promised herself as she
swung the starting handle of her small car and it coughed into
life. Tomorrow, when I've had a chance to sort myself out a
little, I'll write. And think about that new scriptwriter for the
Gerry Gerard vehicle, and start making a few quiet enquiries
about the film rights of that book Priestley's doing so well
with. It should make a good picture. And maybe I'll answer
that letter from Katy tomorrow.

And she drove away through the dust of West Heath
Avenue towards the main Golders Green Road and the long
drive back to Piccadilly, whistling between her teeth as she
went. 'I don't know why I did it, but it seemed like a good idea
at the time –'

Lewis Lackland saw her go, and almost went after her, to talk to her; but then he dropped the curtain of the dining-room window at which he was standing and let her go. How could she help, after all? She may be one of the most successful women in London, running her own film business and the Shaftesbury Theatre and all the rest of it, but she's never had children. How can she know what it feels like to be so anxious about your offspring that every day is shadowed by it? And for a moment he felt a twinge of anger; at my age, still to be fretting over them – it's ridiculous! I ought to be just a serene grandfather content to see them all grown and settled, but as it is –

He turned and looked round the room, quiet and cool, and in spite of his mood smiled a little. He had always liked his cousin Jacob and his rather dumpy little wife Dora, but he had to admit that they were really rather dull people and their home showed it. To live in Golders Green at all was dull, when most of the family lived in the smart middle of London, and a vision of his own elegant white stucco house in Leinster Terrace close by Hyde Park rose in his mind's eye to super-impose itself on this stodgily decorated dining-room. But there, Jacob had never cared about fashion; only about his family's welfare and his religion, and he had told Lewis so when he had bought the house twenty years ago.

'This suits us very well, very well indeed,' he'd said complacently. 'It's just a short walk from Hampstead Heath where the children can play and fill their lungs with God's good air, and the synagogue's near enough to walk to easily – and there are other nice Jewish children living around here for them to play with – and just look at how handsome a house it is!'

And he had shown off the warm red brick and the solid tiled roof and the big bay window at the front of the drawing-room which complemented the French windows at the back of it, and the wide oak-panelled hallway and the tile-floored kitchen and the central-heating system and had puffed up with pride.

Everything in Jacob's world had seemed to be so perfect then, Lewis remembered now as he left the dining-room to make his way back to the garden and Miriam. He had had his cosy house and his cosy family and the certainty of his faith – and what have I got? Three children and only one of them gives me any peace of mind; he thought of Max and again his lips curved, but this time with pleasure. Good old Max. The best son a man could have –

And then, as he came out on to the terrace and saw Jacob standing there, staring down at the garden at his daughter who was clinging to her new husband's arm and gazing up at him with adoration, and he saw the bleak expression on his face, he felt a stab of shame at his own uncharitable thoughts. Poor old Jacob; where were his cosy certainties now? Despite his earnest attempts to keep his children safe within his fold, his choice of a respectable neighbourhood for his home so that his children should meet – and ultimately marry – their co-religionists, there he stood, breaking his heart; who am I to complain about my lot? And he went over to his cousin and slipped an arm into his and the two men stood there silently, each understanding the other well enough without benefit of words.

'Care for a drink, old man?' Jacob said after a while. 'No, not that stuff they're dishing out in the marquee – that damned champagne's more like lemonade than a decent man's drink – I've got some good brandy in my study.'

'Good of you, Jacob, but I was looking for Johanna. Thought she might be in the house, but I can't find her there. She must have come out into the garden again –' And Lewis lifted his chin to stare around the crowded garden, seeking for his daughter's slender shape and dark head.

'Daughters!' Jacob said with sudden venom in his voice. 'Always lead you a dance. Come and have a drink, man, do you more good than frettin' over your girl. She'll do well enough. She'll have to, won't she? Like my Leah –' And he too stared down the garden again.

'Of course she will!' Lewis said heartily. 'Of course she'll do very well. He's a splendid young chap, you know, really splendid.' Not like Jonty Collingbourne, damn him to hell and back, not like him. 'Harry'll take wonderful care of your Leah, I'm sure he will.'

'Are you?' Jacob said and threw a sideways glance at him. 'I dare say you thought the same of that lordship of yours when *your* girl married, hmm?' And he jerked his head towards the rose arbour at the end of the garden, and Lewis followed his direction and saw him; Lord Collingbourne standing very close to a pretty girl in a long white frock that clung to her young figure very revealingly, his head bent as he murmured something in her ear which made her giggle, and even from this distance, show a reddening of her face. 'Oh, I know, Lewis! Everyone does, I'm afraid. They talk about his affairs all over London – it's even in the papers, those gossip columns the servants read – it's no secret, old man. Come and have that drink, for heaven's sake. We both need it. Daughters!' And he tucked his hand into Lewis's elbow and half led, half pulled him towards the French windows. And Lewis, after another glance at Jonty at the end of the garden, let himself be taken away. There was little else he could do.

Johanna could see Jonty too, but was trying not to look. She sat in the shade of the Japanese cherry tree with her nephew Andrew lying on the grass at her feet trying to guide a beetle into a matchbox held clutched in one small dirty hand, and told herself it wasn't important; it really wasn't important. He was just being polite to people at a wedding, that was all. Talking to people you hardly know is what happens at weddings – but does it always have to be the pretty girls he chooses to talk to, and does he always have to stand so close and say things to make them blush? a voice deep inside her mind shrilled at her. Does it always have to be like this, making me feel as though I'll choke with crying?

'Got him!' Andrew cried and pushed home the lid on his

matchbox. 'I've got him! Now I can put him in David's bed tonight and that'll be one for me. He put a worm in mine but beetles is worse because they can run about and that'll tickle him – you won't tell him, Auntie Jo, will you? It's a secret. It's my turn, you see. He did it to me first –'

'I won't tell him, darling,' Johanna said and reached out and ruffled his hair. He was a stocky square child, short for an eight-year-old, but very sturdy and his face was as square as his father's; not handsome – no one would ever expect the children of Max and Emilia to be handsome, for darlings though they both were, neither was particularly good-looking, especially Emilia – but good-natured and intelligent and just nice, and she let her eyes slide away again to the rose arbour where her husband had been standing talking to the pretty girl in the white frock. Jonty's good-looking, God knows, desperately, agonizingly good-looking, but nice? And then as she realized that there was no one standing there by the arbour any more, the tears rose in her already reddened eyes and threatened to spill over.

Andrew, with all the prescience of the young, gave her a vague smile and went away, hopping over the yellowing grass of the lawn towards his mother, who was sitting on the terrace gently fanning herself and staring at nothing in particular. It was good to have time just to sit, Emilia was thinking lazily. Just to sit and not think or do anything much but feel the sun on the back of her neck and watch the children run about so happily; what could be more agreeable? They'd have to leave soon, because Max had a patient coming at seven o'clock, even though today was a Saturday, and she had promised him she'd finish typing his new book by the end of the month and she was barely half-way through, what with one thing and another, so she'd be working late tonight. Not that she objected; far, far from it. Being busy about Max's practice and Max's books and academic papers and Max's home and Max's children was all that Emilia ever wanted out of life; she was a deeply happy, deeply settled person. But all the same it was agreeable to sit here in the sun, fanning herself and filling her nostrils with the mixed scents of roses and crushed grass and cream cakes and champagne and cigars –

'Auntie Jo's crying again,' Andrew said cheerfully as he came up to her. 'Mummy, I've got a beetle in here, but you mustn't tell anyone especially not David, because he's mine and he's a secret. His name's Greta Garbo and he's very beautiful –'

'Crying? Oh dear,' Emilia said and lifted her chin to look round for her sister-in-law. 'Where is she?'

'Under that tree – no, not the one where the Orams are – the other one – see? I expect she's stopped now. She cries a lot, doesn't she, Auntie Jo? Why do grown-ups cry, Mummy? You don't –'

'No, I don't,' Emilia said, and grinned at him. 'At least, not often. Go and find Gran'ma for me, darling, will you? She's probably in the marquee –' And Andrew went thumping off across the grass obediently as Emilia sat and looked at the barely visible shape of Johanna sitting under the Japanese cherry tree, and feeling the familiar irritation rising in her.

Why does she have to be so *feeble*? she thought crossly. The last thing that'll ever bring Jonty to his senses is being feeble. He'll just get more and more selfish and more and more difficult as she gets more and more miserable. If she'd only stand up to him – and she shook her head and got to her feet. No point, really, in upsetting her mother-in-law, Miriam, by asking her to go and comfort her weeping daughter. I'll have to talk to Johanna myself, she thought, and went stomping away over the grass towards her. I could kill my damned brother, she told herself furiously as she went. I really could kill him sometimes –

'Can't say I like the way things are going,' Henry said again. 'Can't say I like it at all. You agree, m'boy, I'm sure.'

'Mmm?' Peter said, and tipped his hat further over his eyes. He'd thought himself so clever finding this quiet spot behind the shrubs where there was a rustic bench on which to stretch his long legs, but clearly he hadn't been as clever as he'd thought. Not if Leah's most boring uncle could find him so easily.

'Agree with me about this Mosley fella and that business last Friday. Hmm?'

'Not sure what you mean, sir.' Peter gave up trying and sat up and at once the rotund Henry Landis plumped himself at his side on the bench, clearly ready to settle down to a long boring prose.

'Why, this fascist chappie, Oswald Mosley, had a mass meeting last week at Olympia. Place was crawling with blackshirts – you must have heard about it, surely –'

'I think I did hear something, sir,' Peter said. 'But I've only just got back. I was in France till yesterday – had to sort out the matter of an actor's contract, you see. New play about to start in rehearsals – it does rather overshadow things for me. Don't think I've read a paper for a fortnight.' He smiled lazily at Henry's gently perspiring red face. 'Shocking, I know, but there it is. Theatre people tend to be a bit narrow, I'm afraid –'

'Hmm, yes, suppose so,' Henry said reprovingly. 'Not that Miss Lackland's like that. Know her, do you? She's got something to do with the theatre. Remarkable gel, remarkable. Was talking to her a while ago – very intelligent woman, got a good grasp of politics. For a woman.'

This time Peter laughed aloud. 'Know Letty? I should say I do! She's my boss as often as not –'

'Your boss?' Henry's brows seemed to snap together audibly.

'My employer, sir. She runs Gaff Productions, you see, and that means plays as well as films. I often direct for her. This new play I'm setting up is for her Shaftesbury Theatre –'

'Yes, well, that's as may be,' Henry said and settled himself more firmly in his seat. 'But as I was saying, this chap Mosley – it's a bad business. Spreadin' a lot of bad ideas, very bad ideas. Anti-semitism, you know, and all that –' And he peered sharply at Peter and nodded his head vigorously. 'Anti-semitic, that's what he is, *and* his disgustin' blackshirts. It's a bad business – it'll lead to trouble, what with Hitler takin' the bit between his teeth in Germany the way he is. It'll lead to trouble for all of us –' And Peter, opening his mouth to say something platitudinous, looked at the old man and saw a glimpse of cold terror in his eyes and closed it again.

He'd never been very interested in politics at all; the theatre was what mattered to him, first, last and in between, and –

until the past few months at any rate – had filled his mind and absorbed his energies totally. But even so, he couldn't fail to be aware of the rumblings that were coming out of Germany; no one could, and now he said gently, 'Yes, sir, I agree. It's a bad business indeed. But I don't think we need really worry about fascism here, you know. We're not a nation that takes to demagogues, by and large.' He reached out and touched the other's sleeve. 'We're too lazy, really. And too stubborn –'

'I wish I could be so certain,' Henry said, and shook his head. 'And anyway, there's not just England to consider, you know. We have family in Germany, in Munich. M'sister-in-law's first cousin and his wife – Otto and Lise, lovely people, know 'em well – they have an art gallery there. Very successful, I'm told. Modern stuff, you know, all these cubists, not to my taste, but very successful. What'll happen to them, I ask myself, the way things are going? It's a bad business, you see, m'boy. A bad business –'

'Indeed it is, sir,' Peter said and got to his feet. There seemed little he could say that would be useful, and he thought wryly of Letty and imagined her listening and nodding politely and listening again, so that the old man was struck by her political wisdom, and wished he could be like her. But that wasn't his style so he lifted his brows at Henry now and said heartily, 'But today's a celebration, sir, hmm? Mustn't spoil it with worrying over what we can't change – come and have a drink, toast the happy pair –'

'Hmmph,' Henry said and stood up too. 'That's the trouble. Everyone says it can't be changed, and so they do nothing. If people'd only wake up now to what's going on there'd be time to change it, wouldn't there? As it is, one day we'll discover it *is* too late and wish we'd done somethin' sooner –' But he followed Peter out of the quiet corner behind the shrubbery and back to the crowded lawn, albeit muttering as he went, and took the glass of champagne Peter fetched for him from the marquee.

It took him ten minutes to escape from Henry's continued grumble of anxiety, but at last he was able to push him on to his cousin Sam Henriques, a cheerful man in his fifties who was as thin as Henry was round and eager to talk business, for the two families shared an interest in the chain of Henriques' chemists' shops, and at last Henry could be distracted and Peter could escape.

Which he did as fast as he could, easing his way into the thickest part of the crowd of wedding guests, lazily sipping his champagne as he went. And came face to face with his mother.

'Peter, my love, I've been looking everywhere for you!' Miriam said and smiled delightedly at him so that her soft chin disappeared into the layers of rosy flesh round her neck. Miriam at fifty-nine was decidedly plump; the roundness of her youth that had so captivated Lewis Lackland almost forty years ago had settled into a firm stoutness that was clearly to remain with her for all her life, and at the sight of her Peter smiled with real pleasure and tucked his hand into her elbow.

'Do you know, Ma, you get more and more like that portrait of Great-grandmamma Abigail every time I see you! The one that used to hang in the hall at Leinster Terrace –'

'And still does, as you'd know perfectly well if you'd come home more often, wretched boy!' Miriam said fondly, and stood on her toes to kiss this tallest of her children. 'I never seem to see you these days!'

'I've been abroad, Ma, as you well know – I told you I was going to be away and –'

Her brow creased. 'You did? I don't remember you saying anything like that –'

'You get worse and worse, you dear old ditherer!' Peter said. 'You just don't listen to what you don't want to hear. And you never want to hear of my travels! If you had your way, I swear I'd still be in short trousers in the old schoolroom sorting out my fishing tackle!'

'If I had my way,' Miriam said promptly, 'You'd be happily settled with a nice wife and a couple of babies like the others. Have you seen anyone here you like? Lots of pretty girls around and –'

'Not such a ditherer after all!' Peter said lightly, and again bent and kissed her soft round cheek. 'You really have a remarkably stubborn streak – I've told you more times than I've eaten hot dinners that I'm not in a marrying mood. I've too much to do to worry about that yet –'

'Yet!' Miriam almost snorted it. 'You can't pull that one over my eyes, Peter Lackland! I was there when you were born, remember, and you're thirty-three. It's high time you were settled. Your father thinks so too – worries all the time about you being on your own. Now, let me introduce you to the dearest girl who–'

'Absolutely not. Not if she's the cat's pyjamas as well as the bee's knees will I talk to anyone you choose for me. You'll just have to be patient, Ma, both of you, and settle for the grandchildren you've got. Look, there's young Jolly over there, being awful as usual – go and fuss over him and leave me in peace. I'm not playing matrimonial games and–'

'I was so hopeful for a while!' Miriam said, paying no attention at all to Jolly, who had come over to them in response to Peter's waving arm. 'The last time I saw you – when was it, back in April? You were in such a strange mood that I told myself – there, at last! Darling Peter's in love! I know the signs as well as I know anything, and–'

'And you know wrong!' He tried not to let the note of sharpness into his voice, for he loved her very dearly and wouldn't have hurt her feelings for the world, but for all that he was irritated and it was difficult to hide the fact. 'Quite wrong – and here's Jolly! Are you enjoying yourself, my dear old chap? Having a good wedding, are you?'

'I'm bored!' Jolly announced so loudly that his grandmother shushed him in embarrassment. 'Well, it *is* boring, people standing round and talking and putting on a show at people–'

'Who's putting on a show at people?' Peter asked, interested, and Jolly scowled so that his really rather pretty face tightened into a grimace.

'Well, Claudia for a start – she's carrying on everywhere as though she was the bride and not Cousin Leah at all! She's only twelve and she's lah-di-dahing at me all the time, and she's only two years more than me – but you'd think she was ever so old the way she's going on – thirty at least!'

'You see, Peter? Thirty is *ever* so old!' Miriam said and laughed. 'No, I promise, not another word, my dear. Jolly, let's go and find Miss Claudia and we shall see what we can do about all this putting on of shows–' And with one more look over her shoulder at Peter she went, leaving him thoughtfully staring after her.

Wily old bird, he thought. Wily old bird – not nearly as dithery as she makes out – and he took a sharp little breath in through his nostrils and turned to go. He'd done all a man could reasonably be expected to do. He'd turned out like a good'un, stood up with his family, and now enough was enough. Back to London, to his cluttered little flat over the delicatessen in Beak Street, that was the order of the day now –

'Peter! You weren't leaving without saying goodbye to us, were you?' The voice made the back of his neck tighten and then get hot and he stood for a moment composing his facial expression before he turned round to answer and when he did he looked his usual relaxed genial self. I should be an actor, not a director, he thought, deep in his mind. I'm getting bloody good at this –

'Well, well! The bride herself and none other. My dear, has anyone bothered to tell you today that you really do look rather nice?'

She made a face at him and it took all the control he had to keep his own in its easy relaxed expression, for the moue she had produced had put a wrinkle across her nose and had half closed her eyes with humour in such a way that he could hardly keep his hands off her.

'Well, one or two have mentioned it,' she said with a mock demure flutter of her lashes. 'But it gets so boring hearing it all the time from the same people. It's so much nicer when other people pay compliments – Harry, darling, here's Peter making shameless advances at me! Paying me the most outrageous of compliments!'

'Is he then?' Harry had come up behind Leah and was standing now behind her with both arms round her so that she stood with her head thrown back against his chest. They looked so right together, so totally happy with each other, that Peter could have wept with the pain of it. 'And what did he say that was so outrageous?'

'He said I looked rather nice.'

'My dear! Such extravagance! Is there no end to this man's lavishness of speech? I'll have to watch out for my honour, I can see that, if Peter is going to continue along these lines! Even the most virtuous of wives must be seduced by a tongue as silvery and mellifluous as – aw, shucks, Peter, I can't keep this up! She does look rather nice, doesn't she?' And he hugged her more closely and bent his head to kiss the side of her neck. 'Ain't I the lucky one though? Wish us well and promise to be the first to dine with us once we're back from Baden-Baden.'

'If I'm in London, of course I will –' Peter said. 'Baden-Baden? That doesn't sound very romantic for a honeymoon.'

'There you see, Harry?' Leah crowed. 'I told him that, Peter, but would you believe it? He said he wanted us to go there because there's a great specialist in these endo-thingummy diseases that will be there at the same time, and he wants to talk to him. I ask you! Whoever heard of combining a honeymoon with work?'

'I want the best of both worlds,' Harry said and winked at Peter. 'Wouldn't you? This way I have the bliss of a honeymoon *and* a chance to meet Professor Ascheim – you know who I mean? He works with Zondek and – well, no reason why you should. But I tell you the man's forgotten more about endocrinology than most other people in the field have ever learned. I couldn't miss the opportunity, could I?' He pulled Leah round to look into her face. 'Darling, you don't really mind, do you?'

'No, you donkey, of course I don't,' she said and again made that enchanting little face and this time Harry bent his head and kissed her in good earnest.

'I know an exit scene when I see one,' Peter said as easily as he could. 'Goodbye my dears, and bless you both. Have a good honeymoon!' And he went hurrying across the terrace to the house and through it to the front door as fast as he could, praying no one would notice how much his hands were shaking.

What bloody lousy luck I have, he told himself savagely as he went down the hill at a half run on his way to Golders Green station and home. What bloody lousy luck. I wait till I'm well past thirty to fall in love for the first time, and then go and fall for a girl who's head over ears for someone else. How's that for rotten timing?

3

'So, tell me,' Letty said as she manoeuvred the car expertly out of Euston's forecourt into the early evening traffic, 'was your father very worried about your coming?'

'Oh, Aunt Letty, he was *ridiculous*, he really was!' Katy said, and gave a little crow of laughter. 'You'd have thought it was Sodom if not Gomorrah I was moving to! He said –'

'My dear child, moving to? I don't want to seem inhospitable on your very first day here, but I asked you to spend the rest of the summer with me – I hadn't meant to suggest you moved in for good and all!'

'Oh, Aunt Letty, of course not! I never thought of any such thing. I mean, I never planned to move in with *you* for always. But I've left Haworth for good, that's for certain. I'll find a place of my own here in London in the autumn and then I'll go there. And you are the dearest most darling aunt in all the world to help me this way. There was I trying to think of a way to persuade Daddy to let me leave home, and then your letter came! Honestly, it was like a dream coming true, just like in the pictures.'

Letty looked at her sideways as she brought the car to a stop at the traffic lights and couldn't help but smile at the vivid little face that looked back at her. A small dark-haired girl with narrow absurdly long-lashed green eyes and a pointed chin beneath cheeks as round as a chipmunk's, Katy was clearly so full of energy and excitement that she could hardly contain herself. She was wearing a smartly belted suit in blue and white checks surmounted with a very cheeky little hat which she wore perched on the side of her head and her face was as well made up as any London girl's. Letty grinned more widely as Katy caught her gaze and said, 'Do you dream a lot? Like on the pictures?'

'Oh, yes, all the time! What else is there to do in Haworth? Daddy said I could work in the office at the mill, but honestly – as if I'd want to do that! I'd be bored out of my mind – not that I haven't been, stuck at home with just Georgie and John and Daddy in the evenings and only the servants all day! It'd be different if Mummy hadn't – well, there it is. But ever since she died it's been so dismal, and I've thought of nothing else but coming to London and working and –'

'Working? What sort of working? Can you type or do anything useful like that?' Letty let the clutch in as the lights changed and the car began to move along Regent Street again.

'Oh, heavens, no! I wouldn't want to *type*,' Katy said with enormous scorn. 'I'd have to be mad to do that. I could have stayed in Yorkshire to do *that*. No, I want to work in the theatre –' And she drawled the last word with great aplomb so that she sounded like the most fashionable of West Enders; and Letty laughed. 'Talk like that, my dear, and everyone in the business worth tuppence-ha'penny'll jeer you to perdition and back. Just say "theatre" – no need to dress it up fancy. So, you want to work in theatre, do you? In what capacity?'

'Capacity?' Katy stared at her. 'How do you mean?'

'What do you want to do? Front of house, lighting, directing, scene design,' Letty said. 'Budget control, advertising and press relations. Or perhaps the originating side, writing, music –'

'I mean acting,' Katy said after a moment, in a small and rather less confident voice, and Letty nodded a little grimly.

'I thought as much,' she said. 'And I also thought that it's obvious you haven't the remotest idea of what the theatre's all about. It's hard work, my dear, not just the glamour of leaping about on a stage in pretty frocks.' Again she looked sideways at her niece. 'And you like pretty frocks a good deal, don't you?'

'Well, yes, I do. And I'm quite good at it, too. Fashion, I mean –'

'Then perhaps that should be the area in which you should look for work. Costume design. Of course you'd have to start at the very bottom. Working in the wardrobe – and that's very hard work indeed. There's sewing and washing and ironing and–'

'Washing and *ironing*?' Katy said, her voice full of consternation.

'Indeed, yes,' Letty said serenely, as at last the car turned into Piccadilly. 'And cleaning shoes and scrubbing down the heavier fabrics – very hard work, especially if it's a period piece you're dressing. But it's necessary work, if you're ever to be a good costume designer. If you're interested, I can see about finding you a job. We can always use likely youngsters – glad to train them. And you're about the right age – twenty, aren't you? Yes – by the time you're twenty-five you could be on the way to a useful career. If that's what you really want, of course. A useful career rather than just the chance to leap about a stage in pretty frocks–'

'Of course I want a useful career!' Katy said with some of her self-confidence coming back. 'I dare say you think I'm just another soppy stage-struck kid wanting to be a star and all that, but it's not like that. It's what I've wanted ever since I was little, and I know it's something I could do. I mean, it's what you always wanted, wasn't it? You wanted to be an actress so much that you ran away from medical school and Grandmamma had to run after you and she didn't find you and–'

Letty had stopped the car now at the kerb, near the entrance to the court that led to Albany, and was leaning back in her seat staring in some surprise at the young face beside her and then she laughed. 'Hey, hey! Who's been filling your head with all this ancient history, young lady?'

'Daddy told me. He told me *all* about it, and how you were going to be married to this wonderful actor and how he died and – oh, I'm sorry, Aunt Letty. I shouldn't have said–'

'It's all right,' Letty said after a moment. 'It was a long time ago. Yes, it was true, I did want to be an actess. And I did try, for a while–'

'Were you good?'

'Good? Oh, I don't know. It was all so long ago. Yes, I suppose I was. Why tell lies about it? I *was* good. I just made rather a mess of it all – well, not in the long run I suppose. Here I am, after all–' And she tilted her chin towards Shaftesbury

Avenue on the other side of Piccadilly Circus. 'My theatre's down there. The Shaftesbury. I don't own it, of course, but I'm the lessee – it's mine for all practical purposes. And there are the films too, of course – and –'

'Oh, I know,' Katy said and caught her breath suddenly. 'Oh, the films are *lovely*, Aunt Letty, and whenever I see one and there's your name up there, Letty Lackland, producer, I want to jump up and down and shout to all the people in the cinema, "And I'm Katy Lackland, and I'm going to be just the same, and have my name up there –"' She stopped, shy for a moment. 'I thought you'd understand about me wanting to be in the theatre better than anyone –'

'I do,' Letty said, and laughed suddenly. 'Of course I do. But I'd be worse than useless to you if I let you think the job was all tinsel and tra-la-la. It isn't. It's sweat and aching muscles and not enough sleep and feet that never stop hurting and feeling sick with terror and –'

'Oh, *yes*,' Katy breathed. 'Wonderful!'

And again Letty laughed and at last opened the car door and got out. 'Come on, young lady, let's get you settled. We'll talk about this later. Over dinner –'

Katy got out and stood on the pavement beside her, staring round, her brow a little creased. 'Where are we going, Aunt Letty?'

'Home,' Letty said briefly as she began to lift Katy's suitcases from the boot of the car. 'Albany.'

Katy was still staring round. 'Albany? Where? There's only shops and restaurants here. Do you live over a shop?' And again she stared at her aunt who laughed even more loudly.

'My dear, you're showing your country origins! Albany is one of the best-known sets of chambers – flats – in London. Down that little alley, there – you see? I'm very lucky to be here at all. They worry a good deal about propriety and so on –like to take a close look at all the tenants before they'll allow 'em in – so you'll have to mind your manners. No racketting around the Rope Walk late at night or –'

'Rope Walk?' Katy had picked up one of her suitcases and was following Letty across the pavement, and then she stopped and turned and said, 'Oh, Aunt Letty, this is

24

wonderful! I never imagined I'd ever be able to come here to London and be with you! And to be here in the middle of it all – isn't it lovely?'

Letty followed her gaze and saw it, just for a moment, as though she'd never seen it all before a thousand or more times; the traffic snarling its way round the Circus, the silhouette against the darkening sky of Eros, tip-tilted on his plinth; the lights flashing and grinning and then flashing again in vivid lollipop colours, reds and blues and greens and glowing golds, and the people strolling by, top-hatted men and their befurred and diamonded companions walking into the Criterion and towards the Long Bar at the Trocadero at the foot of Shaftesbury Avenue; typists and clerks out off on their sprees hurrying into the Coventry Street Corner House where Messrs Lyons offered the most exciting of cream cakes and poached eggs on toast to be eaten to the accompaniment of gipsy bands and the chatter of scurrying waitresses; costers selling hot chestnuts on the street corners and the women with their big baskets selling violets at the foot of Eros's steps – it was all a part of her life and something she took for granted. But seeing it now, reflected for just a moment in Katy's glittering excited eyes, she found a fresh delight in it. And was deeply glad that she had given into her impulse of loneliness after Harry's wedding and written asking her brother to let this youngest niece of hers come to London to spend a few months with her.

She had wished several times, since writing that letter, that she hadn't been so absurd, that she had just settled back into her solitary life in Albany, and even this afternoon, going to meet Katy's train at Euston, had been annoyed with herself for cluttering her life with a youngster. But now she was glad again. This child might be a little absurd in her ideas but she was alive and she was interesting and would add some spice to life. And that was something Letty badly needed.

She unlocked the entrance door to Albany and stood back to let Katy go in front of her and then stood and watched her as she hurried forwards, looking round eagerly.

'But this is so –' she began and then whirled and gazed at Letty with her eyes wide. 'I'd never have thought there could be anything so *quiet* in the middle of Piccadilly! It's lovely, the buildings, and the gardens and – how old is it? It looks very old –'

'Old enough. Late seventeen-hundreds or thereabouts. Regency, you know –' Letty stopped suddenly and stared down the covered Rope Walk towards the Vigo Street end, shadowy in the evening light. 'It's funny – I've never thought of it before but I think it must have been built at about the time your great-great-grandfather – I suppose that's what he'd be –about the time he was a guttersnipe not all that far from here –'

'Who?' Katy tilted her head. 'A guttersnipe?'

'Oh, it's an amusing story – I've always been rather taken with digging out family history, and I used to live with old Uncle Oliver – he's been dead a long time now – and he told me all sorts of tales. There was an Abel Lackland once. A boy from the gutter who was adopted and sent to school and was an apothecary and then became a surgeon. He was the founder of Queen Eleanor's Hospital –'

'I know about *that*,' Katy said. 'Daddy told me. That's where Grandmother Sophie was a medical student – and where you weren't –'

'That's right. Where I wasn't –' And Letty bent to pick up the suitcase again. 'Come along, my dear. We must settle you and get you unpacked and then I think a little dinner. Rules – how would that please you?'

'Is it very fashionable?'

Letty laughed yet again; this child was clearly going to be the source of a good deal of laughter, one way or another. 'Indeed, yes, very fashionable. Sometimes the Prince of Wales goes there. Is that fashionable enough? And of course actors are fond of it. It's very convenient for several of the theatres, so they go there a good deal.'

'Then Rules would be lovely,' Katy said blissfully. 'Really lovely. But not because of the Prince of Wales. Because of the actors.'

Rules was its usual busy sparkling self when the head waiter showed them to her regular table, downstairs, near the back, so that she had a clear view of the whole place, and Katy was clearly in her element as she settled at the table and gazed around. She had changed into a very pretty frock in cream georgette with puffed sleeves and a stand-up collar, and above it her eyes glittered and her dark hair curled ebulliently and Letty thought – she really is a very pretty child. She could look good on a stage, at that – and then pushed the thought away. No need to feed the child's fantasy until she was certain she had some talent. But it would be worth finding out if she had. Maybe she was worth more than a corner of the wardrobe.

'Tell me about this place, Aunt Letty. Is it old, like Albany? Why is it so fashionable? Just because the theatres are so near? Is that why the Prince of Wales comes? Is he here tonight? Where is he if he is? Or does he come later, and can we stay till he does?'

'Yes, it's old, though I don't know how old. Been here a long time, that's all I know. It's fashionable because the food's good and the waiters put themselves out for their regular customers and because no one can ever say what makes a place fashionable. It just happens. And I don't know if the Prince is here, or if he'll come tonight, and we'll stay till we've had dinner and then we'll go because I have work to do tomorrow if you don't. Any more questions?'

'Not just at present,' Katy said, unabashed. 'But I expect there will be. What shall we eat? I'm *starving*–'

'Read the menu. The possibilities are endless. The *pâté de foie gras* is as good as you'll get anywhere – and think about the salmon. They do it well here, and it's the best time of the year for it–'

Obediently Katy settled to study the menu and she was still sitting with her head down over it when Letty saw him across the bustling restaurant and on an impulse waved to him. It wasn't that she didn't want to be alone with her niece, but she was beginning to feel that the child could be quite exhausting in her own way, and having someone to share her chatter could be agreeable.

He came to her table at once, smiling his usual lazy smile and she thought, not for the first time, what a pleasant man he was. Easy-going yet thorough at his job, no trouble to get along

27

with yet by no means at the beck of others' whims, he was precisely the sort of man she most enjoyed working with, and she greeted him with a wide smile which almost startled him. He had always been on excellent terms with her, but she had never been quite as cordial as this.

'Peter, my dear, how delightful to see you! Do join us. Unless you've already dined?'

'Not yet. I came to have a quick chop. I've been working late over the script and it really is much improved. You'll be pleased, I think, when you come to the run through next week – oh! I didn't know that you had–'

'My niece, Katy Lackland,' Letty said. 'My dear, this is another Lackland. One of your remote cousins, Peter. Sit down, Peter, do. You make the place look untidy. Now, a chop you say? And first a little pâté? Excellent!' And she set about ordering their meal as Katy sat and contemplated Peter who returned her gaze with equanimity.

'Are you an actor?' she asked. 'You look like one.'

He smiled. 'I'm not sure what actors are supposed to look like! Do tell me. Are you saying I'm bowling you over with my masculine beauty?'

'No, of course not! I mean, I don't think you're not beautiful – well, good-looking anyway. I mean that you sort of look – well, as though you were to do with the theatre.'

'She's got you in one, Peter,' Letty said as the waiter went away to fetch food and bottles of wine. 'I have to warn you – she's stage-struck to the eyebrows, and determined to leap about the stage in pretty frocks–'

Katy reddened. 'No I'm not! I mean, yes I am, but not just that. I want to be a real actress. Not just a sort of clothes-horse. Although–' She stopped and then laughed. 'I'd quite enjoy that sometimes.'

Peter gave a little bark of laughter. 'A handsome admission. Attagirl, Miss New Cousin! There are a number of actresses I have to work with who would die rather than admit that the only reason they're on the stage at all is their delight in their own adornment – boring creatures that they are! If you're willing to admit you'd enjoy it sometimes, then you're not as boring as they are. And that's a lot to be grateful for.'

'But can they act as well?' Katy said.

'The clothes-horses? Not the ones I'm thinking about.'

'Then that's why they're boring,' Katy said and nodded with great seriousness. 'They're only any good for having their photographs taken. Oh, that sounds very stupid, doesn't it? But you know what I mean. I'm not going to be like that. I'm going to be a real actress. I've done some, you know. Not a lot, but some. Only amateur at Haworth, but you have to start somewhere, don't you?'

'Indeed you do,' Letty said. 'It's how I started.'

'What? As an amateur?' Peter cocked an eyebrow at her.

'Yes, I did. Surprised, Peter? Well, you needn't be. It's my guess I belonged to the same amateur companies Katy did – I grew up in Haworth too, you know!'

'And I'm going to be as successful as Aunt Letty!' Katy said, and smiled at her aunt. 'I am, you know. You can't stop me.'

'Who said I wanted to?'

'You said I'd have to take a job in the wardrobe first. Well, I will if I have to. If it's the only way in. I'll act eventually though – you see if I don't.'

'The wardrobe?' Peter said and again gave that little bark of laughter. 'Oh, Letty, my dear, you can't see this enchanting infant sitting in the bowels of the Shaftesbury wrapped in black bombazine like old Mrs Burley, can you? You couldn't be so cruel! If she's that determined on the business send her over to John Carpenter Street. Let her learn her trade – if she can pass the audition to get in, that is. If she's any good they'll know. And if she isn't they'll chuck her out and then you can bury her in the wardrobe.'

'What's at John Carpenter Street?' Katy demanded, looking from one to the other.

'Guildhall School of Music and Drama,' Letty said absently, staring at Peter. 'I suppose you could try, at that –'

'A drama school? A real – oh, Aunt Letty, could I? Could I really? That'd be – oh, that'd be marvellous! I can't think of anything that'd be more – you wouldn't tell Daddy though, would you? Not till after I'd learned how to be an actress and had a part in something, that is. I mean, he'll have to know sooner or later but if he knows too soon he might make me go back to Haworth and I don't think I could bear that. Not now I've arrived in London –'

And Letty looked at her and that wide hopeful gaze and the smooth youngness of that pointed little face and tried to see the girl she had been herself, thirty years ago when she had first come to London to be a medical student – and aching to be an actress.

'No,' she said slowly. 'No, I won't tell Sam – there's nothing really to tell, is there? Just a few classes –'

'Oh, Aunt Letty, you are the most – I adore you!' Katy cried and leaned over and hugged Letty so wildly that she nearly sent the waiter, who had at last arrived behind her, tumbling over, and they all laughed as he set the plates in front of them with exaggerated care.

'Well, don't go counting any chickens, young lady,' Letty warned. 'There's a long way to go yet. You have to audition, you know, and unless you've some talent you haven't a hope of getting into Guildhall. But we'll make enquiries tomorrow – now eat your dinner, and calm down. All this excitement is enough to ruin my digestion.'

'I'm too excited to eat a *mouthful*,' Katy said radiantly and set to work on her pâté with so eager an appetite that she had finished hers long before her companions had and yet still managed to talk so much that they were exhausted before they reached the end of their second course. Katy Lackland had indeed arrived in London.

4

Lewis had been operating since half-past eight in the morning and now it was well past two, and his shoulders were beginning to ache more and more clamorously. Usually he was able to ignore the twinges and tiredness that were an inevitable part of his day's work, so absorbed in the delicate actions of his fingers that he did not notice what was happening to his bigger muscles, but today he couldn't. The nagging discomfort made him irritable and the theatre sister lifted her eyebrows in disapproval as he snapped at one of the young nurses who had been rather clumsy as she crossed the tiled floor and kicked against a trolley with a small clatter.

He bit his upper lip under his mask as he caught her reproving gaze and said gruffly, 'Sorry, Sister, didn't mean that. Bit tired, I think – I'll close this with interrupted sutures, please, and then you can deal with the skin, John. Make sure it's tidy, now. I promised this girl a scar that wouldn't look too bad and I like my promises kept, but the way I'm feeling at present you'll do a better job than I will.'

And his assistant flushed with pleasure so that his round face went bright pink above his mask as he muttered, 'Yes, sir. Absolutely, sir – I mean, of course you'd do it perfectly well, sir, but I'll be glad to – and yes, I'll make sure it's a perfect cosmetic result –'

'Can't be perfect,' Lewis grunted as his fingers flashed between the glitter of the chrome instruments; he had always taken a considerable pride in the speed with which he tied the knots in his sutures, and now it was second nature to him to move fast, even when he didn't need to. 'The best you can do will be quite satisfactory. Here you are then. Tie the deep tension sutures firmly, please, and then use the silk. And make sure the tails are long. Helps the nurses when they come to take 'em out –' And he stepped back from the table so that John Bartlett could take his place beside the patient and stood there watching for a while before moving heavily across the theatre to the swing doors that led to the lobby and on to the surgeon's room. A cup of coffee, a chance to sit down, time to think, that was what he needed.

Across the lobby the other theatre was working too and he stopped for a moment or two to peer through the little round window in the door to see what was going on. Sir Jacob's list, he thought, as he saw the vast white shrouded shape bent over the operating table, flanked by two much slighter shorter figures. The old Bulldog – looks as though he's doing an amputation there – that'll upset the nurses – it always does; and he yawned suddenly and pulled down his mask. God, he was tired; and as he stood there still watching and saw the muscles strain across the broad shoulders of the Senior Orthopaedic Surgeon to Queen Eleanor's Hospital he felt a sympathetic twinge across his own shoulders and frowned sharply.

Of course surgery was physical hard work; he'd always known that, but he'd kept himself in good trim, made sure he was supple and active. Today's cases shouldn't have wearied him so much; he had only had to pull against the abdominal muscles of a young woman and there was Sir Jacob dealing with the really big thigh and buttock muscles of what looked like a fully grown man and not even sweating – for he could see the wide brow over the line of the mask that Sir Jacob wore defiantly under his nose rather than over it – whereas here he was himself, as fatigued as if he'd been operating all day –

The Bulldog's only sixty or so, an inner voice whispered to him as he turned heavily and completed the journey to the surgeons' room where the sagging armchairs and hissing gas fire waited to comfort him. And you're seventy-two – but he ignored the little voice and pulled off his gown and gloves and dropped them in the skips waiting outside the door before pouring the much-wanted coffee from the small corner gas ring and at last collapsing into his armchair.

Seventy-two, the voice said again as he sipped the muddy brew and gazed sightlessly out of the grimy window at the cluster of sooty roof-tops and chimney-pots outside. They were slicked with the sheen of moisture from the dripping fog that was swirling everywhere, and a few dispirited pigeons were huddled in the lee of a chimney-stack, looking as miserable as he felt, and he looked at them mournfully and then shook his head in irritation at his own mawkishness and set down his cup and reached for the patient's notes. The operation had to be written up before he could go on his ward round, and young Harry would be panting for information; better to get it down now, while it was all still fresh in his memory.

But it was impossible to concentrate; he sat there with the blank page in front of him trying to find the words to start his notes, and all he could think of was Johanna. He tried to see the patient's belly as it had looked when he had set his knife to the tense yellow-painted skin and had moved it in one long wide sweep so that the pinkly glowing wake of the incision opened behind it, as smoothly as though his knife was indeed cutting water, and all he could see was Johanna's bleak little face as she stared at him last night across the dinner-table.

And it had started so well, too, he thought, still looking down at the open folder on his knee and at his hand loosely holding the pen. It had promised to be one of the happiest evenings they had spent together for a very long time indeed; there had been Jonty looking quite cheerful rather than his usual sulky self, and Claudia and Jolly had been, for once, on the most cordial of terms instead of sniping at each other the way they so often did, and even Peter had been there, as well as, of course, Emilia and Max and David and Andrew as scrubbed as he had ever seen them. His lips curved with pleasure as he remembered the way these two young villains had bobbed their heads in unison as they gave him their birthday present – a most laborious and almost unrecognizable painting of Nellie's main entrance, done by both of them. It would look very good indeed hanging in his office at the hospital, he had told them solemnly and shaken them both by the hand in appreciation.

Yes, it had started splendidly, his birthday dinner, with Miriam sitting flushed and happy at the foot of her family's table, clearly enchanted to have them all round her for once, and he had looked at them all and then at her and congratulated himself warmly at having so handsome and well-set-up a crew to call his own. There they had sat at the polished mahogany table, the girls with their marcelled heads gleaming richly in the candlelight that Miriam always preferred for dinner-parties, and the men and boys so proper in their black ties; and then it had all shattered as though it had been made of glass and a mischievous child had hurled a stone at it.

And he had to admit it was his dear Johanna's own fault; Jonty had been so relaxed and casual, seemingly as happy to be with his parents-in-law as they were to have him, and had been expansive and in a mood to show off a little; he'd started to talk about the Prince of Wales, of whose set he was so active a member, and had said something witty about the Prince's special friend Lady Furness, an American lady, and also about the Prince's even more special friend, Mrs Wallis Simpson, and Johanna had lifted her chin sharply, and said across the table to him, '*Mrs* Simpson? She's married, then?'

'My dear old Jo,' Jonty said and laughed. 'You have no memory at all, have you? They came to dinner in Vere Street, she and Ernest, last May! You ought to remember who was there. Heaven knows we give few enough parties, hmm?' And he'd given her a sharp little glance and Lewis had wanted to do the same, for he knew what a bone of contention this was between them; Jonty's wish to be a much more sociable person, entertaining in his own handsome house in Vere Street, and her loathing of the very idea. Johanna's notion of bliss was to spend long months in domestic serenity at the Collingbourne country house at Simister in Wiltshire; for her, the racketting around that Jonty so enjoyed was hell on earth, and though she came to live in London because Jonty insisted on doing so, she couldn't, it seemed, bring herself to be the hostess he wanted her to be. Small wonder, Lewis thought, willing Johanna to look at him so that he could give her the warning look she so much needed, small wonder he gets so irritable with her.

But she didn't look at her father. She couldn't take her eyes off her husband and now said in a tight little voice that was clearly heard, because there was one of those sudden lulls in the conversation that, Lewis told himself despairingly, always happen when people are saying things that shouldn't be said, 'Oh – yes, I remember. He seemed a nice quiet man. Is he a friend of the Prince too?'

Jonty grinned and then winked at Peter, who was sitting beside Johanna. 'Hardly a friend, darling. He really is the ultimate in complaisant husbands, that chappie. Amazin' sometimes, how he manages not to notice what it's best he doesn't see. He's an object lesson on how to do it. Ought to set up a school in the art, make a mint, I'd say. Sort of thing an American'd enjoy, that, hmm? Good way to make money, though he's already warm enough, from all accounts. What do you say, Peter? Good idea, isn't it?'

'I think it's disgusting,' Johanna said loudly, too loudly and again the hush fell as conversation that had restarted faltered once more. 'Married people oughtn't to behave like that. It's –'

And they were off. Sitting there in the surgeons' room at Nellie's the day after his birthday dinner Lewis closed his eyes in anguish as he heard it all again, the barely controlled anger in Jonty's voice as he tried to smooth things over, and then the awful stillness from Johanna as at last she managed to stop herself from talking, but only at the cost of sitting there for the remainder of the dinner with her hands clenched on her blue silk lap, saying nothing at all while everyone else chattered brightly of nothing of any importance whatsoever over the wreck of the Lackland family's celebration. Oh, it had been dreadful, quite dreadful, and Lewis felt the fatigue of his distress over it all seep even more deeply into his tired shoulders.

There was a soft cough and he opened his eyes sharply to stare at the doorway, almost forgetting where he was for a moment, and then his face cleared as he saw who was standing there.

'Oh, hello, Harry. Looking for news of your patient, are you? I'm just about to write up her notes. Come on in – there's coffee on the gas ring there in the corner. Make yourself at home –'

'Not at all what I expected, sir,' Harry said as he came in, and looked round. 'I'd always thought you surgeons have everything very *comme il faut* – this looks as delightfully shabby as any medical man could wish.'

Lewis laughed and leaned back in his chair. He was grateful for Harry's arrival to interrupt his thoughts and that made him more than usually cordial. 'Of course it is! Sister keeps doing her best, tries to order new armchairs all dripping with chrome, and nasty cubist pictures for the walls, but we rise up against her and hurl such abominations where they should go – into the private consulting-rooms the visiting chaps use! These old chairs have been here for ever. Wouldn't be surprised to discover the old founder himself had shaped the cushions with his very own buttocks – we surgeons know how to be comfortable, never you fear. Better than the physician's room, I'll be bound–'

'Much, sir,' Harry said, and sat down, hitching his well-pressed trousers carefully to protect the creases. He looked very dapper indeed and Lewis grinned sardonically at him, comfortable in the open-necked shirt and crumpled linen trousers that he always wore when he operated.

'You look every inch the Harley Street man, I must say, young Harry. Must impress your lady patients a good deal, being attended by a chap as well turned out as you!'

Harry went a little pink, but laughed all the same. 'They expect it of me, sir. Bad enough the poor dears have to discuss the sort of things with me they do – they couldn't manage at all if I looked less than proper, you know!'

'It never seemed to worry my patients,' Lewis said. 'Always looked like a scruff, even in the early days when no one had heard of me. It's all right now, of course. Got my name, and so I can do what I like – did I ever tell you of the three stages of a surgeon's career, Harry?'

'Sir?' Harry said politely, knowing full well what was coming, but not having the courage to say he had heard this famous quip of the old man's several times. He badly wanted to hear about the operation that Lewis had done but it was clear that he wouldn't be hurried.

'The first stage,' Lewis said sententiously, 'is to get on.' He paused and then said even more solemnly. 'The second stage is to get honour.' And even longer pause. 'And the third stage is to get honest—'

'Very good indeed, sir,' Harry said heartily, and in truth, the first time he'd heard it he had laughed a good deal and found it wise as well as witty. Now he could only grin as best he could. 'Ah – about Mrs Porteous—'

'Mrs – oh. This patient of yours. Yes, well, my boy, you were right. A sizeable ovarian cyst. Thing was, it had enlarged backwards, deep into the pelvis. Not much to be felt at all on abdominal palpation, and of course big woman, deep pelvis, not much belly enlargement. But it was big enough – quite big enough to account for her pain—'

Harry leaned forwards eagerly. 'But was it big enough to account for her irregularity of menses? And her failure to conceive? That's the thing, sir. That was why she first came to the department, you see, and because I have a particular interest now in the problem, I took her over. I was so hopeful that we'd found a cause, once I thought I'd identified the possibility of an ovarian cyst—'

'It was a nice piece of diagnosis,' Lewis said looking at him closely. 'For a physician. What do you mean about having a special interest now?'

Harry went a sudden brick-red and let his eyes slide away from Lewis. He made no attempt to answer and after a long pause the older man lifted his brows and said again, 'Well, m'boy? I asked you a question.'

Harry opened his mouth to speak and then closed it and shook his head, still red in the face and clearly troubled and Lewis leaned forwards now and peered at him. 'You must forgive an old man, Harry – and one who is family as well, after all. I don't mean to pry but – how long have you been married now?'

'Uh – getting on for ten months, sir,' Harry mumbled and Lewis said gently, 'Ah! And any sign of a pregnancy yet? Hmm? I had the impression that your good lady had a particular fondness for children—'

'Yes, sir,' Harry said wretchedly and then turned back to Lewis and looked at him very directly. 'Well, you've got it in one, of course. Not much chance of concealing anything from you, is there? They call you old Hawkeye around the hospital, you know, sir. Say you're a tiger for economy—'

'Yes, I know,' Lewis said and smiled briefly. 'I've always been an inquisitive man – it's the best part of being a surgeon, for heaven's sake, getting the chance to indulge one's propensity for sticking one's nose into others' affairs – and as for economy – dammit, man, this hospital's too important to be allowed to waste its resources! Of course I keep an eye on the way they use the equipment and the drugs and so forth. It's part of my job as chief of staff. And stop trying to change the subject. I asked you a question and you've only half answered it. So, let me put it to you directly. Is your interest in this matter of failure to conceive a personal one?'

'Yes,' Harry said and made a face. 'Oh, my God, yes.'

'Causing a lot of worry, is it?' Lewis said shrewdly as he looked more closely at the younger man. There was a tension about the face that he hadn't really noticed before; new fine lines around the wide mobile mouth and a shadow between the brows.

'Are you kidding!' Harry said fervently and then as Lewis looked startled added, 'Yes, a good deal. Lee – well, you'd hardly believe how upset she gets. I told her, it's not as easy as that. I mean, I explained as best I could without upsetting her about the shortness of a woman's fertility cycle – she had the idea, bless her, that one night of marriage and hey presto, she'd be well on her way to motherhood. As it is – it's been bad enough right from the first month when she had her period as usual, but now we've been married the full nine months – well, it's much worse—'

Lewis nodded. 'She'd planned to have a baby by now, that it?'

'That's it. And I've told her, over and over, I've told her, it takes some girls three or more years to start their first baby – but she gets extra agitated because of her age, you see. There's a bit of a gap between us.' He went pink again. 'She's eight years older than I am.'

'And you thought this patient – Mrs Porteous – had similar symptoms?'

Harry nodded. 'Very much so, sir. Heavy erratic periods,

pain, headaches, malaise – though to tell the truth –' He looked even more wretched for a moment. 'It sounds so unkind, sir, and I don't mean to be, for I love her very dearly – but I did think it might be functional with Lee, you know. She gets so very agitated I thought that could account for all the symptoms. Couldn't it? And for the delay in conception? But if I could find a physical cause – well, it would help, I think. She'd accept it better. Feel less of a failure, you see. As it is –' He shook his head. 'As it is, I worry about her a lot. She's just not – well, she's not the girl she was. I try so hard to be sympathetic but there are times I could –' He took a sharp little breath in through his nose. 'I get angry with her and that makes it worse –' And his voice trailed away.

Lewis gazed at him, again seeing Johanna's tight bleak little face in the front of his eyes, and knew exactly what Harry meant. The mixture of compassion and anger, the queasy confusion of love and irritation with which his daughter could so easily fill him, was clearly this young man's lot as well, and impulsively he leaned forwards and touched the other's arm.

'Look, m'boy, you need another opinion on this, don't you? Shall I see her for you?'

'Oh, *no!*' Harry said at once and turned his body sharply so that he was sitting four-square in front of him. 'That would be a disaster, sir, it truly would! She'd never forgive me if she thought I'd mentioned this to anyone else! I told you – she's eaten with shame as it is, the crazy – oh, I can't explain sir, how difficult it all is. Please, I do beg you, *please*, never to say a word to her about –'

'Hush, hush!' Lewis said and shook his head at him. 'No need to panic! Of course I won't! But if I *happen* to see her at some family affair, and *happen* to make some sort of comment, all unprompted, you understand, who knows what mayn't come of it? She'd never know you'd ever said a word, I do assure you. But I won't even do that if you'd rather I didn't –'

'It's good of you, sir,' Harry said firmly, 'but at this stage, certainly, I'd rather you didn't. But if the chance ever arises – well, maybe. I'll see how it goes. Anyway, thanks for sorting out Mrs Porteous. You think there was any link between her cyst and her failure to conceive?'

'You're as bad as the patients, Harry,' Lewis said, but without any real rancour. 'I'm not God. Only God knows that. If she gets pregnant in the next few months, then indeed there may have been a connection. Come back and let me know how she gets on post-operatively and if she gets pregnant and then I'll tell you whether it could have been the cyst that stopped her before. Meanwhile she's rid of a nasty lump, and better off for it. She'll be on her way back to the ward soon and you'll be able to see her once she's clear of her anaesthetic. Tell her what I did, hmm? I'll see her myself in a day or two, but if you see her tonight, I needn't wait after my ward round. And I'm a bit tired –' And he stretched and yawned suddenly.

'Of course, sir.' Harry got to his feet. 'And thank you for your help with this case. Ah – you'll send the notes to the ward with her? Thanks – and thank you too for your advice on – er – the other matter.'

'Any time,' Lewis said and got to his feet. 'And don't worry – I shan't speak on that – ah – *other matter* at all. Confidentiality is something I concern myself with a good deal. Now, on your way, my boy. Time I changed and did my ward round.'

'Yes,' Harry said but he lingered for a moment longer, looking as though he was about to say something more, but then nodded sharply and went clattering his way out through the lobby, where there was now some bustle as the second theatre stopped working and the patient was sent wheeling on his way back to his bed. Not for the first time he was glad he wasn't a surgeon, as the smell of carbolic and ether and blood thickened in his nostrils, though sometimes, he told himself, perhaps it was less painful than being a physician. Surgeons' patients rarely weep on their shoulders, the way physicians' patients do on us, he thought as he escaped into the long corridor outside that led to the ward where he was due to take part in a big round. The way Lee weeps on mine.

But that was something he didn't want to think about. Not till the end of the day's work, and other people's miseries and other people's pain and other people's demands had been dealt with. Then and only then would he have the energy and time to think about the girl he had married so hopefully ten months ago and who was now making him so unhappy.

5

'A tour?' the Principal said and sniffed sharply. 'Hmm. What kind of a tour, may I ask?'

'Sixteen weeks with the option of extensions if the response is good. Start in Paris, go on to Brussels, Cologne, Frankfurt, Stuttgart, Munich, Vienna, Budapest, then back via Trieste, Milan, Lausanne, Basle, Strasbourg and another week in Paris.' Peter rattled off the list, trying to sound interested in it, but it was getting more and more difficult; he'd been through it so often for so many people that it was beginning to sound meaningless in his own ears.

He'd been so very enthusiastic to start with; when Letty had suggested he take a repertoire of Shakespeare plays across Europe to perform in English to university audiences it had sounded a fascinating project, not least because doing the tour would take him well away from London and the risk of meeting Leah, as he was sometimes forced to do at family events. It was no easier living with the knowledge that she was Harry's wife than it had been the day they had married; in some ways it was worse, and he had thrown himself into work with a fervour that had surprised even Letty, who always took total commitment to the Gaff's interest by its employees for granted. So, the chance to work extra hard and at a distance was very attractive. And this tour offered a new challenge; he always paid good attention to the text, of course, when he directed Shakespeare, but he'd need to add a good deal of visual content to productions for people who were not at home in English, and that would add to the interest. With so much to commend it, he had accepted the idea with alacrity.

Now, six weeks into the planning and the casting he was beginning to loathe the whole project heartily; more time had

had to be spent on dealing with passports and visas and travel arrangements than on the plays they were doing and that was boring in the extreme. Now, he made himself look as alert as he could and smiled at the Principal who was staring at him with his lips pursed.

'Hmm. A week in each place, is that it?'

'That's it. Well, near enough a week in each place. Depends on travel arrangements as well as the local demand. We'll have to travel at weekends, you see, and that adds to the complications,' Peter said, and added with sudden venom, 'considerably.'

Unexpectedly the Principal laughed, a little cackling sound that was incongruous coming from his rather bulky body. 'I'm sure it is. I remember doing something rather similar not long after the war, you know. Took a Commedia dell'Arte tour round France. Must have been mad!' But he looked happy for a moment, remembering.

'I'm beginning to think I'm mad,' Peter said, relaxing. 'Incredible what a fuss these damned embassies make! It's not as though we were trying to push ourselves at 'em either. They're panting for the stuff – when my producer first publicized the possibility they fell over themselves, these universities, to invite us. I gather it's had the blessing of their Führer in Germany, that's the thing. Seems keen on culture and all that, and what Germany does seems to affect all the others –'

The Principal lifted his brows. 'Thought it was only German culture he recognized,' he said acidly. 'We sent a student opera company to Germany last year, and they made it very clear they wanted only Wagner because that was this Hitler's favourite –'

'Well, that's as may be,' Peter said glumly. 'It doesn't seem to have affected their demand for Shakespeare –' He stopped then, and frowned. 'Though, mind you, they did say, all the German universities, that they didn't want either *Othello* or *The Merchant* –'

'See what I mean? That chap doesn't like Jews and blacks, so there you are! Still, plenty in the canon without those. Which are you doing?'

43

'*Hamlet* of course. They all want *Hamlet*. And *Romeo and Juliet* and the Roman plays. Oh, and the *Dream*. Very keen on the *Dream*, they are everywhere, though–' And again he frowned. 'We were advised not to use Mendelssohn's music in Germany. Not that we were going to anyway, but still–'

'See what I mean? Jew again, you see. Mendelssohn. All of a piece, these Germans. Still, I suppose they know best what they want. Now then, let me get it clear. You want to audition for four supernumeraries–'

Peter nodded. 'That's it. Two boys, two girls, play as cast, mostly walk-ons and attendants and so forth, bit of liveried scene shifting – you know the sort of thing. They'll be well chaperoned, of course, and you can see the rates of pay –' And Peter leaned forwards to show him again the relevant section of the paper he had already set in front of him.

'Hmm. That all seems very suitable. Well, my dear chap, I think we should be able to help. Even though this is a highly irregular way of organizing an audition. Usually like some notice, chance to warn 'em all of what's wanted, but still, you've explained why and – well, to be honest, there haven't been too many parts offered our young people this year. Must seize opportunity as it arises, hmm? Yes. And they deserve their chances. We've some good young ones in at present, very good, and I think you'll be spoiled for choice and that's the truth of it. I'd – ah – I'd be grateful, however, if you agree to consider only the final-year people. We do a two-year course, you see, and it's a pity to let 'em go too soon. You know how it is with these eager young creatures. They never think ahead, do they? No, they jump at the first thing that offers and then repent later, wish they'd finished their training–'

Peter grinned, well aware of the fact that the Principal was possibly as concerned about losing students with their final year's fees unpaid as about their future welfare, and nodded.

'I quite understand, sir – but of course if the right people turn out to be first years – you wouldn't refuse me, would you?'

'Well, I suppose not,' the Principal said a little unwillingly. 'Can't, in point of fact, can I? A job's a job and I can't stand in their way in these hard times. Always more of 'em out of work than in it, as I always tell 'em when they start here. So I can't very well stop people from taking jobs if they're offered. Still and all, I'd rather you took final years if you could –'

'Of course,' Peter said soothingly. 'If I can –' And the Principal got to his feet and led the way out of his cluttered little office and into the entrance hall beyond. It was a noisy clattering place as students went rushing across the grey terrazzo floor and the sounds of music and singing came filtering through from the scattered practice rooms on the floors above and Peter found his face lifting into a smile as he absorbed the atmosphere of the place.

It smelled comfortingly familiar, the reek of fish glue and size from the basement rooms where the students built their sets and painted their flats mixing with the familiar scent of Leichner's greasepaint and cheap cigarettes and stewed tea and burnt toast – all the lovely backstage cocktail of odours that spelled theatre to him, and with which he'd fallen in love when he'd first set foot backstage, long ago when he'd been taken to see Theo Caspar in Letty Lackland's first production at the Shaftesbury.

He stood for a moment with his head up and his nostrils a little flared remembering how exciting he'd found this sort of ambiance all those years ago when he'd been little more than a schoolboy, as the Principal, unaware that his companion was not immediately behind him, went bustling on his way to the porter's lodge just by the entrance door. And then, Peter almost fell as someone went hurrying past him and bumped him with the big bundle she was carrying so that he lost his balance.

'Oh, I'm so sorry!' the girl gasped as she dropped the bundle and sent papers and pieces of card and boxes flying, and he at the same moment managed to say, 'Sorry!' as he stood up straight again. And they both laughed as they recognized each other.

'Wouldn't you know that you'd be the first person to make my life a misery the moment I set foot over the threshold?' Peter said with mock severity, and Katy laughed and retorted, 'And wouldn't you know you'd be the first person to push himself under my feet when I couldn't see where I was going? What are you doing here? Come to check up on the education I'm getting?'

He smiled down at her with real pleasure; it was always good to see her, for she had remained as she had been that first night he'd met her at Rules with Letty; full of energy and enthusiasm with the sheer excitement of just being alive and being in London. He didn't see her all that often; on the few occasions when he had reason to visit Letty at Albany on matters to do with the Gaff productions on which he was working, Katy was either at Guildhall classes or out with her own friends, of whom she now had a great many in London, but he had seen her at occasional family parties and she had always chattered to him with great delight about what she was doing and what she was learning.

Indeed, he couldn't deny that he had thought of her when he had come to this last stage of casting for his touring company, and had decided to audition at Guildhall in consequence. It wasn't that he had actually decided to take Katy with him, but she had brought Guildhall to mind as a source of lively young actors. Now he put on a mock serious expression and said, 'My dear young lady! Important though your education no doubt is, and hugely though it looms on your horizon, I have to tell you I have other thoughts on my mind. I did *not* come here because of you, or to check on your attendance at your classes. I came to audition for –'

Her eyes widened. 'Audition? For what? And is it for a girl, and can I try for the part, whatever it is and –'

'Certainly not!' Peter said, suddenly realizing what a pit he had dug for his own feet. 'You're much too inexperienced. I'm here to audition final years only –'

'Oh, pooh!' she said and tugged on his sleeve, tucking her huge bundle under her other arm so awkwardly that it threatened to strew itself at their feet again. 'Lots of first years get jobs! Managers are always coming here to audition people and –'

'Oh? First years are auditioned?'

'Of course! You could audition me, and then I could be in your new whatever-it-is and –'

'Have you ever been in first-year auditions, then?' Peter said artlessly and at once she said, 'Of course!' and then stopped, realizing that she had now dug a pit for *her* own feet. 'Well, only once. But they wanted someone to be dull and stodgy and so –'

He laughed at that. 'And of course no one could possibly want a part if it meant being dull and stodgy!'

'Of course!' she said with as much dignity as she could.

'So naturally, you turned it down.'

She looked at him for a moment with her head bent, peering up at him and seemed to consider and then laughed. 'Well, no. I wasn't offered it. I'd have taken it if I had been, of course. I'd take the back legs of a panto horse if anyone asked me to! I'd do anything to get a real job in a real theatre –'

'Not anything, I hope,' Peter said, still amused, and suddenly she went a rosy pink.

'I might,' she said defiantly. 'It depends what it is. But if you mean what I think you mean – well, I might!'

'I can't imagine what you think I mean,' Peter said easily, but he was a little taken aback for all that. He had seen this pretty lively child as just that – a child, but suddenly he had a glimpse of something beyond her youth and vivacity. He had seen an intensity of ambition in her eyes that was as sharp and as steel-hard as any he had ever seen and it made him feel a moment of chill. He was passionately in love with his job, heaven knew; he had been captivated by the theatre when he'd been young and impressionable and he knew he'd never escape its fascination, but would he do 'anything' to get on in the business? That was another question entirely. Maybe this silly girl doesn't realize what she's saying, he thought in a slightly confused way. She's too young to know just how dangerous an attitude that is. She'll learn –

The Principal was at his side suddenly and coughing in a rather impatient manner and Peter turned to him, immediately aware of how rude he had been to linger as he had, and he smiled at him with rather excessive cordiality and said heartily, 'So sorry, sir! I stopped to talk to one of your students – I –'

'Ah yes,' the Principal said, looking with some disfavour at

Katy who looked rather uncomfortable but stood her ground. 'Miss Lackland, isn't it? Yes? Connection of yours, I imagine?'

'We're very distant cousins,' Peter said. '*Very* distant. Now, sir, can we get on? I have several other things I must do today and I don't want to waste your time either, of course–'

'Porter's on his way round tellin' 'em,' the Principal said as he turned and again began to lead the way across the entrance hall. 'I've told him to send people who are interested to the theatre. Just final years, of course–' And he looked a little malevolently over his shoulder at Katy who was following Peter determinedly. 'You, Miss Lackland, are a first year, I think?'

'Sir?' said Katy innocently, not stopping, but walking as closely behind Peter as she decently could.

'Yes. And these auditions are for second years only.'

'But, sir,' Katy said, wide eyed. 'Peter – Mr Lackland said it would be all right if I auditioned with the others. Didn't you, Peter?'

'I have already said I will try to cast only from the final years,' he said dampeningly. 'And so I shall. But–' He couldn't help it; telling the truth was as much a part of him as breathing, and anyway he was beginning to feel that Katy could indeed be the sort of girl he needed for this tour. Cheerful and energetic, which was important for what was likely to be an exceedingly gruelling experience, but also lively and with a versatility and speed about her reactions that made it clear she'd be amenable to good direction. But he was determined not to pre-judge the issue if he could help it. '–but of course as with all auditions, they have to be open to all comers. You'd agree, sir?'

'I suppose so,' the Principal said sourly and led the way into the theatre and down the central aisle to the front row of the stalls.

'Isn't this a beautiful theatre, Peter?' Katy hissed in his ear as they reached the front. 'It's a silly stage, really, all width and no depth, bit of a letter-box, but the sight lines are so easy and the acoustics are lovely. And all the seats are tip-ups and there's a proper circle and everything–'

Looking round, Peter had to agree; it was a charming

theatre, probably seating three hundred or so, a little jewel-box of a place, and he looked from the circle to Katy's face and saw again that expression of greedy ambition on it and thought, 'Heavens, but she's a real actress – no question of that–' and turned away to sit down beside the Principal, determined to be as fair as he possibly could as the students – many of whom were already hurrying into the theatre as the news of an audition for real jobs spread like wildfire through the school – pushed past to the wings via the pass door at the side.

To Peter's relief Katy too disappeared, leaving her bundle on the seat beside him and he settled to watch, sitting in his characteristic way, slumped in his seat and resting his neck on the back of it. Auditions were hard work indeed, and he settled down to a long and probably boring couple of hours.

He was right; they were boring. One after another they came tripping on to the stage, tall and short, thin and chubby, attractive and plain, and went through their audition pieces. Peter knew that the people he chose for this tour would spend remarkably little time actually speaking lines on a stage; most of their working hours would be spent standing clutching spears in the background, or nodding and murmuring rhubarb at each other behind thrones, but he knew better than to prevent each student from doing his or her set piece and was too kind to interrupt even when he knew within the space of a few words that they weren't for him; so there he sat as the minutes and then the hours ticked by, listening to one after the other declaim the 'Mercy' speech from *The Merchant* or Henry's rallying cry of, 'Once more unto the breach, dear friends!' while watching for people who moved well, who could use the stage as though it was as familiar as their own living-room, who had presence and that indefinable quality called personality that could make itself felt even in people who were standing still and saying nothing.

His heart sank when Katy came bounding on to do her piece. He had hoped she'd be wrong, too uncontrolled and coltish to be useful, but as he watched her he knew she was right for his company. She moved easily and without being too mannered, yet she had a natural flamboyance about her that made it impossible to keep one's eyes off her. She exuded life and joy and a certain wittiness, even when her face was in repose, and when she started to sing a comic song – which she had, with characteristic impudence, chosen as her audition piece – he had to give in. Katy would have to be one of the people who would come with him on his tour of Europe, first-year student though she was. Somehow he'd have to soothe the Principal for stealing one of his younger students, and square matters with Letty – who might not be best pleased with his decision – and above all, make sure that Katy herself didn't get too overpoweringly excited. He already had a deep certainty that controlling Katy Lackland would be an exceedingly difficult thing to do, but he also knew she was a good actress and could be made even better. The idea of casting her as Juliet struggled to surface in his mind, though he pushed it away firmly. All the same – she *was* good. And she was coming to Europe with him.

6

'To Europe? Where? And when?' Jacob Landis lifted his gaze from his soup plate and looked sharply at Harry. 'And what for?'

'Mmm?' Harry said. He hadn't been listening to what Leah had been saying; he had, with his usual courtesy, been concentrating on his mother-in-law who had been murmuring to him – equally as usual – about her incipient arthritis, and had left it to his wife to carry the burden of conversation with the rest of her family. Now he looked across the broad table at Jacob and said, 'I'm sorry, sir? I didn't hear what you said.'

'I told Papa we might be going away for a while, Harry,' Leah said challengingly and lifted her chin at him and he shifted his eyes to look at her, and knew that he was defeated.

He'd tried every way he could to persuade her to be just a little more patient, to relax, to stop worrying so much, assuring her that if she did her chances of success were much greater, but she had flown up in such a passion that even he had been startled by it.

They had been dressing for the usual Friday night ritual of dinner at her parents' home and he'd been irritable enough because of that, added to the pressure of a particularly busy day at Nellie's, yet she had seemed unaware of how he felt; she had sat there at her dressing-table at their little house in St John's Wood, dusting her nose with Tokalon powder and never taking her eyes from her own image in the glass, and had started again as soon as he'd come in from the bathroom.

'Why can't we go?' she'd said, just as though there hadn't been the long gap of the day between breakfast, when they had at last talked of the matter, and now. 'You told me yourself you have a month off due to you, and you know I could be ready in half a day. Why can't we go? You told me this man is the best one there is, that he knows more about the illness than anyone else in the world and –'

If he hadn't been so tired he might have been a little more careful, but as it was he'd almost snapped at her as he began to struggle into his boiled shirt. 'I've told you before, Lee, you're not ill. You're just a little disappointed that you haven't yet –'

'Disappointed?' She'd shrieked it at him, totally uninterested in the fact that their little maid, down in the kitchen, could probably hear every sound. 'You call it just a disappointment as though it was like – like wanting a new frock or a hat or something? How can you be so cruel, so wicked, to dismiss me that way? It's the most desperate thing in the world and you're a doctor and you ought to understand and –'

'It's because I'm a doctor that I do understand,' he'd said, exasperated. 'I understand better than you know. I've been making a careful study of the whole hormone business for years now, and I *know* that agitation and anxiety add to endocrine disorder. I've told you and told you, haven't I, how there's evidence that women who suffer severe stress stop having normal periods, and probably stop ovulating? It doesn't matter whether the stress comes from outside or from inside, it's still stress – and I truly believe that much of your problem is the way you keep on and on about it – you never think of anything but babies, babies, babies – you make it hell for yourself and –'

She was crying now, desperately, with great tearing sobs and a flood of tears streaked her freshly powdered face and as ever that dissolved him completely and he hurried across the bedroom to crouch beside her and stroke her and hold her and murmur in her ear and croon to her, totally unaware of how absurd he looked in just his shirt and underpants; until at last she had stopped the painful weeping that had made her whole body shake and managed to take a tremulous breath.

'I'm sorry, darling. I'm so sorry,' she'd said in a small hoarse voice and wiped her face against his shoulder. 'I keep promising myself I'll do as you say, that I'll stop fretting, think of other things, won't nag you, and then you come home, and it all comes bursting out and I just go on and on – I don't mean to, but it's like – it's like being a pot on a flame. I keep on boiling inside and I can't stop it. I know you say all the stress comes from inside me but it comes from outside too. Babies in prams in the street and seeing other people pregnant and things in the papers and in every magazine I pick up – and I feel so empty and yet so full of misery – I wish you could understand, my darling. I do wish you could–'

'I do, Lee, I truly do. It's not that I don't care, it really isn't. It's just that I know there's nothing more we can do and–'

'But you said this Professor Aaronson in Vienna knew a lot about it, and that there was this Doctor Hirshfeld in Berlin and – you did, didn't you? Why can't we go and see one of them? It could be a problem they'd recognize at once, something that just needed injections or something to put right and then we'd have our babies and – there's so little *time*, Harry! I'm thirty-three! If I don't start a pregnancy soon I – it might be too late. You know that as well as I do. It's all right for you – you could leave me and still have plenty of time to find another wife who could give you babies, and anyway, it's different for men. They can go on being fathers for ever, but I'm thirty-three–' And tears threatened to engulf her again.

He'd managed to soothe her at last, and she had re-powdered her face as he changed his tear-ruined shirt and then finished dressing so fast that they'd only been fifteen minutes late at West Heath Avenue, but it had stayed there between them like a physical thing; never before had she suggested that he might leave her, and never before had he been able to comprehend such a fear in her. Yet tonight it had been said. What had been the unthinkable had become the sayable and that had frightened them both more than they would have thought possible.

For once he had been glad that it was Friday and they had to present themselves at his in-laws' dinner-table; usually Friday filled him with irritation, not because he disliked Jacob and Dora and his brother-in-law Gideon and his wife Jenny, and the unmarried sister of the family, Alison, but because of the calm assumption on the part of all of them that Friday dinner must be a family affair. Every Friday of his married life so far, with the few exceptions due to holiday absences, he had sat and listened to Dora's prayers over the candles and Jacob's blessing over the bread and had tried to find the same delight in it they all did, but he'd failed. It had seemed to him a rather absurd mumbo jumbo that had as much relevance to the realities of his life as a fairy tale, yet he had tolerated it for Lee's sake. She found pleasure in it, took satisfaction from the religious observance involved, and he had submerged his own boredom to please her.

But tonight it was different. He had sat there as the candles had flickered and Dora had uncovered her head after saying her soft prayer, had watched Jacob as he stood in his place and swayed slightly over the glass of wine in his hand and the plaited loaf of sweet chollah bread that lay on the table before him, rolling out the sonorous phrases of the Brochah, the blessing before eating.

'*Baroch atah Adenoi Elohanu melech ha olom – ha oretz –*' he said in a voice that sounded deeper and richer than it usually did and for a moment Harry had seen himself not as an individual with his own unique needs, his own special thoughts and desires and ambitions, but as a piece in a pattern, the pattern that was this family. There were the people who went before him, his wife's parents, with their children around them, and behind them he was aware of the countless generations who had uttered this same prayer over the same sort of food on so many Friday nights, and of the generations to come who would do the same. The generations to come, he had thought and looked at Leah, whose eyes were glittering a little in the candlelight as though with unshed tears as she too stared at her father, and he had felt the depth of her pain and her need to take her place in the pattern. It wasn't just a personal hunger for maternity that filled her, he thought, not just what *she* wants. It's all part of this too – and then Jacob had sat down and the little maid had started to serve the soup, and the moment had passed. It was just another routine Friday night in Hampstead, to be got through as best he could –

And now she had come back to the attack and he looked at her almost despairingly as Jacob said again, 'You're going to Europe, Leah tells me? To some sort of medical conference somewhere?'

'There *is* a conference going on,' Harry said a little unwillingly and looked again at Lee, but she was sitting with her head bent, eating her soup. 'In Vienna – but I hadn't really decided whether –'

'Vienna,' Jacob said and put down his spoon with a little clatter. 'How far is that from Munich?'

Harry stared. 'Munich?'

'Yes!' Jacob sounded suddenly irritable and glared at Harry who blinked back in some surprise. 'Munich! It's about – what, two or three hundred miles?'

'I suppose so,' Harry said, still mystified. 'I can't pretend it's a matter I've ever given much thought to. I mean, I'm not that much of a traveller and –'

'It's about five hours or so by train, Papa,' Gideon said quietly. 'But really, you can't ask Harry to – I do see what you're thinking of, but it hardly seems reasonable.'

'Why not?' Jacob demanded. 'Family is family! If you were going to Vienna would you hesitate?'

'Of course I wouldn't,' Gideon said. 'But it's different for me.'

'I don't see that,' Jacob said. 'A son, a son-in-law – family is family.'

'Will someone please explain to me what all this is about?' Harry said and then as the maid came in again to remove the soup plates and bring in the roast chicken, Jacob shook his head at him and hissed, '*Pas devant la bonne*,' and began to talk determinedly of the weather and how much more agreeable it would be if it were as blustery as March was supposed to be, instead of as foggy as it was. And then at last the dining-room door closed behind the maid and at once Jacob leaned forwards and said to Harry, 'My boy, you've heard us talk about Otto and Lise?'

Harry frowned and then after a moment nodded. 'I think so. Your cousins in Germany? The ones who have an art gallery?'

'That's it,' Jacob said. 'Very successful, they tell me, though it's very strange stuff they have there. However – the thing is, I want to get some letters to them. And if you're going to Vienna you could stop off at Munich without too much difficulty, I imagine?'

'I suppose so,' Harry said. 'But – ah – can't you post them?'

'I don't want to risk it,' Jacob said and leaned back in his chair. 'There are people who say I'm crazy, and maybe you will, but I don't want to risk it. I've seen the letters we get here from them, and I tell you they've been opened and closed again. Gideon pooh-poohed it when I first said it to him, but then he saw for himself, eh Gideon?'

Across the table Gideon nodded so that his glasses gleamed suddenly blank in the candlelight, and staring at him Harry felt an ominous little chill.

'Yes,' he said, and turned to look at Harry so that he could see his eyes clearly and they were troubled and not ominous after all. 'I've been watching the situation carefully, very carefully, Harry, especially now the Germans are rearming – and this latest news about Hitler's repudiation of the Versailles disarmament clauses – it's getting more and more worrying. And Papa is right – they do seem to be looking at the mail. I've heard the same sort of thing suggested from other people I know too, so if they're investigating outgoing mail, I imagine they're doing the same to incoming as well.'

'I worry all the time,' Dora said bleakly. 'All the time.' She looked down at her plate. 'It's all so mad, isn't it? Here we are, eating our dinner, minding our business, and Otto and Lise are doing the same in their house in Munich and all the time –' She shivered suddenly. 'It's like waiting for the rain to start when there's a thunderstorm. I feel so heavy all the time when I think about them.'

'I want to make Otto an offer,' Jacob said. 'I want him to come and work here with me. Bring Lise, the children – start again. An art gallery can't be all that different from the chemists' shop business. A business is a business, after all – and we need a good business head at the moment. Gideon and I do all we can, but with Henry to deal with, and Sam and David with no more sense than a – well, anyway, we want them in the business with us. There's more than enough work for us all. And enough income –' And he nodded at Harry, who nodded back. With a chain of over two hundred chemists' shops, he told himself, he was sure there was ample income for any number of the family's members.

'I just hope they'll come,' Dora said fretfully. 'I just hope they *come*. Then I'll sleep better at nights, I can tell you. As it is, I worry all the time. It's bad there, and going to get worse –'

'I'm not one of those people who pay a lot of attention to politics,' Harry said carefully. 'So I can't really say whether – I mean, it seems crazy to me, really crazy, that there should be any – I mean, who is it you think is interfering with the letters?'

'Hitler,' Dora said loudly. 'Their fershtinkeneh lousy dictator,' and she went suddenly pink as Harry stared at her in amazement. To hear that much venom in Dora's voice was as amazing as hearing a cat declaim Shakespeare.

'But surely not –' he murmured and now it was Gideon who displayed unusual vivacity for he leaned forwards and spoke with a sort of urgency in his voice.

'That's the trouble, Harry. People don't believe it's possible that governments can treat their citizens the way this German Government is treating Jews. They say it's a lot of hysterical fuss, that Hitler's good for Germany, he's making their economy work and all that sort of thing – and anyway – they don't say it, but they don't like Jews much themselves. If Hitler puts a few Jews in their place, you can hear them thinking, so much the better –'

Harry stared at him and felt a slow tide of shame rising in him. He was not, as he had said, a young man who had ever cared much about politics. He rarely read newspapers except for information on cricket, for which he was developing quite a taste, and the more amusing snippets that decorated the livelier pages, so Hitler and the doings of his German Government meant little to him. But he knew of the casual insults that were thrown at Jews; had heard the snide comments some of his fellow doctors at Nellie's made about their Jewish colleagues, had laughed with them at the jokes they made about hooked noses and circumcision and financial sharp dealing. Not until he had fallen in love with Leah had he given much thought to Jews and had never noticed how commonplace a matter anti-Jewish feeling was. Now, as a member of a Jewish family, he was becoming more and more aware of it, and he looked round the table at these pleasant, quiet people, comfortable to be with, thoughtful, kindly, sometimes dull, occasionally stupid, just ordinary people, and tried to see in them the images conjured up by the sneers and the jokes that were so staple a part of the medical common room gossip at Nellie's, and couldn't.

And he also tried to imagine their letters being tampered with by British policemen and blinked at the impossibility of it. It couldn't happen here in England; could it happen in Germany? It seemed an absurd idea. And yet – and again he thought of the casual insults and the jokes and heard his own heedless laughter ringing in his ears from his own past unawareness of the significance of those jokes.

'So you see, Harry?' Gideon said softly. 'It's important that we do something. We can't do anything for all the Jews in Germany, but we can look after our own.'

And Jacob nodded and echoed it. 'We can look after our own.'

'And you want them to come here?' Harry said after a long pause, as much to break the silence as really to say anything important, and Jacob nodded again.

'We thought of going ourselves, but with a name like Landis –' He shook his head. 'If they're watching Otto and Lise anyway, then if they start getting Jewish visitors from England they'll get suspicious. I don't know what they'll do, but who knows with such mumserim?' He laughed then at Harry's mystified face. 'Bastards, you should forgive the expression, Harry. That's good Yiddish for bastards. Which is what they are. The thing is, if you're going to Europe anyway, and stopping on the way at Munich wouldn't be difficult for you, then maybe you could see Otto, tell him my message, and who's to notice? A young American doctor in Munich, with a name like yours – no one can think it strange –'

'And you did say you wanted to see that professor at the conference, Harry,' Leah said and her eyes were again very bright as she looked at him over the candle flames. 'Didn't you, darling? You did say it would be worth going, didn't you?'

He looked back at her, at the curve of her cheek against her hair, at the way her brows were lifted so hopefully, at the droop of her mouth and thought confusedly of the way it had been all through these long lost months; of the way their joy in their love-making had become tarnished by her anxiety, how eager she was to share his kisses when she hoped she would be most likely to conceive, and how bitterly she rejected him when once again she found her hopes were wasted and he took a sharp little breath in through his nose and said as easily as he could, 'Well, yes, I suppose so. And we might just as well go via Munich as not, I dare say –'

At once it was as though a light had been lit in the dining-room, as they all began to chatter and laugh, making eager plans for him, and he bent his head to start eating his chicken, chewing it as mechanically as though it were just a mouthful of old rags. He could feel the pool of anxiety that lay inside him all the time these days rise a little and become deeper as he faced up to the real reason he had been so unwilling to take Lee to see the experts in Vienna.

Suppose, he asked his plate bleakly, suppose Professor Aaronson says he can't help? Suppose there is no way anyone can help, and Lee can never become pregnant? What will happen then? But his plate didn't answer.

7

'There you are!' Harry said, and dropped the bundle into her lap. 'Every woman's magazine I could find, and *Punch*, and the *Illustrated London News* and *Blackwood's* and a couple of poetry ones and in case that doesn't last you till we get to Vienna, there's a bookful of crosswords.'

'I shan't need them!' she said joyously. 'I shall sit and stare out of the window and I shall talk to you and when you fall asleep I shall walk up and down the train and talk to the other people and it'll be lovely. I adore travelling and I adore you for taking me and it's all going to be too too wonderful for words!' And she smiled up at him with her face brimming with delight and he looked back at her unhappily, wanting to warn her that she was too hopeful, too happy, too certain that there would be a good outcome to their journey, and knowing that he couldn't. He'd said it all, so often, but she listened and didn't hear, nodded her head at his words and didn't agree. She was totally convinced that she would achieve the baby she so much wanted as a result of this journey, and he hadn't the heart – nor the courage – to tell her again that her conviction was based on the most shifting of sands.

'Well, if it's people to talk to you want, there's plenty on the train. I saw a collection of very serious-looking chaps followed by a horde of press men coming down the platform, and the porter told me they were Members of Parliament going to make a tour of inspection of gasworks or something of the sort in France – they ought to be interesting –'

She made a face. 'Ought to be, but won't. I hope there'll be better than that to keep us company.'

'Well, actors then?' He felt guilty for seizing on this chance to change the subject, knowing he ought to sit down beside her, force her to understand that there were no such things as miracles in medicine, only hope and trial and error, and that this journey could well be wasted, and the guilt made him particularly hearty and excessively jolly. 'I saw great wicker hampers being loaded into the van, and there were all these characters leaping around and calling each other darling and being so effusive I thought they'd melt and run all over the platform in nasty greasy trickles, and some of them were talking with the most desperate intensity about some chap called Stanislavsky, I think it was – *too* much, darling –' And he drawled it in the best imitation of a Noel Coward accent he could manage and she squealed with delight and cried, 'More – tell me more!' And he did, throwing himself around the carriage with great abandon, being, with enormous gusto, the actors he had seen until she had tears of laughter running down her cheeks and was gasping at him to stop.

By the time they had made the Channel crossing and were safely ensconced in the train on their way to Paris where they were to pick up the Orient Express, they had both calmed down a good deal; she seemed less excited, less certain of a happy outcome to their travels, while he, paradoxically, had become more optimistic.

He had stood on deck leaning over the rail of the steamer, staring down at the water creaming away under the keel and told himself it was absurd to be so gloomy, that indeed perhaps Aaronson could pinpoint whatever it was that was preventing his beloved Lee from conceiving, that he was being less than just to his colleagues in assuming they were doomed to fail; and the lift in his spirits that was a consequence of that change of view communicated itself to Leah and sobered her. It was as though she had become aware of the diminution of his opposition and this had made her less defensive, less in need of the blind optimism that she had used to give herself courage. So they were a subdued pair when the guard crying the first call for lunch came shouting his way through the swaying carriages.

He was sitting in his corner seat leaning back with his eyes closed and she had assumed him asleep, though he wasn't, and had let herself sit and stare out of the window with her mouth drooping a little as she thought. There was only one other passenger in their compartment, a taciturn Frenchman who disappeared hungrily the moment he heard the guard's voice in the distance, and as soon as he had gone Leah leaned forwards and gently touched Harry's knee.

He opened his eyes at once and grinned at her and she smiled back and said, 'I thought I'd better ask you if you wanted lunch, darling. They've just called it and though I'm not a bit hungry, you usually are—'

'Are you suggesting I'm a greedy pig?'

'Yes. Because you are. I never knew a man who could eat as much as you do.'

'You're right. I am a pig, and I am hungry and I am dying for some lunch. Come on, then and—'

She shook her head. 'No thanks. I couldn't face it. There's always too much and all that rattling of glasses and cutlery makes my head ache. I've some apples in my bag and there's that chocolate you bought at Victoria — you go and have a proper lunch, darling, and leave me to my crosswords. I might come and join you later perhaps for a cup of coffee—'

'Well, if you're sure—' he said and got to his feet, guilt lifting its head again in him, for he needed, suddenly, to be away from her. He had only pretended to be asleep to avoid conversation, and getting away for an hour of leisurely lunching would help a good deal. But he pushed that thought away and bent and kissed her. 'I could do a good deal of damage to a good French *déjeuner*—'

And she kissed him back and watched him go, smiling, not wanting him to know how glad she was he hadn't insisted on taking her with him. She needed to be on her own for a while, for there were long hours of enforced companionship ahead of them and it would be dreadful if their good humour thinned and disintegrated into irritability and arguments as it so often had during the last few months. When that happened, love-making became a difficult business and love-making mattered dreadfully to Leah now. But not because of any real need to make love for herself or for him — and knowing that, and knowing he knew it too, added to the uneasiness that was growing between them. So, it was good to see him going off to have lunch.

Once he had gone she stretched and kicked off her shoes, pulled off the small hat that clung closely to the side of her head, and stretched again. Even travelling first class wasn't the most comfortable of ways to spend the long hours and it was good to relax, to treat the compartment as though it were her own bedroom, and she put her stockinged feet on the seat in front of her and leaned back, running her fingers luxuriantly through her hair to free it from its neat marcelled waves.

He almost didn't see her. He had been making his way along the swaying train towards the restaurant car with his head down, staring at his feet rather than ahead of him, still ticking off the details in his mind; the seven skips full of costumes and drapes; the personal luggage – and despite the fact that he'd told them all that no one was to travel with more than two pieces, somehow there was a total of sixty-three items to be laboriously checked, counted, supervised from train to boat and back to train again – and the passports. Half the company had agreed that it would be simpler if Gregory Pelham, the tour manager, carried them all, while the other half had announced in ringing tones that *their* travel documents were much too precious to be handled by anyone but themselves, and the resulting disagreement still hadn't been sorted out. 'Whose passports we're carrying for them and whose are still locked in their owners' pockets – and whose have been left behind altogether, which is still a distinct possibility, I'm not sure,' he told himself despairingly.

And then, as he almost bumped into another passenger coming the other way and had to squeeze himself against the doorway of the carriage they were passing, he caught sight of her and stared, not believing it. It was one of those absurd and wickedly cruel tricks of the mind that came to plague him sometimes, he thought, remembering the way he had so often over these past few months seen a slender back disappearing round a corner, or a dark curly head in the crowd and had been certain it was her, only to run to see and discover it was a total stranger after all, and he closed his eyes for a moment and then opened them again and looked once more. This time she was looking at him and after a moment of blank-faced staring smiled with delight and sat up, swinging her feet to the floor.

He paused and then slid the door open as she sat there very upright with a welcoming look on her face and he went in, sliding the door closed behind him to shut out the worst of the wheel rattle from the corridor and stood there for a moment, still uncertain.

'This really is absurd,' he said then rather abruptly. 'It *is* you, isn't it?'

'I'm the only you who's in here,' she said and laughed. 'Peter, do stop staring so! It's no odder my being here than you being there! What are you doing in this train?'

'I'm taking a Shakespeare rep. company out,' he said. 'A university tour over half Europe, God help me. I've been wishing I'd never – and now, here you are! Having you here makes it seem much less dreadful a prospect than it did five minutes ago. My dear girl, what are you doing on the Flèche d'Or? Where are you going? Where's Harry? And–'

She laughed and leaned back in her seat again, glad to relax, feeling, as she always did in his company, extremely comfortable. 'Do sit down, Peter! You give me a crick in my neck, standing there like that. I have to peer up at you–' And after a moment she put her feet back up on the seat in front of her with a little flourish of silken legs, and he, moving a little awkwardly, sat down a little further along the same seat, and leaned forwards, resting his forearms on his knees and linking his hands loosely together in front of him. Sitting like that his eyes couldn't stray to those long well-shaped legs, and it was important that they shouldn't. It really was devilish, the effect this girl could have on him, and he felt his neck dampen under his shirt collar as he realized just how powerful the effect was.

'I'm going to Munich,' she said, and wriggled a little so that she was even more comfortably tucked into her seat, and she linked her hands behind her head to pillow it and smiled again. It really was delightful to see him, she was thinking, exactly what she needed to occupy her mind and stop her from getting gloomy. 'And then Vienna. There's some sort of medical conference there Harry has to go to. In Vienna, I mean, and we're stopping in Munich for – well, we're just stopping there.' For a moment caution had moved in, warning her not to say anything about the other part of their errand on this journey. 'Now, where exactly are you and your company going to? Shakespeare, you say? How very clever you are – I do wish I was clever, like you.'

'You wish nothing of the sort,' he said and grinned. 'You're quite clever enough for anyone and well you know it. Yes, we're doing Shakespeare. For serious English students in a lot of elderly universities. Or do I mean elderly students of serious English in universities? Anyway, people who are very serious about Shakespeare and spend more time with their eyes on the texts they have on their laps than on looking at what's actually happening on the stage. All very dreary, though I shall do my best to make it interesting –'

'And I'm sure it'll be absolutely riveting! Where will you be playing first? And which play? Perhaps we can see it, Harry and I? Now, wouldn't that be amusing? To go back to London and tell people airily, oh yes, we saw *The Merchant of Venice* in Munich. I'd love that because then I'd quote a great chunk of the 'Quality of Mercy' speech which is the only Shakespeare I know, and everyone'd be madly impressed, and think us very stylish! Promise me you'll do *The Merchant of Venice* in Munich just for us!'

'I wish I could! It would indeed be a pleasure to ensure you were stylish – but sadly we're not going to Munich just yet. We've got five weeks in Paris and Brussels and then there's Cologne and Frankfurt and Stuttgart to do before we get to Munich – and even then it couldn't be *The Merchant*. We're not allowed to do that one there.'

'Not allowed? Why ever not?'

'Because of Shylock,' Peter said and suddenly felt his face get very pink. Until the planning and organizing of this tour, he'd never given much thought to the odd fact that, through his mother, a large section of his family were Jewish, while he was not, but now he had to face it and again he felt the stirring of distaste – and another less identifiable emotion – that had so filled him when he had had to tell the Principal at the Guildhall about the restrictions on the tour imposed by one of their host governments. 'They – ah – they have a lot of stupid rules in Germany – you know how it is –'

She had taken her arms down from their comfortable pose behind her head and now sat looking down at her hands, twisting them on her lap. 'Yes,' she said after a moment. 'I know how it is. That's why we're going to Munich, actually –' and then she too went pink and looked at him and tried to laugh lightly. 'Well, I shall have to learn a speech from another play to quote at people, and tell them we saw you here on the Continent, even if we don't. Unless you can rearrange things and come to Munich first? That would be very nice if you could –'

'It would – and I wish I could do it for you, Lee. But it just isn't –' And she gave an odd little exclamation that made him stop speaking and look at her in some surprise.

'You called me Lee,' she said after a moment, looking at him very directly, and he set his head on one side, enquiringly.

'Well, yes. Is that something that –'

'It's what Harry calls me,' she said. 'He's the only one who does,' and at once he bit his lip and shook his head at himself, deeply embarrassed.

'Oh, I'm sorry! I had no intention of being impertinent – do forgive me! It's just that I've heard Harry say it, and thought that – I promise, I never will again. Leah, of course –'

'No,' she said. 'Please. I like it – it sounds friendly. Please do call me Lee. Will you?'

It was a very odd moment. They sat there on opposite sides of a swaying railway compartment, with the dull dark greenness of northern France fleeing past the windows, staring at each other and very aware of the other's physical presence. Even above the noise of the train he felt he could hear her soft easy breathing and the faint thumping of her heart against her ribs, and she in her turn seemed to feel the heat of his body reaching across the space that lay between them, to touch her skin and make it move a little over her flesh, and she shivered slightly.

'Brr –' she said, needing very much to break the moment. 'A goose walked over my grave! But it's really quite warm in here – isn't it?'

'Er – yes,' he said. 'Delightful. Er – will you come and have some lunch? I was just going to myself and –'

'Thanks, Peter, but no. I told Harry I wasn't hungry, so he's gone along on his own. You go and join him, do – I'm just going to have an apple and some chocolate here. We'll be having dinner in Paris tonight before we pick up the Orient Express, and I can't eat two big meals in one day –'

She was chattering foolishly and she knew it and was annoyed with herself. But he had become more disturbing than comfortable to be with and, suddenly aware of her ungainly posture, she took her feet down from the facing seat and tucked them primly beneath her own.

'Have you enough apples and chocolate for two?' he asked and leaned back, putting more space between them, and incidentally putting his face into the shade a little, as the curtain that flapped against the window threw a deep reddish haze on to him.

'Ample,' she said and, glad of the distraction, reached for her bag and rummaged in it, emerging at last with a bar of Nestle's milk chocolate and a bag of small apples. 'They're only little ones,' she said. 'They're Beauty of Bath, the remnants of last year's crop from my parents' garden. You see? All red and yellow stripes. I do love them so, but they don't really fill you much –'

'I don't need much filling,' he said gravely, and took the apple she gave him and the piece of chocolate which she broke off and they sat in companionable silence, eating and watching the trees flash past as the shadows and the bright sunshine flickered on the floor of the compartment.

'So you're stopping in Munich?' he said after a while, needing to say something and not really knowing what else to talk about. 'Have you friends there? Or is it another of Harry's medical conferences?'

She looked at him consideringly for a moment and then seemed to reach a decision.

'We have family there,' she said. 'My mother's first cousin and his wife and children. Papa wants them to leave Germany. He's worried about their future there, and it isn't really – shall we say *satisfactory* to send letters. So Harry and I are going to deliver them. I'm not supposed to tell anyone what we're doing, but you're family too, after all.'

67

'All a bit cloak-and-dagger, isn't it?' Peter said with a sudden edge to his voice. Again there was that stirring of disagreeable feeling in him and now he identified the other component of it; added to his distaste there was a growing anger. 'Is it really necessary?'

'Papa thinks so,' she said. 'And so does Gideon. My brother, you know? There are a lot of people who do. There's a committee now. Just before we left I heard about it. Papa and some of Mother's relations from Holland – all sorts of people are on it. They're trying to get Jewish people in Germany to leave – it's all rather–' She let her voice trail away.

'You'll be careful, won't you?' he said after a moment. 'I'm not sure how things are either. We hear all these tales and I don't know what to believe. But I know things can happen when you're a long way from home – so be careful. I must speak to Harry, too–'

'No,' she said sharply, too sharply, and then tried to smile again. 'No, please don't, he – he doesn't really understand. He's not Jewish, you see–'

'Neither am I,' he said gently. 'In spite of Mother. We were reared in the Church of England.' And she stared at him, her face blank and then looked confused.

'No, of course you aren't,' she murmured. 'I suppose I – you're so much family, you see. I feel as comfortable with you as I do with Sam and David – you know, my Henriques cousins? We are a funny mixed up lot, aren't we?'

'We are indeed,' he said. 'Perfectly higgledy piggledy,' and she laughed and gave him another apple and began to chatter of the plays he was doing, and the tension passed. He felt he had been put back firmly where he belonged, in the niche in her mind clearly marked 'Nice Cousin to be Trusted'. He was no more than a friendly face in a foreign land who had been welcome just because he was so familiar. There was no more between them than that, and the fragile web of intimacy that had seemed to connect them there for a little while had vanished as though it had been blown away by the wind rushing behind the train that carried them on to Paris.

And he ate his apple and watched her face, animated and

eager in the sunlight coming through the window, and felt the old ache of longing settle back into its accustomed place deep inside him.

8

At first he'd been somewhat irritated by them, but now he was beginning to enjoy them. There they sat at adjoining tables, eight flamboyant people, laughing and chattering at the tops of their voices, being outrageously charming to the stewards so that they looked after them more assiduously than any of the other passengers, and generally putting on a performance of being actors that would have been regarded as excessive on a stage, let alone in the restaurant car of a train between Calais and Paris; and he couldn't help but find them intriguing.

By the time he'd finished his *sole bonne femme* and was ready to contemplate a *crème caramel* they had finished their lunch, and after much spirited discussion of who had eaten what and how the bill should be distributed, went trooping out, leaving him feeling a little depressed. Lunch had been enjoyable, and the antics of his fellow passengers had sauced the food agreeably, but now he had to go back to his carriage and talk to Lee, and once more that lift of guilt was there; he loved her, dammit, he loved her very much indeed. Why was her company becoming something he felt he needed to avoid? It was all wrong; and he stared gloomily into his rattling coffee-cup and felt depression settle over him.

Across the aisle the stewards cleared the tables and he could feel them willing him to leave, too, so that they could prepare for the second call to lunch, but he ignored them, keeping his head down, and that was probably why he saw it; a small round black object under one of the seats and as the stewards went sulkily away back to the other end of the swaying carriage he bent down and reached for it.

It was a powder compact in black enamel, and he turned it in his fingers, liking the smoothness of it and thought – one of those actresses. It must have been one of those actresses who dropped it, and at once his spirits lifted as he considered going to find them, so that he could give it back. Perhaps he could linger with them, chatter a little, fill in another half-hour or so before returning to Lee, and he drank the rest of his coffee quickly and was about to wave to the steward for his bill when the door at the end of the carriage slid open and the girl came in.

He had noticed her before; how could he have failed to do so? Of all of them she had been the most vivacious, the most extrovert, the most amusing, and he had been hard put to it not to stare obviously at the round little face with its pointed chin and the narrow green eyes with their ridiculously long lashes. He had felt that if he had stared she would have been aware of his interest, would have turned and stared back at him and that would have been too embarrassing – because it would be something he would have enjoyed.

So he had forced himself to look at the others in the noisy party, the tall young man with the very dark hair slicked against his skull who had been the most drawling of them all, and the large woman wearing quantities of necklaces and brooches who had been so droll, and the wispy blonde with the round baby-blue eyes. But now, as she crouched to peer beneath the seats of the table where she had sat, he could look at her, and he did, liking the way her small body was put together so compactly and the way her hair curled on the back of her neck.

She turned and caught his eye and lifted her eyebrows at him comically.

'Ah – *j'ai perdu ma* – oh, lor, what's the wretched thing called in French? – *ma petite* thingummy – er – *boîte*, is it? – *boîte pour la poudre – pour ma toilette, vous comprenez?* At least I think that's what I mean – ah – *c'est un petit* – er – *objet qui est noir – comme ça* –' and she sketched the shape in the air with fluttering hands, looking at him with her head on one side, hopefully.

For a wicked moment he considered pretending he was French, that he didn't understand, to keep her standing here struggling to explain, but he couldn't and held the compact out to her, smiling.

'Is this what you're looking for?'

At once she clapped her hands together with delight. 'Oh, you are unkind! Letting me make such an ass of myself. Especially when my French is so awful – you'd never think I'd done five years of it at school, would you?'

'Awful,' he agreed. 'And the word you were looking for was *compacte* – not *boîte*, which is box.'

'Well, it couldn't have been that bad, because you did understand me, after all!' she said and then tilted her head again and looked at him consideringly. 'You're an American?'

'Indeed I am,' he said, and then, on an impulse. 'Would you care for some coffee? And I've still a little wine left in this bottle. It was too much for me. Help me finish it?'

She looked at him for a moment, her upper lip caught between her teeth and then nodded and sat down. 'I'd love to. Are you picking me up the way Americans are always supposed to do with strange girls on trains?'

He laughed. 'Is that how you think about travelling Americans? How shaming! And here we are thinking what noble fellows we are, bringing a little New World glamour to the tired old one! I must remember to warn everyone back home that the girls in Europe think we're all wolves on the prowl!'

'*Hope* you're all wolves on the prowl!' She settled herself more comfortably in her seat with a little wriggle and picked up a wine glass. 'It's much more fun to have adventures – and you can't have adventures with noble fellows. Only with wicked wolves.' She grinned at him. 'Actually, you don't look like a wolf at all. More like a –' Again she cocked her head in that characteristic little gesture. '– um – someone frightfully responsible, and wise. The sort of person people talk to. You can't be a parson – if you had been you'd never have asked me to have a drink with you, and anyway you'd have a dog-collar and rimless glasses –'

'Do all parsons wear rimless glasses?'

'Of course they do. Unless they're the sort of hearty chaps who like to work in the poorest part of a dirty city and then they wear thick striped scarves and are frightfully muscular and matey.' She brushed aside the whole race of parsons with a comprehensive gesture. 'No, you're not a parson. A lawyer, maybe. Yes, I think you could be a lawyer. You have a nice serious look – and I could just imagine you with a wig and a gown and those ducky little white bits under your chin–'

And again those restless slender hands made movements in the air and at once he saw them there, shadowy but almost visible, a wig and bands and a black fustian gown.

'But I'm stupid,' she went bubbling on, giving him no chance to speak, not that he actually wanted to; listening to her and watching her was quite amusing enough. 'You're an American and you never wear wigs and gowns, do you? You stand around under huge fans while the judge sits there and fans himself with a dirty hat,' and she nodded at him in great satisfaction, and beamed. 'And the noble young lawyer gets the honest man off and everyone cheers. There! I've got it all worked out, haven't I? Tell me I'm right?'

'No,' he said smiling, and refilled her glass. 'Not at all. Try again. Or shall I tell you all about you?'

'Oh yes! That'll be much more interesting! Do tell me about me – it's my favourite subject!' And she leaned forwards to set her elbows on the table and prop her chin on her clasped hands. Her eyes were very bright and he felt the most absurd stab of shyness as she gazed at him and it made him look away.

'Well, now, let me see. You're not a Sunday school teacher, that's for sure–' She gurgled with delight. 'Not unless it's for one of those awful muscular parsons. They sound as though they'd never notice a pretty girl around the place. No, not a teacher – um – not a hospital nurse, either, though you'd do the sick a lot of good, I guess. How about an actress?'

She opened her eyes wide at him. 'How *ever* did you guess that?' and he couldn't tell if she was really surprised at his prescience or mocking him.

'I listened to every word you and your friends said,' he said and grinned again. 'As I strongly suspect I was meant to. You all seemed to enjoy having an audience.'

'Of course! What is life worth if you haven't an audience? I like to be watched all the time! It's what I'm for!'

'*All* the time?'

'Definitely all the time.'

Again he grinned. 'I can imagine times when it might be less than agreeable. In the bathroom, for example–'

'I look lovely in the bath,' she protested and then laughed and for the first time looked a little abashed. 'Oh, help. You Americans say bathroom when you mean the loo, don't you?'

'Loo?'

'Theatrical slang,' she said with a great air of loftiness. 'I think we'd better change the subject. Where are you going?'

'To Paris. Isn't that where this train's bound for?'

'What are you going to do in Paris?'

'Get another train.'

'Where to?'

'Munich,' he laughed. 'Is this the third degree?'

'Oh, I'd love to have to do that,' she said, sitting bolt upright. 'Can't you just see it. Sitting there, with the cruel light burning, burning, burning in your eyes and the hard man with the carved granite face standing there and shouting at you, and you sunk in your chair, your face white with exhaustion and streaked with tears and yet still looking absolutely marvellous, and refusing, absolutely refusing to say a word that might give your lover away to the G-Men. You know that he's a villain, you know he doesn't deserve to be protected by you, but all the same, you are staunch–' She sighed deeply. 'What a marvellous part that'd be!'

'You want to be in the movies, I take it?'

'Doesn't everybody?'

'I don't.'

'I bet you would, if you really thought about it. If you could get to Hollywood.' Again that tilt of the curly head. 'Where do you live in America?'

'My family live in Virginia.'

'Your family? Don't you?'

'You're quick,' he said, almost ruefully. 'No, I don't. I left Virginia a couple of years ago to live in London.'

'Of course I'm quick. Successful actresses have to be quick. They have to be able to know what's happening in a person's mind even before the person himself realizes it. Then they react properly and show the audience what's going on in the other person's mind by the skill of their reactions. You see?'

'Not really. But if you say so.'

'That's a very unsatisfactory answer,' she said reprovingly, and then softened the rebuke with a sparkling grin. 'You can't be a lawyer after all, not if you say things like that. I'll have to start again, guessing –'

He blinked, taken aback again not only by the speed of her reactions, but her tenacious holding on to an idea; this girl wasn't just pretty and vivacious. She was intelligent as well, and he looked at her with a sharper glance and saw behind the brightness of her eyes and the upturned corners of her mouth a keener edge than he had seen before. He had seen her as fluffy, an amusing kittenish person, but he was wrong. There was more to her than that.

'Well, guess away,' he said lightly. 'I shan't tell you even if you're right.'

'Why not?'

'Strangers on trains should remain strangers,' he said and then, with a sudden need to show her he was more than an audience for her performance, that he was capable of being as amusing to watch as she was – put on a portentous air. 'They should meet and touch,' he declared. 'No more than that. Meet and share a moment which shimmers with promises unfulfilled, words unspoken, mysteries unexplored. They should come together and move apart again, leaving the centre untouched, going away as suddenly as they came, leaving no legacy behind –' He sawed his hands in the air and then spoiled it all by laughing. 'Dammit, I can't keep it up. But you get the picture.'

'It's a lovely picture. I like it a lot. You're absolutely right. No names, no sharing of true confidences, just a couple of ships that pass in the night – if we're going to talk like soppy books, let's do it properly, hmm? – yes, a couple of ships that pass in the night, that's it. I will never tell you my Deep-Down Tragedy, and you won't tell me your Awful Secret. We'll share the wine and gaze at each other and then go back to our seats in this swaying snake of speed, crashing its way though the grey day to the dramas and promises, the threats and hopes and fears that lie awaiting us in Paris – here, I'm quite good at this sort of stuff, aren't I? Not as good as you, mind you, I'll grant you that – but quite good.'

'Excellent,' he said gravely. 'But do you mean it?'

'Mean what?'

'No names. I'd like to know your name. I'll tell you mine first, so that you can tell me yours. I'm –'

'No!' She moved so fast he was hardly aware she had until he felt her fingers warm against his mouth, stopping him from speaking. 'No, really, don't spoil it! It's so much more fun to be mysterious. Exactly like at the pictures. *Lovely*. Don't tell me your name ever – no, I've got a better idea. We'll make up names, shall we? Now, let me think – what name shall I say I have?' And she leaned back, and folded her hands on the table in front of her, but he still felt their warmth against his lips. It was an oddly disturbing shadow of a sensation and he made a little face, in an effort to drive it away.

'Make up names? What's the point of that?'

'It'll be like a – like a clue in a crossword puzzle. I'll tell you a name that is sort of linked to my real one – and you do the same. And we can go on our separate ways, puzzling away at the real answer and then, one day in years to come, when fate flings us together again, we can tell each other the truth. Do you like that idea? I do. Let me think now –'

And she turned her head and stared out of the window, clearly concentrating hard and almost against his will, he found he was doing the same so that he could stare at her image, tremulous in the glass, showing itself against the blur of the passing fields, and as he stared he found a cryptic name for himself came into his mind without effort. When he had been small and had asked his mother why he was called Haversham, she had explained it was because that had been her family name, and then had told him that it was a famous one; that the English writer Dickens had used it in one of his books, about a little boy called Philip Pirrip. The Miss Haversham in the book wasn't at all nice, she'd told the small Harry, but the little boy was, and he had settled down to read *Great Expectations* with enormous excitement. Clever Mamma, he found himself thinking now, and without stopping to think further said, 'Then my name is Pip.'

'Pip? I like that! It's lovely! Just Pip? Is there another bit?'

'Oh –' he said and bit his lip, thinking, and then grinned again. 'Poor Pip. Yes, that's me. Poor Pip.' A man who lacks land is very poor in Virginian terms, he thought and grinned even more widely at her. 'You'll never be able to solve that one, I'm certain.'

'I bet I will,' she said. 'When I want to. But I don't yet. I want you to be Pip. Poor Pip–' And she leaned forwards and touched his hand fleetingly and smiled, and again he felt the ghost of her touch long after she had moved away.

'Now, what shall I be called?' she said and then smiled. 'I think I know. How about – um – Bianca? Yes, Bianca.'

'Pretty,' he said. 'I should be able to work that one out – let me see, now–'

'No, that's cheating! Not yet! You're not supposed to puzzle about that until we meet again in the dim distant future! Don't spoil it.'

'All right, I won't spoil it. What else, then, as well as Bianca? I'm Poor Pip and you're Bianca – what?'

'Oh, help, this isn't as easy as I thought –' And she stared at him and then nodded in satisfaction. 'I know. How about Coolidge? Yes, that's my name. Bianca Coolidge.'

'We once had a President called that. Coolidge, I mean.'

She giggled and clapped her hands together. 'So you did! I'd forgotten that! Well, never mind, it doesn't matter. I'll tell you this much – the link is to do with an American.' And again she laughed as she gazed at him, delighted with herself for remembering the name of the author of that childhood book she had so enjoyed, *What Katy Did*. To marry up the name of Shakespeare's Kate's sister with the name of an American author pleased her quirky imagination and made the silly game more fun.

There was a diffident cough beside them and they both looked up, startled, at the steward who stood there.

'*Excusez-moi, monsieur – mais il est deux heures et il y a les gens qui attendent – ils ont réservé–*'

'What's that?' she said and again the man murmured about '*ils ont une reservation,*' and Harry nodded.

'*Bien,*' he said. '*L'addition, s'il vous plaît–*' and at once the man slapped the bill on the table in front of him.

'Poor Bianca and Pip – parted for ever by the demands of the second sitting for lunch! Ah well –' he said, and paid the bill and unwillingly got to his feet and held out his hand for her, and she too stood up.

The train was rattling over a set of points and swaying even more, and she had to steady herself against the table, and that meant standing very close to him. He could smell her; not heavy perfume, but the faint breath of a clean young body, a little warm, but not unpleasantly so, and he felt a small muscle in his back twitch and his thighs tightened, and he couldn't be sure whether that was to help him keep his balance or to control a more unexpected sensation.

'The ships pass on!' she said lightly. 'Bless you for finding my compact for me –' and she smiled and turned to go, and then after a moment turned back and lifted her face and kissed his cheek, very swiftly.

'We actors kiss people all the time,' she said. 'Don't think anything of it –' And she went away in good earnest this time, almost running between the tables, to the far end of the car to push open the door. She looked back over her shoulder for one moment and then touched her lips with one forefinger and was gone, leaving him to stand there as the stewards, now clearly very tired indeed of his presence among them, pushed past him as they reset his table and showed newcomers to the car to their places.

He turned and went back to his own end of the train, a little bemused and feeling absurdly exalted. Bianca Coolidge – now there was something to think about. What sort of name could that concoction hide? And once he found out the name, could he find the girl? And should he?

9

When they reached Paris neither of them was in a particular hurry to leave the train, both fussing a little over their parcels and hats and coats, so that by the time they did find themselves standing on the platform surrounded by their luggage most of the passengers had vanished.

And at once Harry wished he hadn't been so silly. What harm would it have done if they'd left the train at the same time as the actors and bumped into them? He'd have raised his hat to her and she'd have smiled at him and that would have been that. This way he had deprived himself unnecessarily of another glimpse of her, and that made him annoyed with himself. The annoyance made him edgy and short with Lee, but she didn't seem to notice; she had been unusually silent ever since he'd come back to their carriage, though he in his turn hadn't really noticed, being rather too absorbed in his own thoughts. Now, she let him snap irritably at the porters as well as at her and seemed unaware of what he was saying, though usually she was quick to remonstrate with him if he seemed impatient.

And the reason for that was that she too was confused by her own reactions. Why had she not told Harry as soon as he had returned that their cousin was on the train? What possible harm could it have done? Yet she hadn't; for some reason which totally escaped her, she had said nothing, preferring to sit staring out of the train window pretending to be half asleep as at last it rattled through the sleazy Parisian suburbs. Yet if she were honest, the reason for her silence was not a total mystery; he had called her Lee and for an extraordinary moment there had been something different between them, something that she knew shouldn't exist and yet which she had liked very much indeed. A most confusing experience.

'The Orient Express, *m'sieur?*' the porter was saying to Harry. *'Ah, oui, m'sieur – il partira à vingt heures moins cinq – vous avez vos billets? Ah, merci, m'sieur – je ferais tout ce qu'il faut. Ne vous inquiétez pas –'* And he waved them away from their luggage with much reiterated assurance of his reliability as its guardian and transporter to the Orient Express, a willingness due much more to the size of tip Harry had thought fit to give him than to his essential good nature.

'We've about five hours to kill,' Harry said as he tucked his hand under her elbow. 'That chap'll see our stuff's put on the train for Munich so we don't need to worry about getting to the Gare de l'Est till half-past seven at the earliest. What shall it be, then? The Louvre? Les Invalides?'

She managed a smile. 'Les Invalides? Wasn't that built as a hospital? It was inevitable you'd think of that! No, not Les Invalides, nor the Louvre. I want to be dreadfully frivolous and extravagant. It's not often a girl gets to Paris, after all.'

'The Faubourg St Honoré it is then,' he said at once and she hugged his hand closer to her side and felt a great wash of love for him that comforted her; she had been stupid, positively ridiculous to get in such a state about meeting Peter on the train. Quite absurd.

And at the same time he was looking down on her pretty round face and thinking what a sweet funny dear girl she was, and how much he loved her and how ridiculous he'd been to play such a stupid game with that girl on the train. It had meant nothing, nothing at all, and wasn't worth thinking about. He would take her shopping here in Paris and spend money he could ill afford to buy her fripperies and it would be heaven to do it, and he too tightened his grip on her as they went walking jauntily out of the smokiness of the Gare du Nord to the vivid afternoon light in the streets beyond. They both felt better than they had when they had got off the train – but they had both decided not to bother the other with talk of the encounters that had given them cause to feel uncomfortable in the first place.

Peter too was feeling uncomfortable. He had bustled about as soon as the train had drawn into the station, barely waiting for it to stop before he was herding his company out of their carriages, amid much chatter and exclamation, absurdly eager to get them all away. He had checked up on everything Gregory Pelham, the tour manager, was doing, swearing at the porters unloading the luggage, snapping so much at the actors who were fussing about their parcels that one of the women threatened to burst into tears (and was only prevented by the fact that everyone else was much too busy to pay any attention to her if she had) and generally behaving in a thoroughly unusual manner for one of his normally equable temperament. But his efforts to hurry them were effective; half their fellow passengers were still in the process of leaving the train when his party were climbing into the charabanc which had been provided to meet them.

For the rest of that day, even in the middle of all the fuss of settling his troupe into the accommodation organized for them at the University, and inspecting the theatre where they would perform (and to his relief it was really an excellent one, with ideal backstage accommodation and lighting and sound arrangements) his sense of unease remained with him, and it was compounded by the fact that he didn't really know why. After all, there was nothing new about his feeling for Leah; he'd been in love with her for a painfully long time. Nor was there anything new about seeing her and having to dissemble that feeling. He'd acted his way through any number of such meetings in London. Why had this one on a French train so disturbed him?

But no matter how often he asked himself the question, there was no answer. All he knew was that he had a dragging sense of unease that dogged him, and not only for that day. All through the Paris run – which was very successful indeed – and on through the week they spent in Brussels, where they were equally warmly welcomed by their audiences, it lingered. He became as deeply absorbed in his work as he usually was, sitting through every single performance and taking copious notes to pass on to his actors the next morning, and had to spend a good deal of time dealing with the important minutiae of transporting so many people and so much luggage around

Europe, but all the time, there it was. It couldn't be just because of Leah, he told himself almost despairingly one night when he couldn't sleep for the way he felt. What the hell can it be that's making me so edgy?

It wasn't till the company reached Cologne that he found out.

By the time Lee and Harry reached Munich, after twelve hours on the train, they were exhausted, and not only by the strain of travel. The moment of emotional closeness they had felt in Paris, when they had gone arm in arm down the Faubourg St Honoré buying nonsenses as presents for Lee to take home, had melted away in the enforced physical closeness of their compartment. It had been eroded too, by the fact that in spite of the privacy the wagons-lits seemed to offer, Harry was too aware of the strangeness of their surroundings to be able to make love – which Lee very much wanted to do. But not because of a desire for Harry, as he well knew. She had worked out that she was at the time of her month when the possibility of conceiving was at its highest, and she had said as much to Harry when he had muttered about the difficulty of sharing a single bunk, instead of each occupying their own. At once he had frozen, which had added to Lee's distress; so it was indeed an emotionally bedraggled pair who arrived in their hotel overlooking the lush greenness of the Englischer Garten, a most elegant and well-stocked park not too far from the bustling centre of the city. It took them two days of resting and – at last – resumed love-making to bring them to any sort of state to go visiting.

But at last they did, after telephoning Otto Damont to announce their arrival. They had talked a good deal in London about the right way to set about their meeting; Jacob had been adamant that no one must write in advance to tell the family they were coming. It was all to be casually relaxed, just an offhand sort of thing, nothing any curious watchers could regard as at all suspicious, and though secretly Harry remained unconvinced that there was any real problem, regarding his father and brother-in-law's extreme caution as little more than cloak-and-dagger exaggeration, he had agreed to do things their way.

So they telephoned the Damont Gallery, having found it listed in the directory, shortly after breakfast on a sunny morning that was more like late June than mid May, with Harry doing the talking. It had been agreed it should be done so, though Harry would have preferred Lee to call them; after all, she knew the people. He had never met them, and also his German was less good than it might be. Still, he managed to explain, haltingly, that he was visiting Munich accompanied by his wife Leah on his way to a medical conference, and would like to present his greetings, and at once Otto Damont had moved smoothly into English.

'But how very delightful!' the deep voice had burred in his ear. 'To meet dear Leah's husband will give us all great pleasure. You may dine with us, hmm? Lise, my wife, will be enchanted to see you, enchanted. I will arrange with her at once for this evening if this is suitable for you, yes? Excellent. Please come to the gallery first, which I will show you with much pleasure and then we go together to our home. We live in the suburbs, you understand, and it is not an easy journey for an *Ausländer* – for a visitor.'

'Er – yes, that'll be great. Great,' Harry said, and then, unwillingly again, for he felt remarkably stupid at displaying so much caution, added, 'You're sure that this is not going to cause problems for you? I mean, we don't want to make any –'

'Problems?' At once the deep voice at the other end of the phone cut in smoothly. 'Of course not. How can there be? To see friends is never a problem. *Auf wiedersehen* then. Till tonight –' And the phone clicked and went dead. He stood there for a moment with it to his ear wondering why Otto Damont had cut him short so abruptly, and was about to hang up when it clicked again and another voice said, in perfect English, 'You have completed your call, sir?'

'Er – yes, thank you,' Harry said and then, as surprise hit him, snapped, 'Who's that?'

'The operator, sir,' said the voice and again the phone clicked and died and he jiggled the rest angrily, but there was no response. Slowly he put the phone back on its hook and left the little booth and came out to the lobby of the hotel where

Lee was waiting for him.

'What's the matter?' she said sharply and he looked at her, startled.

'Hmm?'

'You look – I don't know. Bothered. What's the matter. Did you get through?'

'Yes,' he said absently. 'I got through. We're going to the gallery this afternoon and then he's taking us to his house for dinner.'

He hadn't intended to tell her the rest of it, but then, as she set her hand on his arm and made clear she was going to insist on talking more about the call, in spite of the many people around them in the populous lobby, he knew that wouldn't work.

'Let's walk,' he said quietly. 'I'll tell you as we go. Come on –' And to his relief she said no more, tucking her hand obediently into his elbow. He stopped as they passed the front desk and caught the eye of the clerk standing there and on an impulse said, 'The telephone kiosk there –' and he indicated it on the outside of the lobby. 'Is it connected to the exchange through the hotel?'

The man looked and shook his head. 'No, sir. That one is a direct outside line. If you wish to make a call through our own operator, we are happy to oblige you. You may take the call in the small room here at the side of the operator's room –'

'No – no thank you,' Harry said. 'I just wondered. Er – if someone cuts in on a conversation, then, from that box, it is from the central telephone exchange that the interruption comes?'

'Cuts in? I imagine so, sir.' The clerk looked down at his ledger. 'Er – you were speaking English, sir?'

'Yes. Is this a problem in Munich? To speak English on the telephone?'

'Of course not, sir! Why should it be? I merely asked. Er – excuse me –' And he bobbed his head and moved a little ostentatiously away to the other end of the desk to look through a ledger there and after staring at him for a long moment, Harry turned and went, taking Lee along with him.

'What on earth was all that about?' she demanded as soon as

they were on the streets and walking towards the park. 'For heaven's sake, Harry, what's happening?'

'I honestly don't know,' Harry said. 'It's just that – as soon as I said to Otto that I hoped there wouldn't be any problems he sort of snapped at me. Not rudely, you understand – just made it clear he didn't want to talk any more and then I sort of stood there before I hung up – a bit longer than usual, I suppose – and this voice asked me if my call was completed.'

'So? It was the operator, I suppose,' Lee said, mystified. 'Why be so bothered about it?'

'Because it spoke English, dammit! I mean, if someone speaking German was using the phone in England, and the operator wanted to cut in, what language would she speak?'

'English –' Lee said slowly.

'Precisely. And what's more it wasn't a girl. Aren't phone operators usually girls? This was a man's voice. It's very odd.'

'What do you think it means, then?'

'Oh, I don't know. It's just that I thought your father was being a bit of an old – well, I guess I thought he was sort of making it all up. All this anxiety about Otto and Lise and being spied on seemed kind of crazy, but now I don't know – I can't help wondering –'

'Oh, Harry! Is it dangerous?' Lee stopped walking and pulled on his arm. 'If Papa was right and there are troubles here for Otto and Lise, could it – I mean, I don't want to be selfish, but I don't want us to get involved with police here or anything –'

'My dear child, don't be so silly!' Harry said bracingly. 'I have a US passport, for God's sake! And you have a British one, as well as being able to travel on mine. Don't be crazy! No one can hurt us. I'm just a bit puzzled, that's all. But stop fretting, for heaven's sake, or I'll be sorry I said anything. We'll see Otto this afternoon, and he'll explain all about it I'm sure. Now come on. We're here in Munich, so let's sightsee. Where shall it be? The place is lousy with art galleries, it seems. What was it that man was telling me about last night after dinner? The Alte and Neue Pinakothek? Whatever that may be – shall we go there and have a look? Let's – so that when we go to see your cousin Otto we can show him we know all about

85

art! He'll be most impressed. Come on, and stop worrying for heaven's sake. Taxi!'

Three hundred miles away, in Cologne, an untidy young man stood in front of a noticeboard at the University, reading a poster with great intensity. He seemed to find it far more interesting than would have seemed reasonable, considering it dealt only with a week of performances of *A Midsummer Night's Dream*, *Romeo and Juliet* and *Anthony and Cleopatra* that were promised shortly by a travelling English company.

10

The gallery was white-walled, cool and very handsome, with chrome spotlights throwing hard strong beams in well-defined patterns on to the paintings placed with elegant spareness at judicious points, and Lee stood looking round with a guarded expression on her face. The pictures were not at all the sort they had been looking at earlier in the day, at the city art galleries where a goodly display of Renaissance saints jostled cheek by jowl with gambolling round-limbed Dutch peasants, and she wasn't sure how she felt about them. There were patterns of paint which showed no recognizable image at all in strikingly bright colours, and large square-limbed people with expressions of great seriousness on their vast flat faces, and even some canvases which seemed to be made up of assorted oddments stuck on rather than paint applied with a brush. Harry looked as mystified as Lee did as he stood there looking about and waiting for the return of the young girl who had been sitting at the desk in the centre when they came in, and who had bobbed her head silently at his request to speak to Herr Damont, and scuttled away like a frightened rabbit.

'I knew he had modern art,' Lee whispered. 'But this is really very modern, isn't it? I rather think I preferred the things we saw this afternoon.'

'I'm not sure,' Harry said. 'Some of these are fun to look at – look at that over there –' And he jerked his head towards a piece of sculpture sitting on an uncompromisingly rough slab of wood. It was of an odd composite creature, part woman, part man, part animal, and attached to various parts of it were ordinary domestic utensils. There was a flat-iron where the head should have been, while egg-whisks acted as feet, and over the clearly bovine buttocks a tattered apron hung, from the pocket of which a screwdriver, on which was impaled the body of a doll, emerged. 'It's weird. But it's interesting –'

'It's horrible,' Lee said with sudden violence. 'I don't like it one bit – I hope he won't be long, I don't like looking at things like that.'

Harry had moved over to the sculpture and was slowly circling it as he stared. 'Look,' he said. 'There's a crucifix here where – well, never mind. It's really rather awful. I'm not sure whether it's meant to make you think it's a woman keeping a religious object singularly safely tucked away, or a man whose sex has turned to religion. Very rum – oh!' And suddenly he laughed. 'Oh, it really is rather clever. It's called "*Kinder, Kirche, Küche*". That's the German for children, church and kitchen, isn't it? What women are for –' And again he chuckled as he stared at the extraordinary melange.

'You have understood perfectly.' Otto Damont had appeared so quietly that neither of them had seen him, and now he stood smiling benevolently, his hands clasped loosely in front of him. 'It is indeed a witty piece, but also, I think, mordant in its comment on the life of so many women. The baby, so damaged by having its mind attacked by the masculine tools of politics, there in her pocket, and the head that is obsessed only with the foolishness of smoothing linen which will of course be crumpled the moment it is used and the close link between eroticism and religious fervour – it is a very candid comment on our world, hmm? The artist is a man of much perception –'

'Herr Damont!' Harry hurried towards him with his hand outstretched. 'How good to meet you – kind of you to spare the time –'

'It is indeed my pleasure, Herr Doktor Lackland. And here is dear Leah?' He turned to Lee and bent his head over her hand as he brushed the back of it with his lips. 'I have not seen you for many years, my dear. You have indeed grown up to be very beautiful. *Ein sehr schönes Mädchen* – a most delightful girl. Lise will be so happy to see you –'

'And I'll be happy to see her. I remember her, just – so kind. She gave me the most delicious chocolate –'

Otto laughed. 'You remember that? We make the best

chocolate in the world here in München, whatever the Swiss may say! You shall have some more. Lise is in a fever of delight preparing dinner for you–'

'This morning, when we talked on the phone, Herr Damont–' Harry began but Otto shook his head at once.

'Let me show you my gallery, hmm? If you like this piece by one of our newer people you will also, I think, enjoy some of the other items I have here, such as–'

'I'd love to see them,' Harry said with ill-concealed impatience. 'But I just wanted to ask you–'

Again Otto shook his head. It was a very handsome head, big for the size of his body, which was small and neat below powerful shoulders, and it was surmounted by a crest of very thick grey hair, and his beard, a neat goatee, was also grey, though he was clearly not all that old. Harry would have hazarded a guess that he was still hovering around forty. He wore pince-nez attached to his coat by a black silk ribbon and looking at him Harry wanted to laugh suddenly; he looked for all the world like a highly intelligent and urbane bison, with that heavy upper body and tapering legs and neat little feet. But Otto wasn't smiling; he was looking at him with a sort of watchfulness as he turned that handsome head and called, barely raising his voice but making it easily heard at the back of the gallery.

'Else,' he said reverting to German. 'You may, if you wish, leave now! I do not expect more people this afternoon, and I shall indulge myself and close early. You be off, my dear. Your young Günter will be happy, I have no doubt, to see you sooner than he expected. Good afternoon!'

After a moment the young assistant who had been at the desk in the centre when they had arrived appeared from the back of the gallery. 'Thank you, Herr Damont. I will go very soon. If I may I will just complete entering the ledger first,' and she scuttled to the central desk and began to work with a great air of industriousness over a large red ledger.

'Thank you,' Otto said after the briefest of pauses, and turned back to Harry and Lee. 'Now, my dear Harry, Leah, let me show you my paintings – ah, I am sorry! I was speaking in German again – my apologies. It is so rarely that I speak

English these days that I sometimes forget to make the transition. Now, let me see, what shall I show you first? Ah, how about this one, then? My good friend Vassily – Kandinsky, you know. The name is familiar to you? No? A pity. He will one day, I am convinced, take his place in the pantheon of the truly great – however strong the present resistance to his style.'

He had raised his voice a little, and was speaking slowly and with great emphasis as though he wanted the girl at the desk to overhear.

'This one is called "Dominant Violet". You see, there is not only paint on this remarkable canvas, but also sand – yes, is that not remarkable and imaginative? I have great hopes that it will be sold to a Paris gallery –'

Harry and Lee, very aware now of the warning that he was giving them to leave all the talking to him in the hearing of the girl so busily scribbling at her desk, stared silently at the painting, an extremely large canvas decorated with multi-coloured shapes and kite-like formations against a background which indeed was composed of sand glued to the surface.

'Very interesting,' Harry murmured after a moment, looking at Otto for some sort of clue as to what was expected in the way of a comment, but Otto seemed oblivious, moving on to the next canvas which showed a just about recognizable female figure of exceedingly heavy proportions and hair as thick and as solid as her body sitting next to a pile of rocks that were, Harry decided, rather softer and more shapely in outline than she was.

'The remarkable Léger,' Otto said. 'Such power, you would agree?'

'Oh, undoubtedly,' Harry said, and began to want to laugh. To be standing with a man who looked like a bison, looking at paintings so modern that he found them ridiculous, in the middle of a German city he knew nothing about while worrying about the possibility of being spied on – the whole thing was ludicrous. And when Otto moved them on yet again to the next painting, which seemed to him to be of a fishing-net set upon end against a sickly green background and surmounted by what appeared to be a fried egg, though it was clearly meant to be the sun, and announced solemnly, 'This is one of my most valued pieces. Max Ernst's "Edge of a Forest",' he could control himself no longer, and began to splutter with laughter.

'Splendid, splendid!' Otto said heartily and slapped him on the back. 'To be so overcome with emotion that all you can do is express it – this is a very healthy thing. To find a young scientist like you to be so sensitive to visual art – it is indeed gratifying to a lover of painting like myself. Now, let me show you some more – I have many canvases here which will please you – many Americans like yourself have spoken warmly of them to me –'

The girl Else gave a nasal cough and Otto turned and beamed at her. 'Quite finished, my dear? Excellent, excellent! Till tomorrow then –' and the girl bobbed her head and went clattering away over the stone floor of the gallery and they stood and watched her go. She turned to close the door behind her and through its glass panels they could see her eyes fixed consideringly on Harry, and then she was gone. As though someone had pricked him with a pin to release the air that was supporting him Otto gave a small sigh and relaxed so much that he seemed to dwindle.

'Ah! Now at last, we can be comfortable! Come, I have schnapps in my office – we will lock up, and we can talk comfortably –' And he went bustling away to his office leaving Harry and Lee to follow him.

'Please, Herr Damont –' Harry began as they sat down in the cluttered room to which he led them but at once Otto made protesting noises.

'Herr Damont, what is this? I am Otto! Cousin Otto if you insist on being formal, but Otto will do. It is such a pleasure to see you both – here we are – schnapps! Here is to better days and happy meetings.'

Obediently they drank and then Harry started again, almost desperately. 'Why did you have to wait till the girl had gone? Isn't she your employee?'

'Of course she is. An expensive one! In this business you need high-quality staff and when I was offered this one, with a good education and an excellent family – her father is an army officer – of course I took her! Then I discover that a little more is known of my affairs outside the gallery than I like, but it is already too late. She is on my staff, so what can I do?'

'Fire her!' Harry said. 'If what you mean is she talks about your business – though why that means you have to be – well – so worried about talking to someone like me when she's around –'

Otto chuckled. 'Oh, it isn't all worry. I use her too, you know. What I was saying about Kandinsky there – it will all go back to them! Perhaps they will even learn a little from what they are told, instead of shrieking about banning such work – but the trouble is –' He sobered then. 'The trouble is, if it was just business I wouldn't have to worry. As it is, there's business and there's business –'

'I don't understand,' Lee burst out. 'What is all this, Cousin Otto? First Harry being all upset over the phone call and now this –'

'Upset over the phone call?' Otto cocked an eyebrow at Harry. 'What do you mean?'

Harry explained as succinctly as he could and Otto's face was expressionless as he listened and then he nodded. 'I see,' he said quietly. 'I had thought as much. There have been times on the telephone I have heard odd sounds – well, there it is. Now I have information. They are listening in. Well, now I can be wise. I do not talk on the telephone of significant matters, that is all!'

'Who is listening, for heaven's sake?' Harry said. 'Who are these people that girl tells what she hears to? Is my father-in-law right? Is it dangerous here for you?'

'Dangerous? It all depends on what you mean by dangerous,' Otto said. 'It is difficult, this I cannot deny. Jews are not popular in Hitler's Germany. It is nearly two years now since Jewish businesses were made the object of boycott, as a legal political action, you know that? But we survive, somehow, while we have some foreign trade. We survive – but we know we are not popular. And most certainly not in Munich. You must remember that here is the home of his party, hmm? It was here ten, twelve years ago, he tried his *putsch*. It was here he made all his plans, had his most important meetings. How

92

can a Jew be comfortable in Munich? Especially a Jew who is –'
he shrugged and stopped and drank some more of the
schnapps, and his eyes slid away from Harry.

'A Jew who what?'

'Who runs a modern art gallery,' Otto said lightly. 'He
doesn't like modern art, the great Führer, you know that? He
thinks it is decadent, disgusting. The only emotion my lovely
pieces arouse in him and his like is hate. They always hate what
they can't understand, these peasants –' And suddenly there
was in his voice a whiplash of sheer loathing that made Lee
actually shrink back. He saw that and laughed, genial again.

'You mustn't worry your little head over such matters, my
dear,' he said. 'Politics are very tedious –'

'And dangerous,' Harry said. 'Look, Otto, my parents-
in-law are very worried about you all. They want you to come
to England. All of you – they've explained it all in their letter,
but they told me to tell you, they want you very much, and
you must say yes –'

'The business needs you, Otto,' Lee chimed in. 'The shops
we've got, you know? Papa and Gideon are always on about
how much they need someone sensible. The Henriques
cousins, frankly, are more trouble than they're worth. With
you to back up Papa and Gideon it'd all be so much better
and –'

'My dears, my dear people!' Otto was holding up his hands
in amused protest. 'This is all too much. You have no idea
what it is you're suggesting! Me, in chemists' shops? I am an
artist! I cannot just – no, we really must stop this nonsense. We
go home to Lise, we meet the children, we have a little more
schnapps, a good dinner – she promised me there would be a
good stuffed carp – the best *gefilte* fish in Munich, Lise makes
– and a rich casserole of the best goose-livers – you'll see, a
good dinner, a little explanation, you won't worry so much.
Now, not another word – I won't have another word till we
are at home and all is *gemütlich* –'

And he meant it. Not another word apart from the merest
frivolity would he say as they made their way out of the
gallery, which he locked with great care, covering the door
and windows with metal grilles which rolled down from

above, and took a taxi out to the suburbs on the far western side of the city where the Damonts lived. And Harry and Lee had to accept his decision; they sat behind the taxi-driver, well aware of his listening ears, tense and anxious, as the wide tree-lined streets of this most picturesque of cities rolled past their windows. They ought to be having fun, enjoying themselves in exciting foreign parts, and all they could feel was a sense of impending trouble.

Otto wouldn't talk seriously even when they reached his home, a handsome very solid house well furnished with heavy German furniture, but enlivened at every turn with more of the modern paintings which he so dearly loved. They met Lise, a small soft woman, rather younger than her husband and who exclaimed over them with great delight and bustled about her kitchen busily, in spite of having two maids to help her there. She clearly intended to serve her guests only with food cooked by her own hands, and nothing Harry could say to assure her they wanted no fuss made had any effect on her. She wanted to fuss and fuss she would.

Otto introduced his children with touching pride, a tall leggy boy of thirteen called Wilhelm, who bowed gravely as he shook hands and kissed Lee's hand, and two small girls of around ten and eleven who giggled a good deal and hid their faces behind their pinafores when Harry spoke to them. They both wore their thick dark hair in pigtails, they both had wide dark eyes and they were both very pretty indeed.

It was a warm and happy family and as the meal was served, and proved to be singularly delicious, Harry at last felt the anxiety that had so filled him since his phone call of the morning begin to ebb away. He'd been fretting over nothing surely, he told himself as he looked round at the children, all very neat and though a little subdued in the presence of strangers, still lively and contented, at Lise, flushed and proud at the foot of her food-laden table and at Otto himself, looking remarkably imperious as he sat in his place with his broad shoulders set squarely to make him look even more powerful than he actually was. How could there be any threat to these delightful, civilized people? It was unthinkable.

But later, when the children had gone to bed, the girls

curtseying shyly before kissing Lee's cheek in parting (they could not be persuaded to do the same for Harry, however much he asked them to) and Willi again bowing punctiliously, they could talk more easily. And then the sense of foreboding came back to Harry in a great wave that made him feel, in spite of the excellent dinner he'd eaten, strangely empty.

'The problem is, my boy, that no one here really comprehends what this Hitler is about. I have known for a long time that he is a disaster for Germany. So, he brings back employment? Pah – such employment can lead to nothing but trouble. He does it at the cost of the worker's soul, he builds his new Reich on workers' blood. I tell them this – or I used to before some people began to be too interested in me – I tell them there is trouble coming, never mind the *Autobahnen*, the new buildings, the price of bread. These things are cherries on a cake full of poison. I tell them they must look eastwards for the real answers –'

'Otto,' Lise said in her soft voice and he stopped short and looked at her and then turned and shrugged his shoulders, making a wry face at Harry.

'You see, Harry? One word from my Lise, and I stop. I have tried all I can to teach her a little political sense, but will she listen?'

'Of course I don't,' Lise said equably, her fingers moving swiftly through her tapestry work. She was clearly not a woman who would ever waste her time in any way, as prudent and thrifty in her repose as in her busy daily round. 'I know the things that matter, and they are making a good family life and not interfering with affairs that are not for you. I have told Otto and told him, he and his foolish Communists, they will get us all into –'

'Hush,' Otto said. 'You should know better, Lise –'

'Oh, it's all right,' Lise said. 'The maids are both out. No one is listening to you tonight – if they ever are! Such a nonsense, my dear! My poor Otto has such notions in his head. He's convinced, he and his political friends, convinced they are being watched by their own servants. Listen to Otto and everywhere he is followed by men in dark suits – such crazy nonsense –'

'I'm not so sure, Cousin Lise,' Harry said and told her of his experience on the telephone that morning, but though she seemed to listen attentively enough, she clearly did not believe it had any significance. Or would not believe—

'This is another reason why we cannot talk of the matters in your father-in-law's letter, Harry,' Otto said. 'Yes, I've read it. While you were playing with the children. I took the time. Believe me, my Lise will not leave Munich. And nor will I. It is kind of Jacob and Dora to concern themselves, but they must be of good heart. This Hitler will not destroy Germany. It isn't possible. Yes, we must be careful here in Munich, because it is his city, or so the man thinks, but for the majority of the good German people, he has no real appeal. They will use him and his buildings and his *Autobahnen* and his marches until they need such things no longer and then they will throw him away and come back to their senses. They will make their trades unions strong again and—'

'And all be good Communists,' Lise said and laughed and folded up her tapestry. 'Now, my dears, a little *Kaffee*, hmm? And I have made some good *Kuchen* you will love, I know. I'll fetch it—' And she got to her feet and made to go to her kitchen.

But Harry stopped her, putting his hand up to hold on to her arm and said earnestly, 'We *are* right, really we are. We see it from the outside in England. It's not good to be a Jew in Germany now—'

'When was it ever good to be a Jew anywhere?' Lise said, staring down at him and Harry looked back at her and then at the others; at Otto, his grey head gleaming in the lamplight, and his own beloved Lee, sitting curled up on the great sofa with her face shadowed, and felt once more the chill of his outsiderhood. For they all had a look of momentary bleakness on their faces, a sort of knowledge of pain and rejection and hate that had never been his lot. It was as though they were sitting there feeling and remembering for millions of others and he shook his head in sudden irritation and said more loudly than he meant to, 'It's stupid to be this way! You'll be safe in England! This Hitler hates Jews, we all know that! So leave his bloody country and come to England and be safe!'

'It's not his bloody country,' Otto said softly. 'It's mine. And Lise's. And our children's. It is our home. We were born here as much as any other citizen of the Fatherland. Why should we leave our home? And can you be sure we will be safer somewhere else? Even in England? If hate is allowed to thrive here, can't it spread and thrive even in your remote island? No, dear Harry and Leah, tell my good cousins we love them, we appreciate their good hearts but we are staying here at home. We will be all right. You will see. There are other forces here as well as National Socialism. Other forces –' And he nodded and then stood up and rubbed his hands together in great anticipation.

'So, Lise,' he said, and now his voice sounded quite different, light and jolly and full of laughter. 'You will bring coffee and cake, and I will bring out my best *Kümmel* – to improve the coffee, hmm? Yes, – we shall be happy and *gemütlich* and think no more of sad matters like politics. We shall drink a toast –' He was busying himself among glasses at his sideboard. 'We shall drink a toast to all of us – and we – especially to us, because today we have happy tidings, hmm, Lise? We shall tell them, yes?' And Lise went a bright pink and laughed and shook her head and went hurrying away to her kitchen as Harry and Lee looked after her, puzzled.

'It is so delightful – ridiculous but delightful!' Otto said as he came back to them bearing a silver tray and small crystal glasses brimming with the clear liquid of the liqueur. 'At our age we should know better, but accidents are accidents. My Lise – it is early days yet, but *was machst du*? We know the signs well enough – my Lise is again to be a mother. At the very end of the year, perhaps early next, a new little Damont for Willi and Hanna and Lotte to play with! So here is my toast – to a better Germany and a beautiful new baby!'

And he raised his glass as he beamed down at them both and Harry smiled and drank and nodded at him.

But he couldn't look at Lee, sitting there on her sofa on the other side of the room. He didn't dare.

The party had been in loud smoky swing for well over an hour by the time Peter got there. He stood at the top of the steps staring down into the crowded hubbub, felt as much as heard the pressure of the exceedingly raucous jazz band grinding out 'Honeysuckle Rose' and cursed himself for being so bloody-minded. He hated parties like this, full of people shouting at each other and posing and performing and jigging about, hated the noise and the superficial chatter and the reek of tobacco and alcohol, and normally wouldn't go within a mile of such an event. But the professor had so angered him that he'd made up his mind he had to go – and now he was here he hated the professor even more cordially than he had that morning.

And heaven knew he'd loathed him enough then. After the official welcome of the company to Cologne by the faculty of literature teaching staff and the interminable drinking of coffee and nibbling of *Kuchen* he had insisted on taking Peter, as head of the company, on a special tour of his department, and Peter, courteous as ever, had felt himself forced to accept. And had trailed behind the pompous little man in his stuffy black clothes as he droned on and on about the marvels of his department, the only slightly lesser marvels of every other department at the University, and above all the vast benefits being heaped on them all by the wise and benevolent Government under which the citizens and the students of this most ancient and important city basked – on and on he'd gone until Peter had thought he'd lose control and would shout his irritation and boredom at him. But he hadn't, not even when at last they were back in the professor's stuffy office.

He had offered Peter another cup of coffee, which Peter had

refused very firmly indeed and then had said, 'And now, Herr Lackland, there is just one point I must discuss with you. About the comportment of your company—'

Peter's brows had snapped together. 'Comportment? I don't think I fully understand you, Professor?'

'It is a simple if tedious matter to explain. We here at the University of course control our students well. We pride ourselves on our good discipline. However, inevitably we have among us our bad elements. It is not always possible to use the sanction of law, since the law is slower than the wisdom of the State, very often. Soon we will have laws to ban such things, but until we have—'

'I am afraid I don't understand what you're talking about, Professor,' Peter said loudly. His patience was thinning rapidly. 'And if you will excuse me I have work to do for this afternoon's performance and—'

The professor had lifted his hand patronizingly, looking at Peter over his rimless glasses. 'You will be patient, Herr Lackland, and all will be clear. I was saying, there is in this University a subversive element who adopt the filth of the Communists and Jews and flaunt in their disgusting cellars the decadent and reeking ordure that they call music. They play this Negro noise, this Jewish scum, and call it an entertainment. We do not countenance such behaviour and soon, you have my assurance, such people will no longer infect the body of this excellent University. But until the law has caught up with morality and decency, we must do all we can to contain the evil as best we can. Now, your company has been, I understand, invited to attend a so-called party of this nature. You will instruct them they are not to attend.'

Peter stared at him, at the stupid flatness of his pallid face, at his pale blue eyes with their scrubby lashes unpleasantly magnified by his thick pince-nez, at the self-satisfied smirk that curved his lips and all the irritation of the morning coalesced inside him to a cold, hard lump. And there was something else, too. The uneasiness that had been haunting him ever since this tour began moved into the lump and announced itself even more loudly for what it was; anger. He was furiously, icily angry and he stared back at the professor, his eyes narrowed, and said in a voice tight with control. 'Oh, I will, will I? I will instruct them not to attend?'

But the professor seemed totally unaware that such a thing as irony existed; he seemed not to notice the expression on Peter's face, the tremble of fury in his voice. He just nodded, the smirk on his lips stretching into a satisfied smile.

'I am delighted you understand, my dear Herr Lackland. You are a wise man indeed not to allow your actors to abuse the hospitality of the Third Reich. Your refusal to have anything to do with these people will be noted and approved. Now I must bid you good day. I have much work to do,' and he nodded coolly at Peter and sat down at his desk and opened a book and buried himself in it. It was as though Peter were no longer there and for a moment he wanted to lean over and take the man by the shoulders and shake him till his complacency fell from him like a dead skin and his head rolled off his shoulders.

But he didn't; he took a sharp breath in through his nose and turned and went, trying to slam the door behind him, but even that satisfaction was denied him for it closed smoothly and softly over the thick carpet on the floor and was delayed at the close by a spring attachment on the jamb and he went at a run across the hallway outside and down the stairs and out into the roadway, needing hard physical action to burn off his fury. How dared he? How dared that jumped-up self-important pipsqueak speak so to him? It was outrageous, it was disgusting, it was – not to be borne.

And he had gone to the run-through before the performance and told the company so. They had been sitting about, smoking desultorily, the drifting cigarette smoke looking absurd as it wreathed itself round the brocades and furs and stiff skirts of their costumes and the vivid make-up on their faces, and they had listened to him attentively as he gave them an edited version of the professor's *diktat*.

'He said that the Government here doesn't approve of Jewish and Negro jazz and for that reason we're not to go to a party we've been invited to. Does anyone know which party he means?'

'I do.' Katy was sitting cross-legged on the top of the piano.

She was playing one of the fairies in *The Dream* and was wearing little more than a fragment of mustard-coloured chiffon over a matching leotard, and her hair was hidden under a pointed yellow cap with a bell on it. As she spoke, her head nodding vigorously, the bell murmured tunefully. 'There was this rather ducky man who talked to me in the garden yesterday, terribly sweet he was, and madly excited we were here – said he hoped we wouldn't get swallowed up by the professors and that the students'd get a chance to talk to us. And I said I thought that was a frightfully good idea, and we'd love to – well, I mean, I was sure none of us'd want to spend our time with those boring old professors, so when he said there was to be this party, and would we like to come I said that'd be too wonderful! And I told everyone else, and some people said they would come and some said they wouldn't–'

She sat up very straight suddenly and stared at Peter. 'I say, this is odd. He said to me most particularly not to tell anyone not in the company we'd been invited, and of course I didn't. And I warned everyone it was sort of private. Who sneaked?' And she looked round the company with a very disapproving air.

'My dear child,' Laura Fountain, a well upholstered and rather mature Hippolyta in Grecian drapes, shot a malicious little glance at Katy, for whom she clearly felt little affection. 'If you think we haven't better things to do than gossip about parties with pimply students–'

'He wasn't pimply!' Katy said indignantly. 'He was rather gorgeous, actually,' and then she grinned. 'Frightfully gorgeous. All upright and hand-kissing and bowing and heel-clicking. Too giggle-making, truly! But I did promise we'd never say–'

'And I'm sure none of us did,' Gregory, the tour manager, said soothingly. 'No one's had a chance, actually. As far as I can tell, Katy's the only one who's actually talked to anyone at the University since we got here. We've only talked to each other – they must have some sort of spy somewhere–'

Peter felt the anger lift in him again and made no attempt to control it. He was luxuriating in it now and he lifted his chin and said crisply, 'Well, however they found out doesn't matter. The thing is, I'd be glad if as many of you as possible accepted the invitation. I'd like to see us turn out in strength. You'll agree, I'm sure, that no damned stuffed-shirt German is going to tell us who we can and can't talk to –'

There had been a murmur of agreement around the group though Laura had muttered fretfully about the fearful boredom of having to spend time with Katy's tiresome little friends – and that had been that; and now he stood staring down at the sea of people in the smoke-filled cellar wishing he was anywhere else at all.

'Peter!' A voice squealed joyously, easily heard even above the noise, and he peered downwards and saw Katy sitting at a table in the corner and waving furiously at him, and after a moment he smiled and went down to join her. However he was feeling it was clear she was having a splendid time, for her face was flushed and her eyes glittered happily as she looked around the group who were there at the table with her. Six young men, all in sweaters and wearing scarves around their necks, clearly trying to look relaxed and *dégagé* but succeeding only in looking rather self-conscious.

'Peter, darling,' Katy fluted, all very theatrical and delighted with herself. '*Do* come and meet some delicious people. Here is Hans and Frederick and Wernher and Erich and – oh dear –' She shook her head in impatience at her defective memory. '– and Kurt and Johann – there! I got them all right!'

There was a concerted move as the six young men all got to their feet and bowed and then sat down again, and Peter too sat down and took the glass of beer that someone pushed towards him.

'It's good to meet you all,' he shouted above the wail of the saxophone, now working hard at a version of 'St Louis Blues'. 'Nice of you to ask us here like this –'

'It is our pleasure, indeed,' the boy called Erich said. 'It is not often we have the opportunity to meet *Ausländers*. These days a university is a place where minds are closed rather than opened – tell me, Herr Lackland, you know the work of our Bertolt Brecht? A most remarkable dramatist and director, did excellent work in Berlin until a couple of years ago when the Government took over the Deutsches Theater –'

'Ah, yes. The Deutsches Theater,' Peter said. 'Max Reinhardt and all that – indeed, a most interesting place –'

'No, you don't!' Katy said. 'You really can't talk about serious things at a party like this! I want to dance – don't you want to dance, Peter? Come on, let's all dance together –' And she got to her feet, pulling by the hands the students sitting on each side of her. They followed her eagerly, clearly captivated by her vivacity, and at once three of the others stood up too, protesting loudly at the injustice of the situation. She should dance with *them*, not with the two she had chosen, and amid much laughter the half-dozen of them pushed their way into the milling crowd of jigging dancers, leaving Peter still sitting at the table with Erich beside him.

'*Danke Gott!*' the young man said. 'I didn't think we'd be able to talk so soon. Listen, Herr Lackland, I must talk to you –'

'Yes of course,' Peter said and drank some of the beer. It was weak and flat and he grinned. 'Bertolt Brecht, you were saying –'

'To hell with Bertolt Brecht,' Erich said softly but violently, and Peter blinked and peered at him in the difficult light. There was a witch ball hanging in the middle of the ceiling, turning slowly and reflecting flashes of light from the fragments of mirror which covered it, and the combination of that and the smokiness and the redness of the only other light in the place gave the boy's face a remote pagan look.

'I'm sorry? What did you –'

'Look, I have to trust you. There's no time to do anything else – all I can do is beg you to say nothing about this, even if you can't help me. Though I hope in God's name you can, and you will. Listen, I'm in trouble – I need to get away from here, fast. You've got to help me –'

'I don't – what sort of trouble? Are you – is it a police matter?' Peter put his glass down. 'I mean, if you've broken the law I can't interfere. Dammit, why should I?'

'The law?' The boy laughed, a sharp little sound, and Peter picked up his glass again, needing to have something to do with his hands but never taking his eyes from the pale face with the very dark eyes blazing from it. All the smoothness and quietness that had been there when they had been introduced had vanished. This boy was in a state of passionate anxiety that was so powerful Peter could feel it moving into his own body.

'The law?' Erich said again. 'What sort of law is it that these Goddammed Nazis make? It's a law to destroy respectable businessmen's shops. It's the law that says it's all right to burn books; the law to break shop windows if they belong to Jews. Don't talk about the law to me. There are laws that demand to be broken because they're evil laws – but I can tell you this much. I haven't robbed anyone and I haven't killed anyone. All I've done is think for myself –'

He leant forwards and took Peter's sleeve in his fingers, and Peter looked down at them and frowned. Long fingers with broken nails, they were restless and very demanding and he wanted to pull away from them. But he didn't. He just lifted his head and looked at Erich's face.

'I'm a Jew,' the boy said. 'They don't know that, the people I'm with here. If they did they wouldn't dare talk to me. But it's worse than that. I'm – I joined the Party years ago, before I knew it'd do any harm – I was just a kid, for God's sake, fifteen. I pretended to be older, so they took me. And now *they* know, I think. If they get to me before I get away they'll – I've got to get away. You understand me? I've got to get away –' His voice dwindled then, and he sat staring at Peter and still gripping his coat so tightly that he could feel the pressure of the cloth against his skin. The pupils of his eyes were very dilated, making them look exceedingly deep and dark and again anxiety crawled in Peter's belly.

'I'm not sure what I can do,' he said. 'I mean, how can I – I'm just a visitor here.'

'That's the point,' Erich said. His voice had lost its power now. He sounded dispirited and tired rather than terrified and he let go of Peter's sleeve as beyond them on the dance floor the music swept into a stomping cake-walk, and the dancers shouted and leapt about more than ever. 'A company like yours – I could join in, who would notice me? I could go back to England with you, be safe –'

'My dear boy,' Peter said, and the pity in his voice was real and very clear. 'Passports and visas and – you can't travel without them and if you have them you don't need to travel with me, surely! If you haven't, I can't take you – can I? They'd arrest the lot of us – not just you. And you'd be no better off. If it's money, of course, I'll help. I do understand how it is here – at least I'm beginning to – and – yes, I can buy you a train ticket. But I can't actually take you with the company. Have you *seen* the travelling documents your Government demands? Everyone with us is listed, every piece of luggage, you never saw so much paper! It's crazy, there's so much. And at every place we go there are the police, checking everyone in, and checking everyone out. It's misery – but it'd be worse than misery if I suddenly had someone extra who wasn't on the list. You must see that –'

'Money?' Erich said. 'What has money got to do with it?' He laughed then, a thick little sound deep in his throat. 'I'm a Jew, remember? My father sees to it I don't go short. We were never rich, but he's still got some cash. Doctors do – and he's only got me, so he's generous – oh, God, if he knew I'd joined the Party –' And he bent his head so that his hair fell in a dark lock over his forehead and hid his eyes. Peter thought, for a moment, that he was crying.

But he wasn't. He lifted his chin after a while and pushed his hair back from his forehead with a clumsy little gesture and Peter thought – he's young. A baby. If he's twenty it's a lot.

'This was my last chance,' Erich said dully. 'When I saw your poster, last month, I thought – if they come soon enough, I can do it. I can get away with them. My English is perfect. Isn't it? Yes, perfect. I'll be an actor, join them. Then I can wear costume, paint my face, be an actor and even if they look at me, even if it's someone who knows me, they won't know it's me. But if I stay here they'll find me. They always do. They took Thomas and Julia last week. They'll take me too. Tomorrow, maybe. Next week maybe, but it won't make any difference when it is. They'll send me away. To one of their camps. I'll die there – if I'm lucky –' He took a deep shuddering breath suddenly, and stood up. 'I was mad, wasn't I? I knew all along I was mad. I'm sorry I bothered you –' He gave another of those formal little bows and went, turning to run up the narrow stairs. At the top of them, he stopped and turned to look back over the iron railings that bounded them, and stared down at Peter, his eyes still very dark and deep, even at this distance. The lock of his hair had fallen over his forehead again, and once more he lifted his hand in that clumsy boyish gesture to push it aside. And then, abruptly, turned away and pushed open the door and went out so quickly that Peter hadn't a chance to say anything. He just sat and stared after him, trying to get his confused thoughts into some order.

The music had stopped, and Katy and her collection of students came trooping back to the table, all talking at the same time and laughing a great deal, and no one seemed to have noticed that Erich had gone. It was almost as though he'd never been there at all, as though all he had said to Peter had been a dream, and he shook his head trying to clear the muzziness that was there.

He stayed at the party only another half-hour. He'd made his gesture at the smug professor, and that was enough. Now he wanted to get to bed, to lie and think as he tried to work out the changes that the productions of *Romeo and Juliet* and *Anthony and Cleopatra* would need to make them fit the rather meagre stage they had been given. And perhaps, eventually, to sleep.

But when he did get to bed in the big echoing room that he had been given he couldn't think about the plays. All he could see was the boy Erich's face, white and tight in the smoky light as he looked down at him from the top of a flight of stairs. When he did begin to drift into sleep the figure of Erich changed, became a pinioned blindfolded shape, and the landing on which he was standing became a gibbet and he leapt into awareness again, sweating and staring wide-eyed at the dim grey square that was the window of his room. Stop it, he told himself. Stop it. Because some crazy boy tried to use you, and you had to refuse him, you feel like this? It's crazy—

But it made no difference. However hard he tried to make himself believe he had done nothing he need feel so bad about, he couldn't. All he could remember was Erich's voice saying

it. 'They'll send me away. To one of their camps. I'll die there.
If I'm lucky –'
  If I'm lucky.

12

It had been a blazing hot day, and the streets were empty and exhausted in the evening sunlight as Harry made his way up the hill from Golders Green station towards his parents-in-law's home. The gardens he passed were dry and breathless, the trees drooping their heads and the grass yellowing in patches where the gardeners' hoses hadn't reached and he was annoyed with himself for being in the same bedraggled state as they were. It would have been easier after all to insist on collecting Lee at home and coming out here together. He would have felt justified in taking a taxi all the way if she were with him, but on his own it seemed like an unreasonable extravagance, though if one came by now with its flag up – and he looked back over his shoulder down the hill, hopefully. But the few vehicles there were went swishing by and there was no sign of any relief, so he went plodding on.

It had been a more than usually exhausting working day, too. He'd seen his handful of private patients in Harley Street, in the rooms he shared twice a week with a chap from the ear nose and throat firm, and then plunged into the hubbub of ward rounds and treatments at Nellie's. With Chris Parker, the registrar who shared the work with him, off sick with an attack of measles he'd caught from his own child, the number of patients Harry had had to see there was doubled, for there was no hope that Dr Hemmingway would share the burden, and he brooded over that as the road curved towards the top of the hill. Lazy swine, he thought. Wait till I'm a consultant, I'll show 'em the right way to behave to junior people. And it's not as though I'm really all that junior after all. Dammit, I do have the beginnings of a practice of my own.

Thinking about the indignities and burdens his chief heaped

on him, he reached the corner of West Heath Drive and turned into it. And then stopped and sat on the garden wall of the first house, staring down at his dusty shoes. This was silly, and he had to admit it; he wasn't really upset by the old man's behaviour at all. He'd done nothing so dreadful, and well Harry knew it. It was just easier to think resentfully about him than to think honestly about Lee, and how difficult, if not impossible, she was making life seem.

Ever since they'd got back from Vienna a fortnight ago, she'd been so remote, so cold and silent that he'd not wanted to go home at the end of a working day and he had to be honest and say he didn't really want to see her now. When he'd left home this morning she'd been in bed still, something she had never been used to do. In the early days of their marriage she always got up and shared breakfast with him, always made him feel cared for, set up for the working day before it started, but not now. Now she didn't seem to care whether he ate or not, whether he left the house happy or not. She just lay curled up in bed, pretending to be asleep – and again he felt a spurt of anger, and fanned it, needing to be annoyed, needing to justify his unwillingness to walk the last few yards to his destination.

But he had to go and after a moment he got to his feet and went the rest of the way. Perhaps, he told himself optimistically, perhaps she really had been tired this morning? After all, the weather was absurdly hot, even for June, and sleep hadn't been easy. Maybe she was entitled to lie abed if she wanted to, and it had been reasonable, too, to say she wanted to come to her parents' house on her own, early, before he left the hospital. They'd been away on holiday and she hadn't seen them since her return from their own journey; it was natural she should want to be with them rather than wait at home for him to collect her and bring her. By the time he reached the front door of number eleven he had almost convinced himself he was right.

But he was wrong, of course. He knew as soon as he saw them. The little maid took his hat and told him the family were out on the terrace and he went out through the shaded drawing-room to find them and stood in the French windows looking at them. Jacob was sitting in an upright chair, as usual, concerned about his backache, and Dora was stretched out on a chaise longue under a parasol, her head thrown back on the cushions in a posture that spoke very loudly indeed of her sense of being aggrieved. How dare the weather be so dreadfully hot that it makes me feel so weary? shouted her little hands, flopping on each side of her chair. How dare the sun make me sweat? cried her feet, propped up on a stool.

But it was Lee he looked at, sitting on a heap of cushions on the ground. She was facing the French windows and he was certain she had seen him arrive, was certain she knew he was standing there looking at her, but for some capricious and totally incomprehensible reason had chosen to pretend she hadn't noticed. Again anger came up in him, pushing his optimism into total oblivion.

'Evening, sir!' he said heartily, and came out to bend over Dora's chair and kiss her hot damp cheek. 'And Mother Damont. Very good to see you. Did you have a good holiday?' If she wants to ignore me, he was thinking furiously, she's welcome. Two can play the same game without any trouble at all. 'You all look very comfortable, I must say –'

'Oh, Harry, *isn't* this weather frightful? I do miss Bournemouth so. It's so bracing there, even in the hottest weather there's a breeze from the sea. But here it's just too much –' And she waggled her hand at him fretfully. 'It was a lovely holiday. Quite lovely, and I'm sorry to be back –'

'I know the feeling,' Harry said and shot a glance at Lee, but she had bent her head and was watching her own finger tracing the pattern of a crack on one of the flagstones beside her pile of cushions. 'London is no fun at all at the moment. Well, sir, are you sorry to be back too?'

'Not in the least,' Jacob said heartily. 'Home's always best as far as I'm concerned. Best food, best beds, best chairs – who needs all that silly rushing about for holidays? Not me – I've told Dora as much, but there – women –' And he laughed fatly and nodded affably at Harry. 'And I'll bet you're glad to be back too, hmm? Lee tells me the visit to Vienna wasn't all that successful?'

'Oh?' Harry said guardedly and looked at Lee. He had asked her, pleaded with her, begged her to confide her distress about her failure to achieve a pregnancy to her mother, to share the pain in an attempt to relieve it, but she had flatly refused and flared up in a rage when he'd suggested he should tell her parents of their difficulties. Had she really told them now, admitted to them how unhappy she was, and why? Surely not. He remembered the floods of tears that had engulfed her after their day spent at Professor Aaronson's clinic in Vienna, the almost hysterical weeping that had occupied her all night because of Aaronson's inability to give her the promise she so desperately wanted, and turned to imagining her telling her father about that – but imagination boggled.

'Your conference, Harry,' Lee said in that brittle high voice he had come to know meant trouble. 'I told Mamma and Papa how disappointed you were by the lack of real skill among these so-called geniuses they have in Vienna. Useless, every one of them, weren't they? No one seemed to know much more about anything than doctors here do.'

'I wouldn't say that exactly,' Harry said carefully, though stung by the contempt for his profession in her voice. 'The trouble is that patients expect us to be miracle-workers, and we're not. We're scientists and –'

'Oh, scientists,' she said. 'As though they were ever any use to anyone – they're just conceited meddlers, most of the time –'

'Well, hardly that,' Harry said as pacifically as he could, using all the self-control he had not to snap at her and tell her how stupid she was being. 'But it was an interesting visit all the same. Have you said what happened in Munich?'

'Indeed yes, and I must say I'm disappointed in Otto, bitterly disappointed,' Jacob said. 'I'd always thought him a wise man, one with commonsense, but he really is being singularly stupid –'

'Stupid?' Harry looked interrogatively at Lee but she was tracing the pattern on the flagstone again, her head bent. 'In what way stupid?'

'To be so complacent about this Hitler – to pooh-pooh our anxieties that way –'

'Hardly that, sir,' Harry said sharply. 'He knows perfectly well what the risks are. As I understand it, he has hopes that the political situation will change, that the German electorate will come to their senses and get rid of the Nazis, but he has a lively awareness of how bad the regime is, I'd say—'

'Of course he hasn't,' Lee said, looking up at last. 'I heard him as well as you did. All he could do was go on and on about his stupid paintings and his politics and—'

'Lee, you're wrong,' Harry said flatly. 'You're quite wrong. I know you're upset — it was a difficult journey in many ways—' He knew he was treading on quaking ground and chose every word with enormous delicacy. 'And it was an emotional affair, meeting Otto and Lise and hearing their — their family news, but all the same you mustn't misunderstand them. They're brave people, perhaps misguided people, but they aren't stupid people. Don't be angry with them for — matters they can't be blamed for.'

'I'm not angry with them,' Lee said with an air of great indifference that did not deceive him in the least. 'It doesn't matter to me if they want to bury their heads like ostriches. We told them of the risks there are in staying there, and you had that affair of the telephone and being spied on yet still they said they wouldn't leave—'

'Telephone?' Jacob said sharply. 'Spies? This is something new. You told me nothing of spies, Leah! What is this all of a sudden, spies?'

'It was a rather odd affair altogether, sir,' Harry said, grateful for something to talk about that took attention away from Lee. 'I thought it was just something that — well, I'll explain.'

And he did, making the most of the story as Dora and Jacob listened with their eyes wide with anxiety and Lee sat silently at their feet, still obsessively tracing her patterns on the stones beside her.

There was a little silence when he'd finished, and then Jacob said heavily, 'I don't like it. It's all that I feared. He really is in some sort of trouble if they listen in on calls that are made to him. It must be bad. Oh, Harry, what do *you* think is the real reason why he won't come? Leah seems to think he's just blinkered, you know? That he chooses not to see the danger he is in, but I can't feel that's all the story—'

'I don't think so either, sir. No, Lee, don't look at me that way. I'm sorry, but I don't. He's in real trouble with the regime, as I understand it, on more than one count. Bad enough he's a Jew, but he also sells the sort of art they hate. They're banning Jewish writers and painters, especially modern ones, and there in his gallery he flaunts the most outrageous sort, and some of it – a lot, I think – by Jewish artists. He makes a living from what he told me by selling to foreigners, especially the French, and that's why so far they've left him alone – he's good for trade – but they don't like him. He told me he had to fit the most expensive of metal grilles over the gallery door and windows, they've been shattered so often. And on top of that I suspect he's involved directly in politics, the way he talked – he didn't actually say, you understand, but I don't know – he made me think of a chap we have at Nellie's. A red-hot Socialist he is, always on about the way the workers are exploited, thinks all medical care ought to be free, you know the sort of thing. Well, Otto reminded me of him. So one way and another, I think he's got problems, and I think he knows it. But now that–' He looked swiftly at Lee and then went on, 'Now they're having another baby. All a bit unexpected, I gather, but there it is. He told me, privately, that she's not too well – Lise. She's often sick and at her age she needs extra care. She's gone forty, you see, so there's an extra risk there–' Behind him Lee took a sharp breath and he hurried on, cursing himself for forgetting to be cautious. '– so travelling a long way right now is out of the question. I think perhaps at the end of the year, when the baby's born, we could talk to them again. We might go back, Lee, what do you say? I could go back to Vienna, see the people there again, perhaps find them a little more useful. It's worth thinking about–'

It was absurd, having this sort of private conversation in the hearing of her parents, having to dissimulate, put on a show, but at least it was possible to talk to her this way, to make concrete suggestions. Ever since their return from Vienna she had nursed her bitter disappointment so closely that any attempt on his part to talk to her about what Dr Aaronson had actually said got him nowhere. She would weep desperately, burying her head in her arms, refusing to listen. This way, at least she had to hear him.

'I was thinking, you see, about what Dr Aaronson said about that – about the patient of mine I wanted his help with. You remember? He said that the blood tests that had been done weren't able to reveal as much about the hormone balance as he needed to know, that he hadn't perfected the sort of test that would show the facts he required, but that maybe in another year or so, he might be able to do more. You remember that? Well, next year, at around this time, we can try again. And go to Munich again, and this time perhaps Otto and Lise will listen to us – realize how much better it would be to come to England –'

'Next year?' Lee said and laughed that tight tinkling little sound he'd come to dislike so much. 'By then, the poor creature'd be past caring about I imagine! Your patient, I mean – she's old too, isn't she? Old like Lise? And you said she's at risk because she's so old –'

'Lise is almost ten years older than my patient,' Harry said sharply. 'There's a hell of a difference between thirty-odd and forty-odd –'

'But can we let Otto and Lise wait another year before getting them out of Germany? Who can know what'll happen next?' Jacob said fretfully. 'I hear such tales – the committee – they report every time we meet of new happenings, new worries. The universities – they're throwing out Jewish students, and people are disappearing all the time and – can they wait that long? That's the worry –'

The little maid came out on to the terrace to tell them that dinner was served, and slowly the party got to its feet and went indoors, as Jacob went on and on about his anxieties for his cousins. He was sure they would agree to leave if only they got the facts he and his committee were collecting. Perhaps there was some other way of getting over to him the dangers of his situation. Perhaps if they sent another messenger – and Harry said nothing, occupying himself picking up Dora's dropped handkerchief and cologne bottle, settling her at her place at table and holding Lee's chair as she sat down. When she had settled, he set one hand on her shoulder, squeezing it gently, but she made no sign of being aware of it, and after a moment he went to his own place and sat down, irritation again replacing his concern for her. Dammit, of course she was unhappy, but why did she have to make it worse by being so vicious to everyone?

And to make matters worse, Dora revived now she was in the cool dining-room and became quite animated and eager for more information about the family in Munich. She wanted detailed descriptions of Wilhelm and Hanna and Lotte and of the house and the food Lise had given them and what sort of furniture they had and a myriad more details beside, and she directed all her questions at Lee. And then, inevitably, started to talk cosily about Lise. How pregnant was she? Did she look to Lee as though she were ailing? It must be very disagreeable, Dora said, to be pregnant in such hot weather as they were having, and at Lise's age too, when really she should be left in peace. Was she sick at all? Looking thinner or fatter? And on and on as Lee became more pinched about the mouth, answering as briefly as she could, and Harry sat and watched her, praying she wouldn't lose control.

But of course she did, though not with Dora. It was when Jacob returned worriedly to his anxiety about Otto's refusal to leave his home that she snapped in a high clear voice, 'Oh, Papa, really! Why should we go on and on about these wretched people? If they want to behave in this silly fashion, it's their affair, surely. I don't care if they and their boring brats disappear for ever, to tell you the truth. We did our best for them, and they saw fit to ignore us. Well, that's their business. I hope now we need never give any of them another thought again!'

After that they talked only of the weather and the state of the garden. There didn't seem much else that could be said.

13

The hot dry summer gave way to a wet autumn that filled the wards of Nellie's with old people with bronchitis and rheumatism and blurred into a wetter winter that made London life more and more uncomfortable. Everywhere the gutters ran deep and fast and cars sprayed their way past disgruntled pedestrians, splashing them to a fury and leaving them with squelching shoes and cold feet and filthy tempers. For Harry, spending more and more time at the hospital or in his own consulting rooms, the weather matched his mood; life was rushed and physically uncomfortable and thoroughly irritating and there wasn't much he could do to alter things, any more than he could alter the weather.

Not that Lee was difficult all the time. There were days, even whole weeks at a time when she seemed to be the girl who had so enchanted him in 1933 when they'd met and fallen in love. She would laugh and tease and make love with enthusiasm, and he would feel his spirits lift as he contemplated the possibility that at last, really at last, she'd come to terms with the way life had treated her, had accepted her childlessness as inevitable and was going to be happy with what she had, her home and her adoring Harry, rather than breaking her heart over what she couldn't have. But then she'd be back where she started, in a flood of tears, or a raging fury, or displaying an icy unpleasantness that was perhaps the worst part of it all.

When she was like that there was little he could do but escape and he would leave her to her sulks and her sobs and flee to Nellie's telling her he was working, but actually spending the time sitting in the junior common room talking to the other men there, sometimes playing a little billiards, or reading, or just dozing in an armchair. He had become one of the fixtures of the place, and though it was noticed – not least by Lewis Lackland who always knew everything that was going on in his beloved Nellie's – no one talked about it. So the young Lacklands rubbed along well enough, if not as happily as Harry had planned they'd be on that June day when they had married eighteen months ago.

Late one evening in January, when Harry was the only occupant of the junior common room and thinking unwillingly that it was time he went home (not a prospect he relished, because Lee was in one of her periodic states of rage; they seemed to come round as regularly as rent day, he told himself gloomily) Lewis Lackland found him there.

He had been operating on an emergency strangulated hernia and was on his way downstairs to the main hall to tell the porter to fetch him a taxi when he saw the line of light beneath the junior common room door, and clicked his tongue against his teeth irritably.

'Extravagant young puppies,' he muttered and put his hand round the door to reach for the light switch and click it off.

At once there was a protesting shout from inside, and Lewis pushed open the door and snapped the light on again.

'Who's that? Hey? Who's that? Oh, Harry! What are you doing here, m'boy? I supposed everyone had gone and left the lights burning, as usual. Terrible waste of money – but here you are, and it must be gone twelve.' He took his watch from his waistcoat pocket. 'Indeed, yes. It's almost half-past! High time you were away – or have you a special case you're watching over?'

'No special case, thank you; sir,' Harry said and stood up to pull his jacket into a tidiness as he stifled a yawn. 'Hadn't realized it was so late, actually. Time I was on my way, indeed.'

'Can I give you a lift?' Lewis said. 'I'm taking a taxi. Where are you going?'

'Home to St John's Wood, sir. Right out of your way, I believe. You live in Bayswater, I think? No, I'll take the underground as usual. Should still be running. Or I'll pick up a cab in the Strand. Sorry to have hung around so late –'

They went down the stairs together and out on to the dark wet street where it had stopped raining at last, leaving the roadway looking washed and gleaming in the lamplight and Lewis stopped on the kerb, pulling his coat collar up around his ears.

'I love this time of night,' he said unexpectedly. 'It's my time. London is given back to me after midnight. During the day she belongs to everyone else, but now it's just she and me. She belongs only to us at night, the people who work all the hours God gives taking care so that others may sleep. Policemen and doctors –'

Across the road a figure appeared, a woman wrapped in a tight coat, and as her heels went clacking along the paving stones from one pool of lamplight to the next, he laughed and added, '– and the girls of course. Always the girls, but there, I suppose they're working too, taking care of people in their own way.'

Harry looked at him curiously, at the heavy profile above the coat collar and the thick hair that crested it and said impulsively, 'Are you happy, sir? Being a doctor, I mean, and – well, just being what you are? Working all the hours God gives, as you said, and then going home late and –' His voice dwindled away.

'Mostly I'm happy,' Lewis said, seeming to find nothing odd in the question. It was as though at this time of night everything was ordinary, even the most impertinent of questions. 'If it's just my work I have to think about, I'm exceedingly happy. And my wife –' The profile moved and softened as he smiled. 'My wife makes me wonderfully happy. My children, on the other hand –' He sighed then. 'They worry me. But then, whoever expects anything to be unalloyed pleasure? Certainly not me. I've learned the hard way that anything worth having is liable to make you miserable sometimes. What about you?'

'Sir?'

'Are you happy?'

'I don't know,' Harry said without stopping to think and then stood and contemplated his answer in some surprise. 'I really don't know. Does that sound strange?'

'Not in the least. Your wife pregnant yet?'

'Sir?'

'My dear boy, it's a clear-enough question. Is your wife pregnant yet? Have you solved that little problem you told me about?'

Harry cursed under his breath; he'd almost forgotten he'd ever had that discussion with the Old Man and now here he was making a nuisance of himself. 'Er – no,' he said carefully. 'Not really worried about it, though, so you really needn't –'

'Pah!' Lewis made a soft little noise at the back of his throat. 'Of course you're worried about it. I know what worry is, m'boy. It doesn't just go away, you know. Not unless the problem does.' And he lapsed into a little silence, staring down the road towards the corner round which his taxi would appear when the porter, who had gone out to find it for him, had succeeded in his hunt. 'As well I know. You've met my family, I think?'

Harry was bewildered by the suddenness of his changes of tack and opened his mouth again to say, 'Sir?' but Lewis, fortunately, didn't wait for an answer.

'Stupid of me. Of course you have. We all came to your wedding. I remember it perfectly. Well, now, next week, we're giving a small dinner party for the first night of my younger son's new play. He's doing this production at the Shaftesbury Theatre for Letty, you know, and it promises to be an interesting one. It's by that Scottish fella – you know the one I mean. Bridie, James Bridie. Called *The Black Eye* and Peter thinks it'll do well. Bring your wife to dinner, and join us all at the theatre. We'll be a small party, just family, you know. Oh, and Letty of course. Her young niece is in the play – we'll meet her later. It'll all be a bit theatrical. Make a change for you from medicine all the time. Ah, there's the cab at last. Old Webb must be losing his touch – used to be able to get a cab in under five minutes whatever time of day it was. Goodnight, my boy. Remember – next Tuesday, dinner at six-thirty sharp, if we're to get to the theatre in good time. We'll look forward to seeing you both.'

And he climbed into the cab, helped there assiduously by old Webb, resplendent in blue serge and brass buttons and a peaked cap bearing a purple ribbon and a badge on which the words 'Queen Eleanor's Hospital' were clearly emblazoned, as Harry stood and watched him go.

He was uneasy, very uneasy. Could the Old Man be trusted to say nothing to Leah about their problem? He'd offered to help once before, Harry remembered, and it hadn't been easy to convince him that such interference would be unwelcome. Damn, he thought, damn, damn, damn! It ought to be possible either to refuse the invitation or to tell the Old Man in no uncertain terms to keep his tongue between his teeth, but he was, after all, the Old Man, and as such not to be treated like other people.

We'll have to go, Harry told himself dispiritedly as he made his own way to the Strand and a search for a cab of his own. But I shan't look forward to it one bit.

The rehearsals were going exceedingly well, somewhat to Peter's surprise. It had started under an ill omen, this production, with the last play they'd done at the theatre failing unexpectedly after only fifty or so performances, and this one needing to be rushed in in its place; but the casting had gone smoothly, and he'd managed to get a fine actor to play the lead, and there was a nice part that young Katy was perfect for, while the author was blessedly professional and hadn't fussed unduly about the inevitable cuts and changes needed for a first production of a new piece of work. So now he sat in the middle of the stalls watching the last of the technical run-throughs and feeling reasonably content.

It was good to feel that way; for a long time after their return from the German tour he'd been unaccountably depressed. The tour had gone well enough, and had even shown a profit larger than they'd hoped, and at first he'd had mixed feelings about that. They had done so well, with packed auditoria for every performance, not because of their own merit, but because the universities had all made a great deal of effort to ensure their success. Clearly they had seen a certain cachet in having a tour of a Shakespeare season from an established English company, and had displayed the visit in all their newspapers as an example of the sort of healthy cultural exchange that Hitler's government was encouraging. They were fêted everywhere as splendid colleagues of the Third Reich, and that had been enough to fill out the box-office accounts nicely.

Perhaps it was that that had depressed him, Peter had thought, but had to realize it wasn't. A successful tour was a successful tour and something to celebrate not moon over. No, the fount and origin of his discomfort had been that night in the first of the German cities they had gone to. Over and over again he found himself thinking of the boy Erich in Cologne, worrying about what had happened to him, and what more could be done to help him; and then, on an impulse, had talked to Katy.

She had joined Letty's stable of young actresses as soon as the tour was over, with no mention being made of any return to drama school. She had done well on the tour, playing small parts with a good deal of zest, and a surprising degree of restraint when it was called for. She had shown she could take direction, that she had a natural talent for speaking the poetry of Shakespeare as well as a lively sense of comedy, and there was more than enough work for her in some of Letty's peripheral companies. Now, with *The Black Eye* in rehearsal she was in her element; a small but showy part and extra duties backstage as assistant stage-manager meant she was kept busy and was also learning. So she went about the place full of energy and laughter and generally made the people around her feel tolerably good – except perhaps for the older actresses, who rarely contemplated younger ones with anything but the liveliest of disfavour.

She had been working late one evening over her costume; she had wanted extra trimmings on it, for she was playing a village girl, and the wardrobe mistress had been too busy to deal with it, and had gladly accepted when Katy offered to do her own sewing. Now, she was sitting in the big shared dressing-room the lesser characters used, the heap of figured blue cotton on her lap, stitching away as diligently as a tailor. Peter had seen her as he went past the open door and on an impulse had stopped and come in.

'Hello, Katy. Have you managed to learn those extra new

lines yet – the ones Mr Bridie gave you yesterday?'

'Of course I have!' Katy said and bit off the thread with which she was working. 'I love learning lines – listen –' And she gabbled them off like a clockwork train rushing round a tiny loop of line.

Peter laughed. 'We'll need more expression than that – no, donkey, not now. Tomorrow. You're called for the morning rehearsal, aren't you? Yes, I thought so – tomorrow will do. Katy, I've been meaning to ask you – have you kept in touch with any of the people you met in Germany on the tour?'

'Oh, yes!' she said and lifted a glowing face. 'It's such fun! I love getting letters, and it's so boring if they only come from Haworth, though of course it's lovely hearing from the family, but now I get letters from everywhere, and all I have to do is send the merest scribble back and lo and behold, they write again! I never thought having pen-friends could be so much fun –'

'Those boys in Cologne – do you remember? The party the professor said we weren't to go to – do you write to them?'

'Of course!' she said. 'Well, to one of them, anyway. Hans Untermann, he's the one. He's rather sweet. He's studying law and he says I'm his inspiration. Too killing, isn't it? Me, as wicked as they come, an inspiration to a lawyer!'

'Not that wicked,' Peter said. 'Just cheeky. Ah – does he say anything about the others?'

'What others?'

'The ones who were there at that table the night of the party. I seem to remember one called Erich –'

She wrinkled her brows, frowning. 'I don't really remember. Let's see – there was my Hans of course who's got such a silly crush, bless him, and there was one called Johann, wasn't there, and Kurt and Wernher – I remember them because they sounded like a shop in Oxford Street, you know? Kurt and Wernher, linen drapers or something – oh, and wasn't there one called Freddy? I can't remember an Erich –' She closed her eyes to concentrate. 'Though you're right, there were six chaps with us, weren't there? But I can only remember those five. I suppose he just went away – anyway, Hans never mentions him – shall I ask him? Why do you want to know?'

'It doesn't matter,' Peter said easily and stood up. 'I was just wondering. He talked about the Deutsches Theater, seemed interested. That was all –'

At once Katy's face cleared. 'Heavens, yes, I do remember that one! Madly serious sort, wasn't he? The only one who paid me no attention at all – I dare say that's why I managed to forget him. I'm awfully vain, aren't I? Well, I don't know what happened to him. He seemed to wander off somewhere. I dare say he went to find someone else to be serious with. It was fun that night, wasn't it? One of the best nights we had. Not that I liked all the places we went to all that much. It all felt –' She made a little face. 'I don't know. People seemed to be looking over their shoulders all the time, didn't they?'

'I know what you mean,' Peter had said and then had changed the subject to talk of the play and that had been that. Or so he had thought.

But a week later Katy had leaned over the back of his seat as he sat watching the first act runthrough and said, 'Peter – you remember you were asking me about that boy in Cologne?'

'What about him?'

'Well. I was writing to Hans that night anyway, and it was something to write about – to tell you the truth I like getting letters but it's frightfully boring having to write them, there's nothing really to tell them about except the play and they're not the sort to be all that interested – anyway, I asked him and he's written back today, the oddest letter. Would you like to see it?'

'Please,' Peter said. 'Can't read it now – I must concentrate on what's going on. But if you don't mind leaving it with me I'll give it back to you as soon as I've read it –'

'Don't bother,' she said cheerfully. 'You'll see why when you read it –' And she'd gone back to her place backstage and left him thoroughly uneasy, so much so that he stopped the run-through after the first act and sent the cast off for an early tea-break, so that he could read the letter.

It was indeed an odd one; crisp to the point of rudeness.

'*Gnädiges Fräulein*,' the boy had written. 'I am in receipt of your letter of last Friday. I cannot say what has happened to the person of whom you enquired. He is no longer of our faculty. We have no interest in such people. It is better, I think, if you do not write again.'

And that was all. He stared at the curt lines and refolded the letter and took it back to Katy and she shrugged as she accepted it from him.

'Odd, isn't it? And he was supposed to be so taken with me! Ah, well, that's the way it is, I suppose. Distance doesn't lend enchantment so much as I thought it did – not that it matters. I've got some other people still writing delicious letters from Stuttgart and Paris, so I'll settle for them. I say, Peter, about that entrance in Act Three, you know, after the Vicar says that bit about the morning service–'

It had confirmed his fears, his conviction that in some way the boy Erich had been in real need when he had talked to him that night and that he'd let him down badly, but oddly enough rather than adding to his depression the fact that he now knew – or believed he knew – that it hadn't all been his imagination, made him feel better. It was as though it had been the oddness of the episode that had upset him, rather than the real situation that lay behind it. So, now, as the rehearsals of *The Black Eye* brought them closer to the first night, he was able to concentrate fully on work and feel his depression lift.

But it was replaced by something else. An increasing awareness of the fact that he couldn't spend all his time and energy on just his job, enthralling though it was. There was a bigger world beyond his theatre and it needed attention, he told himself. I must read more newspapers, keep an eye on what's going on. Some time soon I think I'll have to get more involved than I have been.

But first there was the first night of *The Black Eye* to think about.

14

It was rare indeed that Miriam allowed herself to be ruffled. She could become agitated when things didn't work out precisely as she wanted, and was quite easily reduced to tears, but she had never been one to become irritated and show it, yet tonight she did. And that made Harry feel a great deal worse.

'But my table!' she almost wailed when Harry, taking his coat off in the hall, explained in rather halting words that he was alone because Leah had been stricken by the most frightful headache and sent her apologies. 'I mean, I do understand, of course, but I wish you could have let me know sooner –' And she had gone hurrying away to tell her parlourmaid to remove one setting at table and arrange it for nine rather than ten as neatly as she could. But Lewis had just laughed and taken him by the elbow and led him into the drawing-room.

'Bless her, she's got a bad attack of nerves for Peter. She's more worried that he is, and it really is absurd. It's by no means his first West End production, and even if he doesn't have a huge success it won't matter unduly. I mean, he's well established in his business, so he won't come to any harm. But there, mothers – she gets more and more anxious about him rather than less –' And he grinned as cheerfully as though he himself never worried at all about his children, though he was as tense tonight as Miriam was, if the truth were known. But he hid it better and Harry was unaware of it, and could concentrate on his own problems.

Which today had been considerable. For some time now Lee had seemed more at peace with herself, but today she had woken to discover that this was yet another month in which she wasn't pregnant. Sometimes it seemed to Harry that their entire life revolved around the waxing and waning of her cycle and though he sympathized he was finding it more and more difficult to display as much concern as she needed when disappointment followed disappointment. Today he had been in a genuine hurry to get to the hospital; because they were dining tonight with the Old Man, and the injunction to be in good time had been repeated in a note from Miriam confirming the invitation, he had arranged to start his day's work early, instructing his few private patients to be in Harley Street well before nine.

So, when she had emerged from the bathroom with her face white and tight he had ignored the warning signs and kissed her briefly and fled, not asking her how she was, or showing any awareness of her misery. It was small wonder that by the time he got home she had worked herself into a state of near collapse with a very real headache born of the hours of furious weeping in which she had indulged.

But there had been no possibility of refusing to go to Bayswater himself. An invitation from the chief of staff of Nellie's to one of its more junior doctors was like a summons to the judgement seat. Bad enough that one of them was going to fail; he couldn't fail too, and he had tried to explain this to Lee, but she had been unable or unwilling to see his point and had flown into as spectacular a rage as any as he had ever seen. Now, standing in Lewis Lackland's drawing-room and drinking his pre-prandial sherry, he felt himself filled with an uneasy mixture of anxiety about Lee and relief to be away from her. It didn't augur well for the evening.

But in fact it turned out to be a very pleasant one. The rest of the guests arrived together to create a flurry of excitement in the middle of which Miriam revolved blissfully, quite forgetting her irritation at the damage to her neatly arranged dinner-table. Emilia, full of easy chatter and as relaxed as it was possible to be, came into the drawing-room first, followed by Max, and Harry at once fell into eager conversation with him; his own speciality might be surgery and therefore a million miles away from Max's practice as an alienist, but for all that he had a lively interest in matters psychological, and Max was a very agreeable man to talk to, and when Johanna and Jonty came in after them, closely followed by Peter and Letty, he felt as comfortable as he had for a long time.

He was lucky indeed to have so many agreeable relations here in England, he told himself, as they all went in to dinner; they could have been the most dismal of stuffed shirts, as so many English people were thought to be at home in Virginia, but these people were far from that. They were his friends as well as blood kin and he settled himself next to Letty at table with great satisfaction.

She looked searchingly at him as the soup was served and asked casually where Lee was, and when Harry murmured that she had been felled by the most severe of headaches accepted it and said no more; but she had noticed the tension round his mouth and the incipient line between his brows and worried for him; he was clearly not as happy as he might be, but she knew better than to pry. People's pain, in Letty's world, was a deeply private affair. You never asked about it or expected it to be shown to you, just as you never displayed your own. So she talked instead of the play they were to see, and how high were her hopes for it.

'It's a first West End opportunity for Katy, too,' she said. 'She did well for Peter on the European tour I sent out, and she's entitled to her chance. Tricky when it's a member of the family, of course, but I think the company realizes her talent is real. No one could really accuse us of nepotism on this—'

'I'll look forward to meeting her,' Harry said politely, not really all that interested in the girl but aware of Letty's close attachment to her.

'Oh! I thought you already had?' Letty said. 'Ah, well, then that will help. You must let me know what you think of her performance – your opinion should be worth a bit more because it won't be coloured by previous knowledge. She's a beguiling little wretch, and I sometimes fear that even my judgement is overturned a little by her charm.'

'I doubt it,' Harry said. 'If I learned one thing about you in that year I lived with you, it's that your judgement is as sound as the most melodious of bells. You're not one to have the wool pulled over your eyes—' And he sounded bitter for a moment, and Letty looked sharply at him. But her discretion won, as usual, and she said nothing. Whatever it was that was worrying him was his affair. Perhaps, one day, if he was in need of a confidante he would remember her and how fond she was of him. If he didn't, well – again that had to be his affair. And she turned to talk to Peter on her left as Harry politely turned the other way to talk to Emilia.

The street outside the theatre was humming when they arrived in a string of taxis, and Harry felt his spirits lift absurdly as he climbed out and helped out first Letty and then Emilia, who had travelled with him. Busy and exciting though his own life was in many ways, it was not one normally spent under the glare of spotlights and to arrive at a glamorous first night like this, and be shepherded along the narrow pathway that had been cleared between the people who stood craning and pointing and gasping over the famous faces they saw, was a rather heady experience. He tried to imitate Letty's nonchalance, for she sailed into the theatre with her head up, apparently completely unaware of the staring eyes, but he couldn't, any more than he could share Emilia's amusement at the absurdity of it all. He found himself walking awkwardly, stiff-armed and jerky, just as he had when he had first walked on the hospital wards as a raw medical student. He felt dull and stupid and wished, suddenly and very powerfully indeed, that he was at home with Lee. Perhaps it would be all right now to sneak away, go back to her – but at that point they arrived under the awning of the theatre and Lewis seized him by the arm.

'Come along, m'boy. We have our seats in the dress circle, and there are drinks set aside for us in the bar up there. Come along, now, hurry along – ah, Emilia, there you are! Now, my dear, you too! And Johanna – up to the dress-circle bar with you –'

He hustled them all along, for all the world like a mother hen with a set of particularly unruly chickens, and the moment for escape passed and Harry lifted his chin with a stubborn air as he shrugged out of his overcoat. Damn it, he was here now; whatever Lee would say when he got home, he might as well stay and enjoy the play –

He did quite enjoy the first act, though the play seemed to him to be a bit wordy, but settled in his seat after the first interval feeling a little sleepy. He'd had sherry before dinner, and good claret during it and in the circle bar there had been a couple of bottles of champagne set aside for them as the management's special guests, and he had had his fair share of that. So, as the play wound on its way he found his eyelids slipping a little, and he slumped low in his seat, hoping to settle his shoulders against the back so that if he should happen to doze off, his head would remain firmly upright rather than obviously falling to one side or the other. It was a trick of posture he'd learned long ago to help him through the duller lectures he'd had to attend; it was surprising how easy it was to look as though you were wide awake when you were actually well settled in slumber.

And fall asleep he did, and dreamed, an odd jumpy little dream in which he was on a train and a girl was chattering at him, and he woke with a start as a little ripple of laughter went round the theatre and found himself staring down at the stage. He had completely lost track of the action; when he'd fallen asleep there had been the leading actor there together with a rather serious older woman, both droning on about something to do with a past experience they had shared, but now the stage was much busier. There was someone in a parson's outfit and a man in the heavy clothes and dirty boots of a gardener or a farmer, and a girl in a blue gingham dress trimmed with ribbons. It was something she had said that had made the audience laugh and so wake him and as he stared at her she spoke again in a rather obviously bucolic accent and he felt an odd lurch of recognition. He'd seen her before somewhere, and couldn't think where, and he eased himself more upright in his seat and fumbled for his programme.

Someone on the stage said the name of the character being played by the girl in gingham; Ellen; she was playing the part of an Ellen and he peered at the close-printed pages in the half-light and found her. Ellen Rushbrook, it said, played by Miss Katy Lackland, and he nodded with satisfaction. That must be why he thought he'd recognized her; a quirk of family likeness –

Yet as the scene ran on he became more and more convinced

that it wasn't that. This girl in gingham with her hair in tight pigtails that hung over her shoulders and make-up that made her particularly rosy and countrified was familiar for another reason and he sat and stared at her the whole time she was on stage and frowned, struggling to remember.

And then suddenly, did. She turned her head quizzically to look at the main actor, now on the far side of the stage, and laughed, a soft little gurgle of a sound and even as the audience laughed too, clearly finding her delightful, recollection washed over him like a sea wave and he actually felt himself get red, and was grateful for the darkness.

He spent the rest of the play in a stage of great confusion. That little adventure on the Flèche d'Or had been amusing, no more, he told himself, refusing to remember the way the girl had lingered in his memory for several days after the journey was over. She had been nothing to him; a pleasant half-hour spent foolishly in a train, no more. It was perfectly natural that he should have to struggle to remember her now. So why be in such a fever of excitement because he was going to meet her afterwards? Why be so impatient for the play to end so that he could go round back stage and greet her as 'Bianca Coolidge'? And he grinned in the darkness as he teased out her pun; Bianca was the sister of Kate in *The Taming of the Shrew*, of course; that was the origin of that, but why Coolidge? And then in his mind's eye saw a book of his sister's lying on the floor in their schoolroom. *What Katy Did* by Susan Coolidge, and again he grinned, delighted with himself and impatient to tell her how easily he had cracked her alias.

But it took longer to get to her than he had hoped. By the time the crowds in the front of the theatre had thinned out enough to let them reach the entrance it was eleven o'clock, and Lewis stood on the kerb with his watch in his hand, waving imperiously for the few available taxis, and trying to organize his group sensibly to be taken home. Letty had vanished, murmuring something about going to find Peter, who had not been with them at all since they had arrived (they had all taken it for granted that he had spent the evening backstage with his actors) and the seven of them hovered a little as Lewis again waved vigorously at every passing taxi, whether it had its flag up or not.

'Er – won't we be going round to talk to them?' Harry ventured as Lewis, scowling, saw yet another taxi swish past him with a fare already ensconced.

'Go round? What for?' the Old Man grunted. 'I've had enough of that sort of thing, m'boy. Peter's dragged me to more of these wretched first nights than I care to count. Just a lot of hubbub and smells round there – don't want to bother with that–'

'Well, sir –' Harry began and then at last a taxi came along without a fare, and at once Max shot out into the street and made it stop.

'Look,' Jonty said, speaking for the first time that evening. 'You go with your parents, Johanna. I'll find my own way home – want to drop in at the club anyway–' He seemed animated for a moment and Johanna, standing beside Harry, opened her mouth to say something, but he was gone, pushing through the knots of people standing gossiping on the kerb and leaving her standing very still and straight as Max returned to shepherd them all towards the waiting taxi.

'Now, let me see,' Lewis fussed. 'You girls – Miriam, Jo, you sit there, and Emilia, my dear, can you manage too? Excellent, excellent. That leaves the two jump seats for Max and me and you, Harry, can sit–'

'No need, sir,' Harry said hastily, pushing him gently so that he had to get into the cab. 'I'll manage well on my own. Take the tube, you know. Thanks for the evening, absolutely delightful – thank you so much–' And he stepped back and Lewis poked his head out of the taxi window and called, 'All right, m'boy, all right. See you at Nellie's in the morning. Wish your wife better for me–' And the taxi was gone leaving Harry standing staring after it, a little chastened by Lewis' reminder about Lee. He ought to go home, immediately, tell her he was sorry, soothe her, hug her, perhaps make love to her to reassure her that all was well–

'Damn,' he said beneath his breath and turned sharply to walk along to the alley at the corner where the little sign, just illuminated by a dull lamp, said 'Stage Door' and a small disembodied hand pointed the way with an elegant forefinger.

Inside the stage-door keeper sniffed unappetizingly at him when he asked to see Miss Lackland and looked suspiciously at the card which Harry gave him, but seemed reassured by the sight of both his name and his doctorate and went slap-slapping away down the cold stone corridor to lead him to the dressing-rooms. People hurried by, looking oddly exotic in spite of the fact that they wore ordinary clothes and he thought – actors; they always look different. Not dull like doctors, and he wished heartily he was one of them. An odd thought and one that he had never had before, but then, tonight was odd altogether. To have an adventure on a train had been odd enough. To find himself following it up in this fashion was even odder.

The stage-door keeper stopped outside the door and lifted his hand to rap on it, but suddenly Harry said, 'Just a moment, I want to write a note on that card,' and took it from him and scribbled on the back, 'May I see you? Poor Pip,' and thrust it back into his hand, together with a half-crown which seemed to cheer the old man considerably.

Harry stood outside in the chilly corridor waiting for him to reappear, for he had vanished inside in response to the muffled answer that had greeted his knocks, his overcoat over his shoulders and his hands thrust into his trouser pockets. He was whistling softly between his teeth as he leaned against the wall, taking in the atmosphere of the place. It smelled strange but not unpleasantly so; a mixture of soap and Jeyes Fluid and make-up and a fishy sort of glue smell and just a hint of cats. It was stuffy and the electric lights spaced widely along the ceiling were dull and threw a rather sickly glow. It all should have been depressing but it wasn't; he felt filled with a huge and very enjoyable excitement and more alert and alive than he'd felt for ages. He had no idea what he expected would happen when he saw her again, how she would react, and for a moment that didn't matter. The only place to be in the whole world was here outside a dressing-room door in the grimy back reaches of the Shaftesbury Theatre, waiting, wanting, and not knowing what for.

The door opened and he turned his head sharply, but it was only the old man who came out. He nodded gloomily at Harry and without a word sniffed again, even more unpleasantly, and went shuffling back the way he had come leaving Harry staring after him.

And then suddenly, there she was, standing behind him. He felt her there and whirled to look at her.

She was wearing a tight black coat with a fur collar which was pulled high under her pointed chin. There was a small tightly fitting fur hat to match it on her head, and she peeped out at him between the two thick layers of fur looking as bright-eyed and eager as though she were in fact the creature on which the fur had grown.

'Well, well,' she said and giggled. 'Dr Haversham Lackland, my very own cousin! And here was me thinking my Poor Pip was a lawyer! I wasn't all that wrong though, was I? How did you find me? And how is it you didn't find me sooner? And have you been thinking about your Bianca? I do hope so – because I've thought a lot about you –'

15

He didn't mean to have an illicit affair, and indeed, if anyone had suggested he was doing so he would have denied it most indignantly. How could anything so amusing, so innocent, so light-hearted, be labelled with so portentous a word? Yet that was how he came to think about it deep in the secret recesses of his mind.

It had been quite extraordinary how they'd been able to pick up precisely where they had left off. It was as though they were still on the train. She had been funny and outrageous yet quite unthreatening as she led him along the dingy corridors and back to the stage door chattering all the way. She seemed to find nothing at all strange about their meeting again, but he was most struck by the fact that they were actually cousins, and had the same name.

'Isn't it delicious?' she crowed. 'Too ridiculous for words! There we were inventing absurd aliases for ourselves and all the time – well, it's too screamingly funny! Wait till I tell the others and –'

'Oh, no,' he said at once. 'Don't tell anyone else. About the Flèche d'Or, I mean. People can be so – I'd really rather you didn't –'

'Oh. All right,' she said after a moment's pause but quite sunnily. 'I dare say you're right, actually. Secrets are so much more amusing – now, are you coming to the party with me?'

'What party?'

'The first-night party, of course, silly! There's always a first-night party – everyone drinks a lot and we all have to come down and –'

'Come down?'

She sighed with a most exaggerated air. 'Oh, dear, you

people who aren't in the business – my dear old Pip, acting is frightfully hard work, you know! You have to get yourself all sort of worked up, and imagine you're someone you're not – I mean, I'm not a soppy country yokel by nature, am I? Yet all evening I've had to be just that, and it takes a lot of sort of inside fire to make it happen. You end up feeling as high as a kite and then you have to come down. You see?'

'I see.' He grinned at her. 'Adrenalin.'

It was her turn to look puzzled and he took a good deal of pleasure in explaining to her the medical basis of her need to 'come down', telling her in a slightly lordly manner about hormones and the effects of arousal as she stood there in the street staring up at him from beneath her fur hat and looking suitably impressed.

But when he'd finished she laughed again and said, 'Well, that's as may be, dearest Pip. All I know is that there's a delicious party waiting for me, and I'm going. Will you come too?'

For one mad moment he had actually considered accepting but then commonsense had stepped in and he'd shaken his head.

'I can't. I must go home. To my wife –'

Quite what he had expected her to say to that he wasn't sure; he'd just known he must tell her, and tell her soon. But her reaction startled him, for she showed no concern at all. It was as though he'd said something about having a dog or a canary in a cage to go home to; it was a fact that was marginally interesting but of no real relevance to her.

'Oh, well, another time perhaps? I dare say it is rather late for you – people like us, in the business you know, are used to being up half the night and sleeping all day, and of course for you that would be awful wouldn't it? – but we must meet again, dear Pip, mustn't we? It would be too silly to disappear again as we did on that train! Will you give me tea one afternoon? I adore going to tea at the Ritz. Tomorrow? Then we can read the notices for the play together and if they're nasty you can comfort me and if they're nice we can show off like anything to the other people there! Won't that be fun? I'll see you there at half-past four. Don't be late, now – I can't abide it when people are late. Goodnight, Pip–'

And she had stood on tiptoe and kissed his cheek and her lips and the fur of her hat had brushed his skin together so that he hadn't been quite sure what he had felt of her, and what of her setting; it was as though the reality of her wasn't there at all somehow. The frame was clearly visible but the picture it contained was shadowy and tantalizing. He wanted to know more of it, more of the real her–

But she had gone then, running away down the street towards the corner, turning and waving cheerfully as she reached the faint glow thrown by the dull little lamp on the wall there and then was gone, leaving him to make his own way home thoughtfully and in a state of considerable confusion.

He couldn't, of course, meet her for tea tomorrow. He'd have to send a message to her somehow, to say so – did she still live with Letty? Perhaps she didn't; perhaps she had a flat of her own now, he told the blank window of the tube train as he sat there swaying his way back to St John's Wood, making excuses to himself, and pretending he wasn't. If she had her own flat, that meant he didn't know how to find her so he couldn't not keep their appointment, could he? He'd have to go to the Ritz, wouldn't he? It would be too rude, too uncousinly not to. And anyway, where was the harm? He wasn't doing anything he shouldn't – he'd tell Lee, of course he would–

But when he got home Lee was asleep, worn out with the exhaustion of her headache and further tears all evening, and somehow in the cold light of the next morning it didn't seem a reasonable subject to start talking about. She was calmer, then, had got up to share breakfast with him and though she looked puffy-eyed and dull and far from her once cheerful self, was so patently trying to make amends for her behaviour of the night before that all he could do was respond to her as she wanted; with affection and gentleness. To tell her he had arranged to have tea that afternoon with a pretty girl cousin would hardly have been fair–

And that was how it all started. Once they had shared that first tea-party, eating cucumber sandwiches and cream cakes and poring over the notices for the play (which had been lukewarm, though she personally had some approving comments) and heaping on the heads of the hapless critics and their editors the nastiest fates they could devise, it had seemed the most natural thing in the world to repeat it. And sometimes to have late suppers after the play, and even occasionally to meet in the mornings to drink coffee in Bond Street and help her choose new fripperies at the shops there.

He hadn't meant to be devious, to hide his jolly friendship from Lee, but once the first meeting had taken place and he hadn't told her, it became impossible to explain. To say offhandedly, 'Oh, I'm squiring Katy Lackland around town these days. She's an actress you know, rather pretty and very young –' was an impossibility. So he didn't say it.

But he still went on with the meetings and they became more and more delightful to him. They were worth the effort of rearranging his appointments and his ward rounds so that he could get away to be with her for an hour. It was worth working late at the hospital several evenings a week so that he could finish just about the time the curtain came down on *The Black Eye* and meet her afterwards and go across to Rules to eat winter oysters and drink a glass of Chablis – and it was all so easy. Lee had always accepted the fact that doctors' working hours were not like those of the businessmen in her family. She had never demurred when he had to work late and didn't do so now, greeting him as trustingly whether he came home at seven in the evening or at midnight, and this made him feel uncomfortable sometimes. But then, Lee always managed to dispel that discomfort by her behaviour; no sooner had he reached the stage of feeling uneasily certain that he must stop meeting Katy this way, innocent though each of their meetings was, than Lee would plunge again into one of her attacks of aggressive depression, weeping, complaining and generally driving out of him all the very real sympathy he felt for her distress. Her tears would have the effect of making him grateful for Katy, rather than guilty about her, and more certain that he couldn't tell Lee about her.

And so, as the winter crept greyly by and the play settled down to a comfortable run, in spite of its lukewarm critical reception, the strands of his liking for Katy tightened about him and became a warmer fabric; she was still the witty vivacious child she had seemed the day he had first met her, was still the most amusing of companions, but now was something more; a real friend with whom he could be comfortable. He could talk to her of work, of people with whom he had to deal at the hospital, of his anxieties about patients, about the silly things they did that made him laugh and the way they expressed their gratitude to him when they were made well, and she would listen and exclaim and ask intelligent questions, and it was all balm to him, so much so that it was some time before he realized that he was talking less to Lee than he had been used to.

She had once been the recipient of all these confidences, but now he no longer needed her in that capacity, and she seemed not to notice that this was so. She went on becoming more and more wrapped up in her own needs, only really showing an interest in Harry when she had worked out that she was most likely to conceive; and then she would court him and coax him and make love very satisfactorily. That at least helped to bring them closer again, if temporarily, and so they rubbed along well enough as the year slid painfully into a heavy summer.

The Black Eye closed in September, and to her intense delight Katy was offered a part almost immediately in another play which was to open in January of 1937 at the St James' Theatre. The play was *Black Limelight* and her part was a decidedly sparkling one, giving her an opportunity to throw an impressive fit of hysterics, and to display worldly wisdom and sophistication of a high degree. It would, she told Harry gleefully, be a marvellous opportunity after being a sweet country lass for so long at the Shaftesbury, and wasn't it wonderful that Letty was going to let her do it?

'I thought she might be a bit put out at my not wanting to go into another of her plays,' she said as they once again sat over tea at their favourite Ritz. 'But she said it'd be good for me to try my wings elsewhere and it's a super part – so there you are! They're paying me six pounds a week, too! Isn't that lovely? What with that and my own money – you know, that my mother left me – well, I can have a place of my own! Isn't that lovely? It's been wonderful living in Albany of course, but it's really time I had my own home, isn't it? I'm getting a bit old to be living with what amounts to a chaperone, however nice she is, and of course Aunt Letty really is an absolute darling –'

'Old?' he said and laughed. 'Go on, whisper it to me. How dreadfully old are you?'

'Twenty-two,' she said. 'And don't you dare laugh. I'm not a child any more, and I won't be regarded as one. I don't look like one, do I?'

She jumped to her feet and stood with her feet apart and her arms akimbo, and he looked up at her lazily and grinned. She was wearing a white silk afternoon frock with huge tightly cuffed sleeves that drooped prettily about her hands (the nails of which she had painted a very bright crimson) and which was buttoned with very mock demureness to the throat. She had a hat which drooped beguilingly over one eye, its white silk grosgrain decorated with white violets, and she looked delectable from the topmost violet to her kid-shod silken legs.

'You know damned well you don't,' he said. 'And you don't have to prove anything to me. This is old Harry, remember? I'm on your side whatever you do! Go ahead and get your flat. I'm sure you'll be fine.'

She sat down again and smoothed her frock over her knees. 'As long as you remember, then,' she said. 'I didn't say I was old – just that I was old enough to live alone.' She slid a sharp little glance at him again from beneath slightly lowered lids. 'I'm old enough for a great many things.'

'Like what?' he said and beckoned to the waiter to bring more hot water for the tea.

She said nothing, just looking at him, and after a while he looked back at her again and was startled; there was an expression on her face that he hadn't noticed before. It was a sort of considering look, not precisely calculating, and yet – and he blinked and at once the moment was gone as though it had never happened. She was just her usual laughing self, teasing and chattering and making him feel comfortable.

'Why only more tea?' she demanded. 'The people at that table there have the most beautiful cakes with cherries on them. I yearn for cakes with cherries on them and if I don't have them immediately, I will probably fall into a swoon all over you and you'll have to carry me out and cry for help and—'

'Such stuff!' he said. 'I should merely lay you flat on the floor until you came round of your own accord, which of course you would quite quickly, and wait till you sat up again as a sensible person should. Meanwhile I should have ordered the cherry cakes and eaten them all myself—'

'That's the trouble with doctors,' she said and made a face at him. 'They know too much.'

'We know everything,' he said portentously and waved again to the waiter.

'Everything?' she said, almost casually, but not quite. 'Like sex and so on?'

'Eh?'

'Sex,' she said again, more loudly so that the people at the next table looked up and to his mortification he blushed.

'That's what I thought you said.' He knew better than to shush her; that would make her react in quite the worst sort of way. 'Of course I do. There are men and there are women and—'

'Do you think it's true that sexual sophistication changes a person?'

She was quite solemn now; there was none of the coquettishness she had so often shown, and he looked at her, puzzled yet again by the mercurial nature of her behaviour. She could swoop from frivolity to seriousness and back again at the flick of a whisker, and now it was clear she was genuinely interested in her question and wanted a genuine answer.

'It depends what you mean by sexual sophistication,' he said carefully. 'It's not something I've thought about a great deal, frankly. I've heard some people say that the longer the young are protected from awareness of sex the better – the old tree of knowledge idea, you know – and others who say that it's possible to be innocent without being ignorant. Why do you ask?'

She bent her head to start cutting carefully into the cherry cake the waiter had brought, deliberately not looking at him.

'It's this new part. The girl I play – she's rather – well, she's an experienced person in some ways. She's – lived–'

'How do you mean, lived?'

'Oh, don't be tiresome, Harry!' she flared suddenly. 'You must know what I mean. It's perfectly obvious. There are girls who are – who are just girls and then there are women, and you know perfectly well what sort of living changes a girl into a woman, or what people *say* makes the change. I'm just wondering if it's true–'

Now she did look at him and suddenly grinned, almost shyly, and it was an odd expression to see on her carefully powdered and lightly rouged little face. 'I mean, what about darling Aunt Letty? She's no end of a woman, isn't she? It's not just her age either. It's something else. She has that sort of – well, *look*. As though she's experienced and suffered and lived. Yet she's never married and being the age she is I can't imagine she'd have had love affairs. They didn't in those olden days, did they? Do you think she did?'

He pondered the question carefully and then shook his head. 'To tell you the truth it seems all wrong even to think of her that way. I mean, she's a woman of course, and frightfully nice – I do like her enormously – and she was so good to me when I first came here and – but to think of her that way–' He laughed then. 'I daren't!'

She giggled too. 'Nor dare I. Even though I asked. But when it comes to imagining her actually in bed with someone – well, you can't, can you? But she did have a lover once. It was dreadfully sad. He died of TB you see, before they could marry, and that was how she came to be where she is – anyway, the thing is, this part I have.' She dismissed Letty and her history as abruptly as she had brought her into her conversation. 'The thing is, I have to decide what to do about my preparation for it. Do I or do I not need to become sexually sophisticated to do it well? What do you think? You're a doctor, you should know about these things. Does it change a girl?'

He stared at her, not sure now whether she was still being serious or had returned to her frivolous state but she was staring at him with her eyes wide and limpid and her face quite still. There was no hint of a smile on it; just an expression of earnest enquiry.

'Are you saying that–' he said and then stopped, not sure how to go on. 'Are you suggesting that for the sake of preparing for a part in a play you'd actually, er – consider taking a lover? A physical lover, I mean?'

'Of course,' she said and still didn't smile. 'I'm an actress, you see. We have to do everything necessary for our art. Have you heard of Stanislavsky?'

He shook his head, bewildered yet again by the change of tack. Keeping up with the workings of Katy's mind was sometimes exceedingly difficult.

'He's Russian, too marvellous and he does plays in Moscow and he says people have to feel a part, really *feel* it before they can do it well. They have to live it in every fibre of their being, thrill with it, breathe and eat and lust with it–' Her voice had deepened and become rather loud again and he looked over his shoulder, feeling the heat break out on his forehead. 'I was hearing about him from this chappie in the new company, who met him once when he went to Moscow. He said Stanislavsky said you have to do as much as you can to be like the person you're playing when you work up a character. It's not just the matter of learning lines, you see. You have to *be* – so I thought, well, this character, she's different from me in some respects–' For the first time she looked embarrassed and her eyes slid away from his. 'And I thought I'd ask you, as a doctor, you see, whether you agree. I've asked Wernher and Jean-Pierre too–'

'Who?'

'My pen-friends, of course! In Paris and Strasbourg. They're the only ones I still write to. I met them on that tour and they got such crushes on me – madly sweet – anyway I still write because it's so delicious to get letters. I'm asking everyone who's sensitive and understands these things, and Jean-Pierre's a student of philosophy, and Wernher – well, he's just nice, and you're a doctor. So I'm asking you too, and you still haven't given me an answer!'

He shook his head then and tried to smile, but it wasn't easy. The apparent artlessness of her questions had had the oddest effect on him, making his skin dampen across his back and the muscles of his thighs and buttocks tighten.

'And I'm not going to,' he said as easily as he could. 'I'm a doctor, Katy, not an actor! I deal with real life, not the art of make-believe. I've never – ah – investigated the psychological effects of sex. Only in some cases the physical ones. To do with the matter of reproduction. That's my speciality, you see, women's diseases. Or at least it will be when I'm sure I've learned enough. I work in the gynaecology wards, though not as a surgeon. Yet. When I've learned a bit more, ask me again. Meanwhile, my dear, I think – well, let me say as a cousin, that you really need to be –'

'No lectures, Harry!' she said lightly. 'I won't be lectured. I like answers to what I ask, and no more. You have no answer. All right. No harm done. Forget all about it – oh, darling Pip, *do* look at that woman over there. The one with her back to you. She looks so young from the back, doesn't she? Not a moment more than twenty, wouldn't you say? Now wait till she turns round and you see her face – there! Isn't she frightful? She must be at *least* thirty. And dressing like a schoolgirl! Honestly aren't people too too screamingly amusing?' And she was off into a cascade of chatter about every other person in the populous Ritz winter garden as Harry sat and listened and watched the expressions move like cloud and sunlight across her animated face and tried not to think about the implications of their conversation.

But it was very difficult to avoid doing so, and not only that afternoon. For the rest of that week, the whole conversation kept repeating itself in his head. It was very irritating, and not a little exciting, too.

16

Everyone in London seemed to know Theo Caspar was coming, and that there was going to be the biggest and best of private parties given for him at the old Gaff Studios in Chelsea, which were to be made over in a spectacular manner to accommodate it. Every newspaper and magazine carried long gushing articles about Theo and about the very glamorous reception being arranged for him, and his handsome face reproduced four feet high looked down with sultry intensity from every other hoarding and from the sides of buses and vans.

All of which irritated Peter considerably. He had never been at all interested in personal publicity, but he cared a great deal about publicity for his work, for it was, after all, its life-blood. If people didn't know about his plays, didn't talk about the actors, they were unlikely to be sufficiently interested to buy tickets to see them. And what was the point of putting all that work into a production if audiences remained unaware of it? Yet here was this wretched man, absorbing a vast amount of public interest just when Peter's play was being launched at the Shaftesbury, and not only that, was absorbing much of Gaff Productions Ltd's attention too.

Trying to get hold of Letty these days was like trying to catch a firefly. She was never available to come to the telephone and never called back when he left messages, and he became more and more angry as the week wore on. He had important matters to sort out, a great many details to get right about the new tour, and without Letty's countersignature on a number of documents he was stymied. He fumed and muttered and became uncharacteristically bad-tempered with everyone. And then, finally, took a cab to the Gaff Studios, though he rarely had cause to go there, generally seeing her at her small West End Office, determined to sit there all day if necessary to get what it was he needed.

And, of course, was at once disarmed by the fact that Letty this morning was actually there and had time for him, and came hurrying out to the reception area, hands outstretched in greeting, as soon as she knew he was there.

'Peter, my dear!' she said, and shook his hand with both of hers, holding it in a warm grasp that was very unlike her usually fastidious behaviour. 'I owe you the most grovelling of apologies. You've been trying to reach me all week, and I've been unconscionably busy and therefore rude to you. But I know you'll forgive me because who knows this business better than you do? My dear, come into my office and Mrs Alf shall fetch you her best coffee and we shall talk and sort out everything—'

He looked at her with his brows raised, trying to look fierce and angry, but failed completely and made a rueful face and then, rather outrageously, bent and kissed her cheek.

'I'll forgive you,' he said. 'I'll deprive myself of all the marvellously blistering things I was going to say to you, and settle for blistering myself with coffee—if it's anything like the brew you usually drink.'

'It is, it is,' she said gaily, leading the way back down the broad corridor to her office. 'I've got Mrs Alf trained at last— my dear, how are you? You look tired—'

'I am. Mostly from trying to get hold of you—no, all right. Not another word. Just lots of silent reproach every time you look at me—'morning Mrs Alf! Are you both well?'

Mrs Alf, who enjoyed a special status at the Gaff Studios by virtue of being married to the company's longest-serving employee, nodded at him and smiled and nodded again as she busied herself pouring coffee from Letty's special equipage in the corner of the big sunny room, and bustled about to bring him not only coffee but a plate of his favourite digestive biscuits and an ashtray as Letty sat watching benevolently, and he laughed as he sipped the scaldingly hot bitter brew and looked at the two women over the top of his cup.

'All right, all right,' he said. 'Point taken. All apologies

145

gratefully accepted. How's Alf, Mrs A? Thriving, is he?'

'Thrivin'? I wouldn' know, ducks, an' no error! Not 'ide nor 'air of 'im 'ave I seen this past week, one way an' another. Gets 'ere by seven in the mornin' when I'm still flat aht asleep, and doesn't get 'ome till close on midnight, an' even when I'm 'ere 'e ain't got no time for me. It's all Mr Theo's party this and Mr Theo's party that – I told 'im, I did, much more o' this, an' 'e'll be a bit of an 'Ollywood star 'imself. 'E'll be bleedin' well divorced, that's what 'e'll be–' And she sniffed loudly and went away, muttering under her breath.

'You see, Peter?' Letty said. 'It's not just you. Everyone's getting rather agitated about the amount of time it's all taking up–'

'What I can't see is why you're making such a fuss about him, I mean, damn it, Letty, I know he's an old friend, one of the family, started his career at the Gaff and all that, but really, isn't all this a bit excessive?'

'It's good business,' she said crisply. 'I've got as big a deal as any I've tried simmering nicely, and it all depends on Theo now. I've got the screen rights to Genevieve Laine's *The Last Foundation* – it's outselling Priestley and Bennett and every other damned novelist in the business – and I can get international distribution if I get a big front name. And you can't get much bigger than Theo Caspar. I need him for this film, and I'm damned well going to get him. But he's a vain devil these days – he likes the best butter to oil his works. So I'm laying on plenty of the best butter, and it should improve my bread no end if it works! And it's got to. You see?'

He grinned and set down his coffee cup. Already he was feeling a good deal better.

'How can I help but see? But in the middle of all this buttering, have you any time to dish out a little for me? I have to settle the universities tour now, if it's to happen, and it's important it does. You may want to get your film together, Letty, but I want to get this tour right–'

She leaned back in her big revolving chair with its heavy leather upholstery in which she looked every inch the powerful business woman she was and tapped her teeth with her pen.

'Why, Peter? What is it about this one that's got under your skin so much? After that last tour I seem to remember you were pretty fed up. Implied, even if you didn't actually say it, that you never wanted to do such a job again. Now here you are, with a new play just opened and every likelihood it'll run – it's better than the Bridie piece was – and you're itching to get on the road again. I'd have thought you'd be glad of a little peace and quiet –'

He looked at her, his face smooth of any expression, carefully guarding himself against giving anything away while he tried to think. Should he tell her what was in his mind? Would it be safe to do so? Would she understand? As far as he could tell work was the be-all and end-all of Letty's life. She breathed, ate, slept Gaff Productions Ltd. If she thought that some of his energy was being deflected while he was ostensibly working for the Gaff, would she be so irate she wouldn't let him take the tour out at all? He couldn't risk that, so he smiled now and looked back at her with his eyes wide and innocent.

'Oh, I get bored if I'm too quiet,' he said easily. 'And it was an interesting tour. I realized that, once I'd got over the initial tiredness. I learned a lot on the right and wrong ways to do things, and it'd be a pity to waste the knowledge, it seems to me. There's a challenge in it too, taking good English theatre to all those heathen Continentals – poor devils need a bit of education –'

She stared back at him, consideringly. Was he being totally honest with her? There was something about that limpid stare of his that made her suspicious. Peter had never been one of those people who told you all about themselves with every facial expression. The theatre was full of such people, and she was well used to them, and the fact that Peter was a man who could keep his own counsel had always been one of his charms. She found him more restful than most of the directors and actors she had to work with. But now, was the counsel he was keeping something important to her? Was he so eager to do this tour for reasons of his own rather than the Gaff's? It was hard to be sure; but she decided she had to trust him. After all the years they'd worked together, what else could she do?

'Well, I can manage half an hour now,' she said, and pulled her chair closer to her desk. 'Let's see the paperwork –' And she held out her hand and at once Peter was there beside her, his document case open.

They worked together for twenty minutes in an amiable silence broken only by her occasional crisp questions about the documents he put before her, and his equally crisp replies, and then, when she'd finished, she leaned back and looked at him a little challengingly.

'Right, Peter. That's you on your way. You've got all the authorizations you need, and the money to set the tour up. When do you want to start?'

'I thought I'd see the rest of the year out,' he said. 'Go in February, say. I know it's not the ideal time from the travel point of view, but it's good for audiences. University students tend to get a bit bogged down with their exams at other times –'

She frowned. 'So why the hurry to get on with the documents now?'

'Because dealing with civil servants and diplomats takes time,' he said as he gathered his precious papers together. 'The mills of bureaucracy grind slowly, but they grind exceeding small –'

Because I need the time to get other things sorted out as well, he was thinking. I've got to make sure I've got the lines clear for the committee –

But there was no sign on his face that he was thinking of anything at all but the neat disposition of his documents. She seemed to accept that, for she sat watching him for a moment and then said abruptly, 'Well, now, that's sorted out, I can lean on you. I need some help, Peter, with this party for Theo –'

'My dear Letty, as far as I can tell everyone in the place is working flat out on it already!'

'That's as may be. But they can't do what you can do. Look, I want a cabaret. Nothing elaborate – in fact I want it to look extempore, but I want it to be the best bit of professional work you can get. See if Sonny and Binnie'll do a number, get a chorus together – Hutch, too, if you can –'

'But Letty, I'm not musical comedy! I'm a straight director.'

'That's why I want you to do it,' she said and got to her feet. 'Because you'll make it a good piece of work, and not that awful over-fussy stuff the musical comedy people always go in for. Just a half-hour or so, the best you can get for me. I'm relying on you, Peter! And you can pay whatever they ask – I'm not skimping on this one. No hard bargaining –'

'It's possible to be too eager to please!' he said sardonically and she grinned at him.

'I told you. It's big business, this. To invest a couple of thousand in a party is well worth it. I stand to make a quarter of a million on *The Last Foundation* if it works. The film market's running away with itself, and I'm damned if I see why Hollywood should get all the jam. Theo may be a big Hollywood draw, but he's an Englishman. It's high time he made some money for us. Isn't that worth a bit of effort?'

'How can I argue? You're in charge –' he said and then shook hands with her. 'It's all right, Letty. I may think he's not really worth all the fuss, a face and not much more is all he is after all, but if you want it, you shall have it. I'll start this week. When's the precise date of this excessive evening?'

'The seventeenth,' she said. 'And make sure it's the most excessive evening you can manage. With taste, mind you –'

There could be no doubt that the publicity had worked. Outside in the street the crowds were seven deep, and spilled right out and along the Embankment for almost a quarter of a mile, and they were noisy and exceedingly happy. So was Letty, standing in the reception area of her highly decorated studio as the guests arrived, and beaming at all of them with enormous satisfaction.

'So glad you could come,' she murmured as one after another of the famous faces arrived, having run the gauntlet of the cheering crowds outside. 'So delighted to see you –' And they passed on to the big studio beyond where champagne was being dispensed in gargantuan quantities and food and gossip were being dished out with equal lavishness, and it wasn't difficult to find someone to gossip with lavishly, too, whoever you were. The studios were large enough for Letty to have been able to indulge herself by inviting almost every person she knew; there were not only representatives of theatre and films and the new passion, wireless (for it seemed that all the bright young men of the BBC were there talking at the tops of their voices), but also all her family and most of their friends too.

Harry, arriving a little later than he meant to, and therefore in the thick of the most fashionable who would rather die than be on time for anything, blinked at the sight of the glitter that awaited them and tucked Lee's hand firmly into his own elbow, feeling the need to protect her from the press.

'Heavens!' she said. 'It's like being in a film! Is your aunt going to take pictures of all of us and use them? I don't think I could stand that –'

'No, I'm sure she isn't,' Harry said, though he could in fact see men with cameras wandering about all over the place. 'Not film pictures anyway. I dare say there'll be lots of newspaper ones. Look, isn't that your parents over there? And Peter – look, talking to Jonty Collingbourne –'

And Katy, he thought, seeing her standing there chattering to Jonty with great vivacity as Peter stood beside her smiling a little. And Katy – and for a moment as she looked again at Jonty Collingbourne and he bent his head to say something into her ear he felt a stab of pure anger. How dare that polished idiot talk to Katy in that obscenely intimate manner? And he started forward, as Lee gave a little squawk of protest.

'I'm sorry, my dear,' he said, looking down at her. 'I didn't mean to rush you – we'll say hello to Letty, shall we? And then see who we want to talk to –'

It took him almost half an hour of gently urging Lee in the right direction to manage it. First they had to say hello to Letty, and then to her parents, and then to various other relations who were littering the fashionable crowd – every one of the Tollemaches seemed to be there, and gave an impression of adding up to a veritable regiment – but at last he managed it. They found themselves standing next to Peter, who was still with Jonty Collingbourne and sipping his champagne as he listened to Jonty talking loudly about his fellow guests.

'– not really the most top-drawer people, are they? I mean, dammit, the place seems to be crawling with the oddest types!

It would have been so much better in the old days, when we could have had David and Wallis here – wicked, all that, really wicked. I still can't get used to the idea that they've gone. Six months, and still I think about 'em and how outrageous it all was – damned press meddling –'

Jonty, who had been a very racy member of the Prince of Wales' set, still felt keenly the loss of his own status since the Abdication of last autumn, and talked about it still at every opportunity. Peter caught Harry's eye and gave him the shadow of a wink.

'I don't suppose they mind as much as all that for themselves. From all accounts they're enjoying life well enough where they are. Probably rather more fun than being at Buck House. Er – is Johanna with you, Jonty? Haven't seen her for far too long. When she visits the parents I seem not to be there, and when I do, she's away somewhere else –'

'Er – no, not tonight,' Jonty said, and his eyes seemed to blank a little as he looked around him. Katy was now talking to another group of people a little further away and he eyed her thoughtfully and then emptied his glass and set it on the tray of a passing waiter and picked up another. 'Well, must circulate, you know, must circulate. Talk to you later, hmm?' And he drifted away towards Katy's group, leaving Harry looking after him with considerable anger bubbling in him.

'Hello, Lee,' Peter said quietly, and at once she looked at Harry, but he seemed not to have heard and she shook her head at Peter slightly, wanting to warn him. Why it mattered now that Peter should not call her by her diminutive name in Harry's hearing he couldn't have said. She just knew it would be better not to, and she looked down at the glass in her hand, her face a little pink.

She was looking quite wonderful, Peter thought, trying not to stare too obviously. Her dress was in a beautifully cut oyster satin which showed an exceedingly large area of her back, but since the back in question was smooth and charmingly supple it suited her very well indeed. Her hair was equally well cut, showing the shape of her head to great advantage over a face that was, when the colour of embarrassment had faded, delicately pallid. She was thinner than she had been, with shadows in her temples and beneath her eyes, but that suited her. She looked somehow bruised and vulnerable and he wanted very much to touch her.

Katy turned as Jonty moved in to join her group and began to talk rather loudly again, once more referring to the absence of David and Wallis, and she caught Harry's eye and at once slipped away to come and join them. She slid her hand into Peter's arm as she came up to them and smiled up at him.

'Hello, Peter,' she said. 'It's me again. Are you having fun?'

'Oh, lots,' he said, with a slightly sardonic note in his voice. 'I've got to go in half an hour to soothe a bunch of thoroughly selfish prima donnas of all three sexes and make sure they give a decent show. I've got a boss who's behaving like a duchess out there, waiting for an emperor to arrive, and now I've got you to put up with. I'm having a wonderful time – never think otherwise, please –'

'You're breaking my heart,' she said. 'Now introduce me –' and Peter looked surprised.

'But surely you know – oh, perhaps not. Harry, Leah, this is Katy Lackland. A cousin, you know, who came to live with Letty after you two married, and you left Albany, Harry. I was sure you knew each other.'

Katy ignored him completely and turned to Lee with a wide smile, and held out her hand. 'Hello,' she said. 'I had to come and talk to you, as soon as I saw your frock. I guessed at once who you were because people have told me how pretty you are. I positively adore that frock. Where did you get it?'

Lee, a little startled but not displeased because Katy herself was looking delectable in a tightly fitting sheath of silver lamé, stammered a little as she gave the name of her *couturière*, Mary Bee, and Katy nodded at once.

'Oh, yes, *doesn't* she make the most delicious clothes? I yearn to be able to afford one – as soon as my new play really settles in, I dare say I will. You must take me to her and introduce me. She's called Hannah, isn't she, the woman who runs it?' And she slid her hand into Lee's elbow and drew her away from the two men, leaving them standing there in the

middle of the most fashionable party in London that year and
staring after them. But neither was looking at the girl he ought
to be looking at.

17

'*Déjà vu*,' Theo said and made a face. 'And I'm not sure I like it.'

'Mmm?' Letty was a little abstracted now, with the first peak of the evening behind her and the need to gather her energies for the assault that was to come still before her. 'How do you mean?'

'Have you forgotten?' he said and looked down at her. 'It was the first time that I came here. Twenty years ago. I was a pathetic peaky creature then, such a bundle of nerves, I could hardly walk, let alone talk, and you were showing your war film. Just after the Armistice. Don't you remember?'

She remembered perfectly well, could see in her mind's eye the way he had looked then, the strained pale face with the smudges of shadows under the eyes and at the temples and the opaque eyes that seemed to hide so much pain. He'd been a war hero, newly back from the trenches, and had seemed to embody so much of those difficult and dramatic times that she hadn't been able to hold on to her common sense. That had been the start of that fearful crush she had got on him – and even now she could only cope with it all by labelling it firmly as a crush. She couldn't admit to herself that she had been very painfully and very genuinely in love with him.

'Not really,' she said now, as lightly as she could. 'I certainly can't imagine you as ever being pale and peaky. Not looking at the way you are now.'

He smiled with a practised flash of very even white teeth, and looked at her with a comical twist of his mouth.

'My dear, you should know the difference between real tinsel and false tinsel if anyone does! You started me in this business, and you still know more about it than anyone I ever work with in Hollywood. So don't try to pretend with me, Lady Letty—'

'I wouldn't dream of it,' she said and turned to lead him further into the thick of the crowd. 'And I've no time to dream, anyway, and neither have you. You've got work to do. All these people waiting desperately to be bowled over by your manly charm — come on. You're not here just to look suntanned and unbelievably beautiful. We need some sparkling chat as well.'

'What for, Letty?' He pulled back on her hand a little, making her stop and look at him. 'Come on, my dear. This is old Theo, whatever may have happened in between. You're not throwing a party like this just for the sake of old times. There has to be a good old-fashioned ulterior motive underneath somewhere, so let's get it out and have a look at it. What's the proposition?'

She looked up at him consideringly for a moment, letting her eyes slide appreciatively over the planes of his face. It was as incredibly beautiful as it had ever been, but improved; twenty years had added strength to the boyish handsomeness that had launched him on his screen career; there was the excitement of experience as well as beauty in that face now and she had to let her glance move away, aware that her appreciation of him was showing too nakedly.

'*The Last Foundation*,' she said after a moment and he stared at her and then whistled softly.

'So it's you — I heard that Warner's as well as United Artists had been trying to get that, and were livid because someone else already had their hands on it.— well, well, I should have guessed. Are you going to offer me the priest's part?'

'Which else? Unless you see yourself as a girl in the grip of an illicit passion—'

'Very funny. As if I haven't had enough of illicit passions to last me a lifetime—' And his face was bleak for a moment as he looked over her shoulder towards the group of people where Roger, the young man he had introduced as his secretary, was in the middle of an admiring crowd. 'Do I get a profit-sharing deal if I do it?'

'It's open to discussion,' she said cautiously, not wanting

her excitement to show. Was she to get Theo as easily as this? It didn't seem possible. But at the same time, she wasn't going to let him take all the cream there was. 'There should be plenty of mileage in this for all of us. The book's sold half a million copies alone.'

'It's going like popcorn in the States,' Theo said. 'Okay, Letty. You're on. If we can fit it into the schedule – and of course if you can pay what the studio'll demand to get me. But they want to please me at the moment, and if I want to do it they'll let me go.' He grinned then, a sharp self-deprecating little grimace. 'I don't know how long this is going to last, so I have to make the most of it while I've got it. One of these days, they're going to wake up and ask themselves who the hell *is* this aging face that they're giving all this money to.'

'Not quite yet,' she said, and felt the shake in her voice and hoped he hadn't noticed. 'You're still a bankable name. And if your Americans give you the elbow, I'll always take you on. You started here –'

'So I can finish here. Thanks,' he said sardonically. And then set an arm round her shoulders and hugged her. 'No, I didn't mean to sound bitchy. I appreciate it, darling, I really do. It's good to know I still have people here at home who love me.'

Love you? she thought bleakly. Goddam it, yes. But it's only a crush. That's all it is, only a crush.

It was getting harder and harder to believe it herself.

On the other side of the vast room people were beginning to arrange themselves to watch the cabaret that had been announced by the bandleader, sweating on his little podium. They hurried to collect cushions from the heaps of them set ready at the sides to perch in madly *dégagé* poses as they pretended not to notice what effect such postures had on their clothes, while carefully arranging them to look exceedingly smart for the photographs they hoped would appear in the next day's gossip columns.

Peter was incarcerated behind the screens that had been provided to act as curtains for his stage, after asking Harry and Lee to hold a space for him at the end of the row. He would have to come out front once it got going, he told them; if he stayed backstage he'd only get over-involved with what they were doing. He'd been rehearsing them for almost a fortnight, and now they were on their own for good or ill, and he made a rueful little face at them and disappeared, leaving them in an oddly uncomfortable little group.

Not that they were uncomfortable about the same things. Harry was edgy because of Katy's determination to play the role of artless little cousin who was meeting them both for the first time, while Lee was equally edgy because of her awareness of Peter's presence. She didn't know why being with him should make her feel as it did, but there it was; he seemed to be different in some way from the way he'd been before they'd met on the Flèche d'Or; in the old days he'd been a relaxed and agreeable cousin, just good old Peter, but now he was more remote, somehow, showing her a deference that she found both intriguing and alarming. When he was with them she was uncomfortably aware of his physical presence, and when he wasn't she was even more uncomfortably aware of his absence. It was all very odd.

As for Katy, her discomfort was more of an excitement than anything else. She had made up her mind to it that she was going to get her own way, and now she had met Harry's wife she saw no reason to modify her decision. She seemed a nice-enough girl, Katy thought, studying her covertly under the umbrella of her own cheerful chatter, but by no means desperately in love with her husband. She seems rather cool towards him, actually, Katy told herself defiantly, a chilly fish altogether. I'll bet she won't care what he does, as long as he doesn't let her know he's doing it. And she let her hand slide casually along the polished floor so that it touched Harry's. So why shouldn't I? Why shouldn't he? We're grown-up sophisticated people; we don't have to worry about the old-fashioned notions that trammel others. Art is all-important, it's dangerous to the spirit to force it to be inhibited and – on and on her mind babbled, repeating all the pat phrases, all the fashionable arguments she had heard at Chelsea parties, at jolly luncheons at the Ivy, in all the girlish huddles in the dressing-rooms at the theatre; this is 1937, not 1837; we're much more sensible today about sexual hygiene, and anyway it's only sex, nothing to get so excited about, only sex – and she hugged her excitement to herself and threw Harry a wicked little look. But he was staring glumly at the screens in front of them, and seemed not to notice her. Ah, well, she told herself. Ah well. Men are never as quick about things as girls. I'll just have to explain to him, that's all. He understands really, anyway. I told him at the Ritz – he'll understand and it'll all be lovely –

And as the screens were at last pulled apart and the performers came tripping out on to the stage to loud cries of welcome and wildly applauding hands she fell to thinking about her carefully laid plans, and the way she'd left the flat all ready. Tonight would be as good as any other – if she could just get chilly Leah out of the way. Tonight –

The cabaret was all it deserved to be, considering the eminence of the performers Peter had managed to recruit, and it left the party-goers in a high good humour. They clustered round the food tables and the bar afterwards, all talking at the tops of their voices so that the huge sound stage rang with it, and Lee, standing to one side waiting for the food Peter had insisted on going to fetch for her, felt the beginnings of a headache. And knew she couldn't do anything about it. To tell Harry she wanted to leave for such a reason would irritate him, and justifiably. Over the past year she'd had too many headaches – too many of them self-induced – to be able to claim all the sympathy she needed. She'd promised herself that she'd learn to live with her sense of deprivation, would stop punishing Harry for it, and now she was grimly determined to do just that. But it wasn't easy and she stood there staring with an unfocussed gaze at the milling crowd of glittering people and wondered miserably how much longer she could go on coping with herself.

'Well, if it isn't dear Leah,' a voice murmured beside her. She looked up to see Lily, the youngest twin of the Tolle-mache sisters, and her belly lurched at the sight of her. She and her sisters had always been the most malicious of all of them, even more than the vast tribe of gossip-sustained Oram girls.

'How nice to see you,' she murmured with the brightest

smile she could muster. 'Are you well?'

'Considering, I suppose so,' Lily sighed and fanned herself rather ostentatiously. 'Though it's frightfully hot in here, isn't it? And when I'm in this state I always feel it so much more.'

I won't ask her, I won't let her tell me, Lee thought urgently, almost frantically. I know what she's going to say and I won't listen. I won't—

'Yes, it is rather warm,' she said and turned to look over the heads of the crowd still milling round the tables. 'Someone's gone to fetch me some lemonade, but it's obviously frightfully difficult – I'd better go and see if I can help and—'

But Lily wasn't going to let her go that easily. She set a sharply taloned little claw on Lee's arm and purred, 'Oh, my dear, I'm sure your Harry will manage perfectly well without you. Do stay and have a little prose with me. Tell me all your news—' And she set her head on one side roguishly. 'If you have any news, that is? Really *interesting* news?'

'Not really,' Lee said desperately, wanting to get her arm out of the other's grip and not knowing how to, though she stepped back a little. But Lily moved closer still.

'I made sure you'd have something jolly to tell us tonight. I said to dear Mamma as we arrived here, I said I do hope we see the family in the middle of all this vulgar brawl, and how lovely it would be to see dear Leah. Haven't seen her since her wedding, I said, and I thought perhaps you weren't entertaining because you just weren't up to it. For the same reason that I'm not.' And she smirked a little. 'Isn't it too hectic of Arnold and me? There's my darling little Freddy – there he is barely two-and-a-half, and here I am on my way again! But there, Arnold's such a family-loving man – perhaps your Harry doesn't care for babies as much as Arnold does? Such a pity when a girl is as clearly cut out for babies as you are—' And again she threw that sharp little look at Lee and watched expectantly, her head tip-tilted like a greedy bird's, watchful and malicious.

I won't, Lee thought, I won't, it mustn't show. I'll just say nothing, make a joke, walk away, leave her here. I won't let her know how much she hurts – but she felt the tears thickening in her throat, felt them pushing as sharp as a needle against the back of her nose and knew if she tried to speak her voice would break up, and that the dam would burst too and the tears would run down her face. So, she shook her head and then took a breath and shook it again and flapped her hand vaguely, as though she suddenly didn't feel well, and turned to move away. Behind her the screens that had been pulled back after the cabaret was over offered the hope of a refuge and she plunged towards them awkwardly, not caring what Lily thought.

Peter saw it happen. He had been pushing his way back towards the corner where he had left her, leaving Harry and Katy to follow with plates of food as he carried the drinks to her chosen corner, and he knew at once that Lee was distressed in some way. A rather bony woman in an unbecoming red dress was talking to her in what seemed an almost threatening manner. Certainly, Lee was shrinking back as though she was, and as Peter at last managed to free himself from the hubbub Lee turned and seemed almost to stumble away. The woman in red – whom he now vaguely recognized as one of the more remote Tollemache cousins – was about to follow her but he came up behind her and said loudly, 'Oh, dear, is the heat getting to Lee? I must go and look after her –' And he almost pushed Lily aside. She stared at him challengingly and he stared back, his face hard and still and after a moment she shrugged and turned away.

'Such an odd girl, Leah,' she said rather loudly. 'Rude, if you ask me,' and she went away, planting her rather large feet on the ground in a manner that made it clear she was eaten with curiosity, but for once hadn't the courage to push the matter further. She looked back once at Peter who stared at her more forbiddingly than ever and at last disappeared into the mêlée of people.

He set down on the little stage the tray of glasses he was holding and stood there for a moment considering. Whatever it was that had upset Lee and made her disappear behind those screens, it had clearly been something rather awful. He had felt her distress as much as seen it, had read misery in every line of her body and the way she had stumbled away, and though he wanted very much indeed to go to her and help her he was held back by a sort of diffidence. It was something intensely private, of that he was certain; every line of her face and body had seemed to show that, and to intrude on that privacy might make her feel worse rather than better. But if she was unhappy and alone and needed someone to talk to –

He made up his mind suddenly and pushed his own way behind the screens and stood there in the darkness that they threw, readjusting his eyes after the brightness of the big party-filled sound stage, and said as quietly as he could, 'Lee?' Behind him the roar of the party went on, only partly muffled by the screens, and he thought he could hear her breathing and he said again a little more loudly, 'Lee? I'm not sure what's the matter, but I came to see if you needed any help –'

There was an odd little sound and after a moment he thought anxiously, she's crying – and now he pushed forwards in the dimness as his eyes became more accustomed to the lack of light, and then saw her. She was a small huddled shape standing in the far corner, like a child who had misbehaved, pressing herself against the wall. Her shoulders were held as rigid as it was possible for them to be, and tears were coursing down her cheeks.

'Oh, Lee, my dear,' he said softly and went up to her and took hold of those tight hard shoulders, and she looked up at him in the dimness and he could see the little light that there was glinting on her wet cheeks. 'Lee –' he said again, and couldn't help what happened next. He put his arms around her, holding her closely, wanting to take the tightness out of her and into himself. It was as though hugging her would ease her pain, would actually remove it from her, and that was something he knew he had to do.

And then, without knowing what had happened, he felt her face against his. Her wet cheek was on his neck and her breath was on his skin, warm and damp and quite agonizingly exciting and he said her name again, hearing his own voice thick in his ears.

'Lee –' he said and then again and again. 'Lee, Lee, my own dear Lee –' and her face turned, her wet skin sliding against his, and he felt her lips on his cheek now, not her breath, and as though his own mouth was attached to a pulley and was no longer in his control, his head turned and he was kissing her, holding her as tightly as he could as she, in her turn, clung to him with all the desperation of which she was capable.

18

'But why should she?' Harry said again, and this time he stopped. They had reached the main entrance to the Gaff and could see out of the great glass double doors into the street. There were people still standing there shivering against the night-time chill but determined to wait for glimpses of the famous guests, and beyond them the river dimpled and gleamed in the rich blueness of the night. The Embankment was festooned with strings of lights, and from the sound stage behind them the throb of jazz being played exceedingly well by London's most fashionable dance band of the moment sparkled to match the dancing of the lights and their reflections on the river. 'Why should she?'

'I'll explain later,' she said. 'Yes, there is something to explain, and I'd hoped you wouldn't ask me to, but what can I do?' She looked up at him beseechingly. 'I'd much rather not meddle, honestly, darling, but sometimes people have to, don't they?'

'I'm going back,' Harry said. 'I can't just leave, can I? Not without seeing if she really –'

'She's with someone else,' Katy said after a moment, and then put her hand into his and, pulling gently, led him out into the street. There was a little flurry as a few people surged forwards to peer into their faces to see if they were important enough to be asked to sign autographs, and then, as they saw they were not and dismissed them, Katy and Harry could get through to the street beyond. She didn't wait for him to take any sort of initiative but waved her arm imperiously. The silver-lined evening cloak which she was wearing over her silver sheath of a dress slid away from one bare shoulder and the light from the lamps beside the street gleamed on her skin so that it shone like satin. Her eyes glittered as brightly as her dress and the taxi driver was all jocularity as he drew up beside them.

'Cor, my night for lovely ladies, ain't it? Right, squire, now where're you takin' 'er, then? Lucky geezer you are—'

Harry seemed to be unaware of the man as he climbed into the taxi and it was left to Katy to give the address and after a moment's consideration she did and clambered into the taxi beside Harry, who was sitting in the corner staring out into the street.

'What do you mean, she's with someone else?' he demanded and she looked at him as the taxi picked up speed, after turning in the middle of the road to make its way westwards from Chelsea Reach.

'Are you sure you want me to tell you?' She was genuinely upset herself now. It was one thing to assure yourself that the married man you rather had your eye on was attached to a woman who wasn't really all that attached to him; it was one thing to make naughty delicious plans about such a man and be blithely certain it wouldn't hurt his wife; it was quite another actually to have the evidence of your own eyes to prove that you were right. 'Don't be silly, Katy,' he said sharply. 'If you can't tell me whatever it is you have to say, then—'

'Oh, all right, all right!' she said and leaned back in her corner of the taxi so that her face was hidden, and tried to think. It had all been so quick, that was the trouble; perhaps she hadn't seen what she'd thought she had? She closed her eyes and in the alternate darkness and redness the flickering lights outside threw behind her lids she replayed the whole scene; coming back to the corner with a plateful of lobster patties to tell them that Harry was struggling to get some of the most delicious salmon that was there, and would come as soon as he had managed to snaffle lots for them, and seeing first Lee, and then, in a matter of seconds, Peter, disappear behind the screens, after talking to some awful old trout in a hideous red frock, and then deciding to follow them. She watched herself set down her plate of patties beside Peter's tray of drinks and then slip into the space enclosed by the screens. She saw herself as she moved forwards softly in the dimness until she could see more easily and then saw it again—

'Oh, damn it all to hell and back,' she said now. 'It didn't seem so awful when I was just thinking about me, but now – well, I suppose, I mean, they *are* cousins, aren't they? Maybe she just wanted to–' and then she shook her head. 'No, it couldn't be that. Not the way they were when I saw them.'

'*Who* were when you saw *what*?' Harry's voice was controlled but dangerously so, and she looked at him swiftly and saw the glitter in his eyes and took a deep breath and said baldly, 'He was kissing her. Peter. He was holding Lee behind the screens and kissing her quite dreadfully. I mean, he really meant it. You know?'

Harry sat and stared at her. It was as though she hadn't spoken and as the taxi turned a corner and made her lurch against him she said, 'Harry? Are you all right?'

'All right?' he said after a moment. 'I – yes, I'm all right. Whatever that is.'

'I'm sorry I had to be the one to tell you, Harry. I mean, if it isn't something you already knew? No, I suppose it wasn't – looking at you. But you know, it isn't all that awful really. I mean, so she was kissing him and all that – lots of people kiss people, don't they? I'll kiss you, see?' And she leaned forwards and very deliberately kissed his mouth. His lips felt hot and dry beneath her own and she put up one hand and touched his cheek. 'There, you see?' she said lightly. 'That wasn't so awful, was it? Just being kissed. I dare say that was all it was with Lee and Peter–'

She gave a sudden little giggle then. 'I say, you know – I always wondered about Peter. Madly attractive really in his own funny old way, but I never once saw him with anyone. Not to say *saw*, you know what I mean? I did wonder – well, we all did, the girls you know, whether he was a bit the other way. It's always like that in this business. The nicest men just aren't interested in girls, such a bore. But I said all along he wasn't like that. And here I am, perfectly right! Isn't it funny?'

'Yes,' Harry said. 'Funny.'

'And I don't suppose it's all that important anyway,' she went on hastily, uneasily aware of the stillness in him. 'As I said, my dear, just a kiss after all.'

'And she told you to tell me to go without her?' Harry said, and now he seemed to be thawing a little, as expression came back into his voice. He was puzzled now rather than stunned.

She blushed in the darkness. 'Ah. Well, now – oh, dear, I'm afraid I was a bit naughty there,' she said. 'I meant well, mind you –'

'Look, Katy, I can't handle this!' he burst out. 'First you tell me she told you to tell me to leave and now you –'

'Yes, that was very wrong of me.' She said it with an air of handsome honesty and leaned forwards to set her hand on his. 'It really was. But I didn't want a scene, you see. I mean, it's one thing to have a little fun for yourself, when you're a man, but it's different when your wife does, isn't it? It's always like that – the girls say it all the time. Chaps who go out with them and think it's no more than a joke get fearfully waxy when they find out their wives are doing the same –'

'So you –'

'So after I saw them, I thought I'd come and find you and tell you not to bother with the salmon after all, and that Leah said you were to leave on your own because she'd already gone. I know it was wrong of me, but you wouldn't have thanked me to tell you in the middle of all those people that I'd seen your wife in the most incredible of clinches, now would you?'

'No,' he said after a moment. 'No, I suppose I wouldn't.' And he leaned back in his seat trying to get his whirling thoughts into some sort of order.

The taxi lurched, slowed and then stopped and Katy leaned forwards to peer out of the window. 'Oh, bliss!' she said. 'Here we are already – lovely – do pay the man, Harry, and I'll go on up and switch the lights on and all that – the third floor!' And she was out of the taxi in a flash and up the steps, fumbling for a key in her little bag, as slowly he got out as well and obediently paid the fare. The taxi-driver winked lewdly at him as he drove away and Harry felt his face redden as the cab went chugging nosily down the street.

It was a quiet street, lined with identical little stucco-fronted houses behind tiny privet-hedged front gardens. There were plane trees at intervals along the kerb beneath which a couple of prowling cats stalked and from behind several of the curtained windows muffled music came into the street. There was an air of raffishness about it all that was oddly comforting and after a moment he turned and stared up at the house into which Katy had vanished. And then, moving slowly and heavily, like a much older man, he climbed the small flight of steps that led to the open front door. Ahead of him a flight of stairs led upwards into the gloom and not knowing quite why he was making the ascent, he started to climb again. There seemed nothing else he could do, for he felt numb and angry and tearful, all at the same time.

Ahead of him at the top of the stairs was a door, half-open, with a deep golden light coming from behind it and he moved forwards and pushed it fully open and stared in. The room was a big one, surprisingly so for the size of the house, and he realized after a moment that it was actually two rooms which had been knocked into one. The ceiling was heavily draped with billows of brightly coloured Indian cotton so that he felt as though he were stepping into a nomad's tent; the floor was piled high with cushions and there were bamboo tables cluttered with all sorts of oddments of ornaments scattered about, and in a corner a light glowed before a particularly scowling figure of Buddha. Beside the Buddha was a small saucer from which a curl of aromatic smoke arose.

He looked round, startled, and then saw Katy. She had made very good use of the time he had taken to climb the stairs, for she was no longer wearing the silver sheath but a wrap of some sort of floating silk. It was coloured in flame and orange and green and blue and in the tawny light thrown by the lamps dotted about this exotic room she looked extraordinarily exciting. He stared at her and then to his own amazement and her chagrin, burst into laughter.

'What's so funny?' she demanded furiously, setting her arms akimbo and so quite ruining the effect of the flowing gown.

'You are,' he said and spluttered with laughter again. 'This room. The lights. That damned smell – what is it? Incense? It's all terribly, terribly funny – I've never seen anything funnier –' And went off into a great peal of laughter as she stood there and stared at him.

And then after a moment she began to laugh too. She looked round at the room and then at his twisted face and her own creased with a grin too, and she began to giggle and then to laugh as loudly as he was. But even as she laughed, she was very aware of all she was doing as she came over to him to pull his coat from his arm and throw it into a corner, and then, as they both went on with their breathless gales of amusement, helped him out of his jacket too.

'Well, I suppose it is quite funny,' she managed to say at last. 'But all the same it's better than being like everyone else. I'm so *bored* with all those chrome tables and stiff old chairs and cubist paintings – I wanted to make my flat something frightfully different and gorgeous – and I didn't want to spend too much money because I need a lot for my clothes and I'm half-way into next year's allowance as it is. And I can't always be sure I'll be making lots of money working, can I? The new play doesn't start for ages, and – well, anyway, I thought this was much more jolly than any other flat I've ever been in.' And she tugged on his arm so that he lost his balance and fell among the great heap of cushions that filled the centre of the room, and very deliberately fell beside him.

The laughter stopped as abruptly as it had begun as he lay there and looked at her. Her face was rosy with laughter and the mascara with which she had plentifully adorned her lashes had smudged a little, but that didn't repel him. Indeed it had quite the reverse effect for he found himself staring deeply into her eyes and thinking – she's exciting. She's very exciting. She was breathing rather fast now, partly because of her exertion and partly because, he knew, she was feeling the same excitement he was. Her breath smelled lightly of wine and cigarettes but it wasn't disagreeable, any more than the slightly grubby look of her face with its messy make-up was, and he took a deep breath and rolled over on to his back, needing to get his head clear. He'd had a fair amount of wine himself, at the party, now he came to think of it, and wasn't nearly as clear-headed as he usually thought himself.

'Lee,' he said after a moment. 'I just can't understand –'

Beside him she moved sharply, making an odd little noise between her teeth and he turned and stared at her, to find her almost glaring at him.

'I'll never understand men, never!' she said. 'What on earth are you fussing about? So your wife kissed someone! Is that so awful? I told you – people kiss people all the time and it doesn't mean a thing – it's just fun –'

'Maybe they do in your world,' he said heavily and was, just for a moment, aware of his own pomposity. 'But in mine they don't. People like us, Lee and me, we don't go rushing around being unfaithful and –'

He stopped aghast. Unfaithful? His Lee, unfaithful to him?

'Oh, pooh,' Katy said and rolled over so that she was lying on her front and could bring her face very close to his. 'Have you been unfaithful to your precious Lee?'

'Of course not!' he said indignantly.

'Well, then, why should you think she's been unfaithful to you? One kiss doesn't mean anything, any more than half a dozen cream cakes at the Ritz do. She could as soon say you were unfaithful to her on such evidence, couldn't she?'

'Of course she couldn't,' he said, very aware of the closeness of her body. She was, he suddenly realized, wearing very little under that flame-coloured robe. The flimsiest of underwear, perhaps, if anything at all. 'How could she? We've done nothing.'

'And nor has she. Any more than we have,' Katy said and then very deliberately added, 'Yet,' and leaned further forwards so that her face was no more than an inch away from his.

It seemed the most natural thing in the world then. There she was, and inside him was excitement and distress and anger and – he stared up at her, at the dark smudgy eyes so richly green in their depths, at the roundness of her cheeks and the softness of her mouth, and deliberately he fanned the anger that simmered in him. Lee, the wife he had loved so much. Lee, who had tormented him with her tantrums over her childlessness without any consideration for how *he* might feel about it. Lee, with her headaches and her tears and her refusals to make love when he wanted to and her insistent demands that they should only when she thought she might have a good chance of getting pregnant, Lee daring to kiss another man when she had given him so much to be unhappy about—

Considering her total practical inexperience, Katy was remarkably adept. She kissed him with an enthusiasm that was extremely arousing, and he felt his body respond to her with a promptness that amazed him, even allowing for the fact that he and Lee lately had been – but Lee was not to be thought of, and he closed his eyes tightly and kissed Katy back with an eagerness that pleased her hugely. She threw herself into his arms and held on to him, allowing her hands to move across his chest without any hint of shyness at all.

Had he been less tired, less angry and hurt with Lee, less aware of the amount of Letty's good wine he had taken, it might not have happened. But all those things were there to contribute to Katy's determination. She knew what she wanted and why she wanted it. Not for nothing had she spent long hours talking to the more racy members of the *Black Eye* company about their experiences. Not for nothing had she lain awake for many hours thinking of what they had told her and of what she had read in the sort of books people loaned her from their Charing Cross Road purchases. Not for nothing had she planned her strategies so carefully. Harry really had very little to do with what happened. He was there, and he co-operated, but it was Katy who made the running. All of it.

So much so that when half an hour later he lay there gasping and spent, staring up at the ceiling above him and very aware of the way his clothes were spread all around him, he was first amazed and then almost distraught with shame.

'Katy?' he said hoarsely after a moment. 'Oh, my God, Katy, I'm so sorry – I shouldn't have – I can't imagine what I was thinking of–'

'You weren't thinking at all,' Katy said with great satisfaction. She was lying curled up on the cushions, quite naked, her shoulders pulled back so that her rather pointed little breasts could easily be seen in the amber glow of the lamplight, and she grinned lazily at him as she settled herself even more comfortably. 'You were just feeling. Weren't you? Lots and lots of marvellous *feeling*. Oh, Harry, *isn't* it wonderful? Now I'm sophisticated, properly sophisticated. I've experienced everything! I've lived!' And she stretched like a cat, lifting her arms in the air and wriggling her long hands about ecstatically. She almost purred.

He propped himself up on one elbow and stared down at her, his forehead creased. He knew himself to be four years her senior but now, suddenly, he felt much, much younger. Lee, who was actually eight years older than he was, had never made him feel so callow, or so foolish, and he frowned sharply as he stared at the small round face with its pointed chin and the deeply satisfied smile on the full mouth.

'Is this – are you trying to tell me you planned all this?'

She smiled even more widely. 'Of course I did! I told you, it was time. I couldn't go on being the way I was, all awkward and virginal, could I? Too boring – and I do like you so much, Harry –'

'Like me?' He sat up then, reaching for the clothes scattered around him, feeling exposed and ashamed. He needed to be dressed, as fast as he could be. 'I – for most people it's love that matters. Not just liking.'

'Then most people are stupid,' she said firmly and sat up to curl her arms round her knees and watch him scramble into his clothes. There was an amused glint in her eyes and he was feeling younger by the moment. 'Because it's fun when you like people. I have a suspicion that when you love them it all gets too – oh, important. And soppy. Doesn't it?'

He turned his head to look at her, as his fingers, shaking a little, awkwardly buttoned his shirt. 'Important isn't the same as soppy,' he said.

'Isn't it?' she said. 'Are you sure?' And again she laughed and then rolled off the cushions and pulled her robe on over her head. At once she looked neat and comfortable, even demure, and he marvelled again at how much in control of the situation she was.

He was dressed by now and he smoothed his hands over his hair awkwardly, needing to tidy himself. 'I think it's time I went home,' he said. 'I – whatever you say, I feel bad about this. I took advantage of you, and I didn't mean to –'

She came to stand beside him and despite his attempts to hold himself rigid and so repel her, curled her arms round his neck. 'Don't be silly,' she whispered. 'Oh, it was lovely. I enjoyed it, and it hardly hurt at all, though I knew it wouldn't. I'm really awfully physical, aren't I?' She gave a soft little chuckle. 'I'm afraid I'm always going to be rather awful about sex. I *do* like it. It says in the book that first time girls never do, but I did – it was marvellous – really super–'

His back became even more rigid. 'First time–'

'Of course,' she said and lifted her face and kissed him. 'You don't think I'd have let anyone I like less than you do that for me, do you? Of course I wouldn't. You're a darling, Harry, and if I'm not careful, I might even start loving you! And that would never do – I've got my new play to think of–'

He tried to speak, but couldn't. The words wouldn't leave his throat and he just shook his head and pulled her hands away from his neck and turned to go plunging away down the stairs to stand outside in the street taking deep breaths of the early morning air. Across the chimney tops that faced him he could see the sky lightening and thought confusedly, tomorrow – it's almost tomorrow today, and oh, my God, what am I going to do about Lee?

19

He really had intended to go straight home, but when it came to it, he just couldn't. To face Lee knowing she had been hiding with Peter behind screens like a common-or-garden flirt was bad enough; to do so after what had happened with Katy was even worse. That he'd have to eventually he knew, but right now he just hadn't the courage.

So, when he found a late taxi in the nearest main road after walking aimlessly for ten minutes, and persuaded the driver to take him, even though he'd been on his way home to bed, he didn't give his address in St John's Wood. Instead he told the man he needed a drink and asked him if he knew anywhere he could get one at this time of the night.

The driver, who had been somewhat given to sulkiness hitherto, at once brightened up. 'Take yer to a place I know down Jermyn Street,' he said promptly. 'Members only, o'course, so it'll cost yer a bit for immediate signin' on an' all that – an' I'll expect a bit fer me own time an' trouble takin' yer, like – could lose me licence for it, see what I mean? Touting, the bleeders call it – but if yer willin' yer'll get yer drink there an' a bit more besides, if yer see what I mean –' And he winked heavily and Harry closed his eyes and sat back in the corner of the cab and said wearily, 'Anywhere you say –'

The streets were eerie in their emptiness as the cab went rattling past shuttered shop windows and blank-faced houses with no other human being to be seen anywhere, and the combination of that and the reaction to all that happened and the sheer physical fatigue that filled him – for it was now almost four in the morning – made him oddly relaxed. He felt detached, like an observer of his own actions, and he gazed dreamily out at the passing scene and thought of nothing at all.

And when the driver pulled up outside a rather dull-looking front door in Jermyn Street and got out and tapped on it and muttered something to the person who opened it, and then beckoned to him, he got out as meekly as a child and went in.

The taxi-driver took two pounds from him and departed in high good humour and the man who had let him in made him pay another three 'for temporary membership, sir,' as he murmured unctuously – and asked him to sign the register, which he did, still in a sort of half trance. And at last he was led into a large brightly lit room from the dim little hallway that had been the entrance area, was shown where the bar was, and was left to his own devices.

At which point he seemed to come to his senses. He stood there looking round at the bright blue velvet sofas and deep armchairs and the little gold painted tables and the obviously expensive people who were sitting about and chattering and laughing together and thought dazedly, What the hell am I doing here? And almost turned to leave, to reclaim his coat and hat and seek yet another taxi in the deserted streets so that he could go home to Lee. Whatever the storm that lay ahead, sitting around in this absurd place wasn't going to help him.

'Well, I'll be a monkey's uncle!' said a drawling voice behind him, obviously putting on a mock cockney accent, and he turned to look at the speaker. 'If it isn't the good doctor! M'wife's family's crawlin' with doctors, you know, Lucan. Very worthy people, the lot of 'em, and this one's as worthy as the rest. What are you doing in this sink of thingummy, old man? Not your style, surely, is it?'

There were two men standing there looking at him and he blinked; one was a total stranger but the other was familiar and after a moment he realized who it was.

'Hello, Jonty,' he said, trying to sound relaxed and friendly, and horribly aware of being very embarrassed. The Old Man's son-in-law, damn it, he was thinking. Of all people to run into, the Old Man's son-in-law, and he remembered the last time he'd seen him at that dinner-party before the first night of *The Black Eye*. If I'd never gone to that bloody play I'd not have met Katy again, and if I hadn't none of this would be happening – and even as he thought it he knew he was being stupid. Of course he'd have met Katy again. It was all so inevitable. Like this meeting. 'Just came in for a drink—'

'You a member?' Jonty seemed highly amused, and all too aware of his discomfort. 'Can't imagine what the Old Man'd say if he knew one of his pet young sawbones was hanging around this sort of establishment. Let alone what m'wife'd say.' And he laughed, a sharp ugly little sound. 'Going to tell her you saw me here, hmm? Or tell her father so that he can? Give her something else to grizzle about?'

'I've no intention of saying anything to anyone.' Harry tried to gather his remaining shreds of dignity about him. 'Where you go is no business of mine at all—'

'Glad to hear it,' Jonty said. 'That means where you go is no business of mine, either. I'd never tell anyone in the family we ran into each other in a fancy cathouse, so—'

'In a what?' Harry said.

'Cathouse, dear boy. Isn't that what you Americans call places like this? There, I was just trying to put you at your ease instead of talking about brothels, which is good English, and you don't understand a bloody word I'm saying—'

He was, Harry now realized, very drunk. His face was rather pale but there was a spot of bright colour over each cheekbone and his eyes had a hard glint that was uncomfortable to look at. His air of studied rudeness was part of his drunkenness too. Harry had often come across this sort of reaction in a heavy drinker in the casualty department of the hospital, and being able to categorize this man so made him seem less threatening. He relaxed and grinned, flicking a glance at Jonty's companion, who had stood beside him impassively throughout. The man just stared glassily back, and was, Harry decided, as drunk as his friend.

'You'll have to forgive me,' he said as good-humouredly as he could. 'I dare say I've been in England so long I no longer speak good American. Well, now, if you'll excuse me—'

'Got a booking with one of the girls, then?' Jonty said and laughed loudly, a braying sound that grated on the ears. 'That'll take the load off your wife's back, I dare say—'

Harry felt his face redden and his hands tighten to fists, but he took a deep breath; just as in the casualty department when dealing with drunks one didn't risk losing one's temper, so must he hold on to it now.

'Good night, Collingbourne,' he said evenly. 'I dare say you have other things to do.' And he nodded sharply and turned away to walk towards the bar at the end of the room. For a moment he feared the two men would follow him, make even more of a nuisance of themselves, but after a moment Jonty laughed again and Harry heard him say something to the other man that made him laugh – the first sound he'd produced – and he could see, in the mirror that backed the bar which he'd now reached, that they were going. And took a deep breath of relief.

What he wanted to do more than anything now was leave this unpleasant place himself, but discretion was needed. To leave too soon after Jonty was to risk bumping into him in the street outside and that was the last thing he wanted. So when the barman lifted his brows interrogatively at him he ordered a Gin and It and sat there staring with glazed eyes into the mirrored glitter of blue and gold, waiting as patiently as he could. Ten minutes or so, he thought confusedly. Just ten minutes or so, and he let his gaze become even more unfocussed.

And drifted again into that relaxed almost trancelike state. He'd had too much to cope with altogether in the past few hours and was dangerously near to snapping, not that he fully realized it. He only knew that sitting there propped on his elbows and staring into a vague shifting mirrored image was comforting, and his drink sat untasted before him on the bar.

It was in fact half an hour or so after Jonty and his friend had gone that someone tapped on his shoulder and he turned his head and said a little muzzily, 'Mmm?'

'Doctor Lackland?'

It was the man who had taken his money when he arrived and Harry blinked at him, trying to clear his tired brain.

'I'm so sorry to bother you sir,' the man said with the sort of deference that experienced servants of dubious clubs use to cover their deep contempt for the people they serve. 'But I have an urgent message for Lord Collingbourne. It occurred to me that you might know where he's gone?'

'Gone?' Harry said stupidly.

'Yes, sir,' the man said with heavy patience. 'He left about half an hour ago, and I saw you talking to him. His – er – his wife has called. There is illness in the family, I gather, and she is anxious to find him. I told her he'd been talking to you, but that he'd gone. Now she's just phoned again. I just thought that perhaps you might know where he is.'

'I'm sorry,' Harry said. 'I don't,' and shook his head to clear it again, and got to his feet. 'Illness, you say? Is she –'

'She told me she wanted her husband, sir, that was all,' the man said and backed away politely so that Harry could make his way towards the door. 'I'm sorry to have bothered you, and I do hope I was not indiscreet in mentioning you were talking to Lord Collingbourne –'

Harry stopped and stared at him. 'Eh?'

'Lady Collingbourne knows her husband is a member here, sir, and comes from time to time to have a drink. Perhaps I shouldn't have mentioned that you were here, too –' And he looked at Harry with wide limpid eyes and behind that cool gaze Harry could see the flicker of malice, and wondered briefly why the man should find such delight in behaving so. And decided it was because he had been talking to Jonty. Jonty clearly was a man who made enemies; people who seemed to be his friends must share in the hatred he created in others.

'Guilt by association,' he said absurdly, and the man said, 'Sir?'

Harry shook his head. 'It doesn't matter. My coat and hat, please. I'm leaving. And I don't give a damn what you say to anyone about the fact I was here tonight. I'll never be back, that's for sure –'

'Certainly, sir,' the man said imperturbably and led him to the street door, handed him his coat and hat with a small and clearly insulting bow, and saw him out.

And Harry stood in the clear daylight of the early June morning and felt very sick indeed, and didn't know whether it was because of his exhaustion, or the wine he'd had at Letty's party all those hours ago – was it only hours; it felt like days – or apprehension about what lay ahead of him. Because now he had to go home.

The phone's insistent ringing had filled Peter's dream with anxiety, translating itself into the frantic signalling of a fire engine and he dragged himself out of sleep with a rapidly beating heart and a dry mouth. It took a few moments after he'd picked it up for him to realize just what it was that Johanna was saying and he had to make her repeat it twice before he understood.

'Who's looking after him?' he said, his voice hoarse with tiredness. 'Have you called Pa?'

'No, I haven't.' Even through the thin clacking the telephone made of her voice he could hear the fear in it. 'He's the best, of course he is, but to get him out of bed in the middle of the night at his age – so I called Nellie's and they sent an ambulance at once and it's all right – I mean there's a good staff on at night – he's having the operation in half an hour and I just wanted to find Jonty – I'm so scared, Peter. I don't know what to do, and I've phoned everywhere he goes and no one knows where he is, but –'

'Jo, calm down! Have they told you the operation's a risky one?'

'Well, no. They keep saying it's just an ordinary appendicitis and Jolly'll be all right and they've got it in plenty of time, and they don't even think I need tell Papa till it's all done, they're so sure it's nothing to worry about, but how can I be sure? They could be just saying it and I want Jonty and –' Her voice thinned out, took on a note of hysteria. 'What shall I *do*, Peter? He's off somewhere the way he always is, and I can't find him and suppose they're wrong and Jolly doesn't wake up from the anaesthetic and I'm here all alone and –'

'Jo, be quiet!' Peter said. 'You're getting hysterical again and I won't allow it. You really must stop expecting the worst all the time. I'll come and sit there with you and –'

'No!' she wailed. 'I want Jonty. That's why I phoned you, Peter, to find him for me. One of those clubs he goes to, they told me he'd been there with Harry and I tried ringing his house but there's no answer so I thought maybe –'

'No,' Peter said, almost without thinking. 'Lee took a sleeping pill. She won't have heard it –'

'What did you say?'

'Nothing, nothing important – look, you say Jonty was with Harry? All right, I'll go and find Harry and ask him where Jonty is. When did you phone his house?'

'Half an hour ago. Then I phoned the club again in case he was still there and they said he was but he couldn't come to the phone and – oh, it was so hateful. The man was so sneering on the phone and everything and – Peter, where's Jonty? I do need him so –'

'I'll find him,' Peter said. 'Just calm down and I'll find him. Stay there at Nellie's and wait. Stop phoning people and wait for me.' And he cradled the phone and sat there on the edge of his bed staring blearily at the light that was already creeping in round his curtains, and tried to think what to do.

To find Jonty he'd have to find Harry. Oh, God, but that was ironic! After all that had happened last night, after finding that Harry had gone so abruptly from Letty's party that the assumption had to be that somehow he'd seen them together, and then taking Lee, in a state of abject misery, home to bed, to have to go now deliberately to find Harry – it really was the most awful mess.

All the time he was washing and shaving and dressing he tried to sort it out in his mind; how was he to greet Harry when he saw him? Pretend that nothing had happened at last night's party, that it was the most natural thing in the world for a man to leave his wife abruptly, go off on his own and let someone else escort her safely home? Or should he go in full of righteous indignation, upbraid him for his neglect of the dearest girl a man could hope to have as a wife and – no, that wouldn't do, because there was always the very real problem of what had happened between them, he and Lee. It had been innocent enough, God knew, just a miserable lonely girl being comforted by her cousin. That was all –

Like hell it was, he told himself as at last he closed the front door of his flat behind him and went hurrying down to the street to see if he could find an early taxi. It was a long way from Beak Street to St John's Wood and at five in the morning it was hardly likely that the tube would be running, but as he ran along towards Piccadilly, his feet slapping noisily against the empty pavement and echoing against the shop fronts he was passing, his luck was in. A late driver was on his way home and willing to go out of his way to accommodate a chap who'd be equally willing to pay for the favour. He reached St John's Wood just after quarter-past five.

And then, as he stood on the doorstep and the quietness of the broad tree-lined road came back as the taxi went chugging away, he realized that he had allowed his sister's hysteria to push him into the most absurd behaviour. What could he possibly do? Ring the bell, wake the entire household, get Harry and Lee out of bed to ask Harry if he had been at some nightspot or other and seen Jonty? It was ridiculous, impossible, and he stood there on the step uncertainly, not knowing what to do.

That was why the first sight Harry saw when his own taxi drew up outside his home was Peter and he stood with his hand in his trouser pocket, arrested in the act of getting out the money to pay the fare, not certain that he was actually seeing what his eyes told him he saw. The way he'd been this past couple of hours Peter could have been a mirage, the product of his own exhaustion, and he closed his eyes and then opened them again.

But it was Peter, for he turned and looked at him with his head up and Harry paid the man, and stood there waiting for the change – which the driver found with some disgust – trying to decide what to do. Attack Peter for daring to kiss Lee? But even as he tried to imagine himself squaring up to him he saw an image of himself in that absurd room in Fulham, lying in a tangle on a pile of cushions with Katy naked and laughing beside him, her small pointed breasts well displayed, and the image of himself behaving towards Peter as an outraged husband shattered into a myriad shards and vanished.

It was as though the decision was made for him. He pushed open the little gate that led into the minuscule front garden of his house and walked up to Peter, amazed inside at his own acting ability. He would never have thought himself capable of what he did then.

'Morning,' he said. 'What are you doing here?'

'Looking for you.' Peter looked at him sharply. He didn't

seem all that the worse for wear, in drink terms, certainly, he thought. Harry's face was white with tiredness and his hair was rumpled and his white tie was hanging unknotted round his collar, and there were heavy shadows beneath his eyes which were bloodshot, but he was clearly in full control of himself.

'At this hour of the morning? What on earth for?'

'My nephew, Jolly. He's gone down with appendicitis and been taken into Nellie's. My sister's in a state, wants her husband and can't find him. Apparently she phoned one of his haunts – er – a club he belongs to. They told her you'd been with him there – Johanna thought maybe you'd know where Jonty was, could get a message to him–'

Harry was so taken aback that he could only stare. Quite what he'd expected he didn't know, but to be faced with something as mundane as this–

He shook his head. 'How on earth should I know where Collingbourne is?' he said. 'I hardly know the chap. I ran into him tonight, but that was all – talked to him for five minutes or so, no more.'

He frowned then, seeing again in his memory that sleek unpleasant doorman at the club. He'd clearly taken a real delight in creating problems for Jonty, telling his wife where he'd been, that Harry had been with him – and for what? Just to vent some personal spleen? It all seemed so stupid and suddenly to his own amazement, he yawned hugely, a jaw cracking gape that took him by surprise.

'Sorry,' he mumbled. 'It isn't that I'm not concerned about your sister – I mean, I'm sure everything'll be fine with your nephew. Appendectomies are ten a penny – everyone who has one does very well. But I've had a long night and I'm very tired. Desperately tired–'

'You must be.' Peter couldn't help it. 'That must have been some party you went on to.'

'Party?' Harry said and stared at him challengingly. 'What party? I was sent for by a patient. Lives in Jermyn Street. After I'd dealt with him I stopped at the club next door for a drink. I'd earned it. The man was ill, it took a lot of time and energy to deal with him. So I stopped for a drink–'

Peter reddened. 'Oh,' he said and then bit his lip. 'I'm sorry. Didn't mean to pry. But Lee – I found her there – at the party – very upset. She said you'd gone and left her, just like that. She was very worried. I saw her home –'

Harry was hating himself more and more by the minute. 'Damned waiters! I told the man to find her and tell her, said I had to rush. The message I got was that the patient had collapsed and was very ill – I couldn't hang about. I made sure she'd get a message. Damn waiter – thanks, old man. For taking care of her. Most grateful –'

He bent his head to fiddle with his key ring, not wanting to look Peter in the eye. The confusion of feeling was thickening into a fog now. He should be angry with this man for what he'd done, taking Lee behind those damned screens, kissing her, pushing him, Harry, into Katy's arms, but here he was thanking him and – again he shook his head.

'You must forgive me,' he said gruffly. 'I must get some sleep. Been up all night. Hope you find your brother-in-law soon. Hope your sister and her boy are all right. Sure they will be, quite sure –' And he opened his front door and walked into the house, and just before closing it in Peter's face said again, 'You must forgive me,' leaving Peter standing there on the top step, staring at the blank panels of the door.

20

The only one of them who seemed untroubled by what had happened on the night of Theo Caspar's party at Chelsea Reach was Katy. She went on about her usual business, greatly pleased with herself and as happy as it was possible for a girl to be. Even Letty noticed her contentment, and remarked acerbically to her on one of the afternoons when she came visiting at Albany that she 'looked like the cat that had got the cream'. And Katy had laughed and actually considered, just for a moment, telling her dear Aunt Letty just why she was feeling so pleased with herself. But decided, with rare discretion, that it might be better not to do so. For all her romantic history, Aunty Letty was, after all, old; she wasn't a modern woman, with modern sensible ideas about sex hygiene and sophistication. She was old, old, old, at least fifty, and in Katy's eyes that inevitably cancelled out many of her other qualities.

Not the least of which was her involvement with Theo Caspar. Everyone in theatre was talking about the fact that this most glamorous of Hollywood inhabitants was in London, and staying at Albany with Letty Lackland, and for Katy this was very important. She had of course got a glimpse of the great man at Letty's party, but no more than that. The chance to talk to him, to get to know him well, to persuade him of her charms – that was something that Katy very much wanted; she wanted it enough to be less bothered than she might have been by the total silence from Harry.

She called him on the phone, but his parlour maid always said he was out; she called him at the hospital but the secretary who dealt with his affairs there always said he was busy, and he never returned her calls. But with Theo to think about and to stalk, that wasn't as annoying as it might have been for Katy. So she was happy enough.

Harry, on the other hand, was far from happy. The lie that had slipped so easily from his lips that morning hung around his neck like an albatross, and stopped him from doing anything at all about the tale that Katy had told him about seeing Lee and Peter together. He had, perforce, to tell Lee precisely what he had told Peter, and furthermore he had to tell her as soon as he reached their bedroom, for she woke as he went in, and sat bold upright in bed and stared at him accusingly.

'Harry? *Where* have you been? What happened last night? I've been frantic —' she'd said and the same words about the mythical patient in Jermyn Street had come out and she had put up her arms to him and hugged him, apologizing for being so cross when of course he couldn't help it, and he had sat there beside her on the bed, staring at the wall over her shoulder and aching to shake her, to force her to tell him what had happened behind those damned screens last night —

And as it had started, so it had gone on; he biting his tongue on his lie, and therefore on his doubts, Lee being undeniably sweet and good and almost like the girl he had married — but not quite. He would sit and look at her at the end of their dining-room table as she chattered brightly through their meals, and ask himself why she was being so good now, when for so long she'd been so moody, so miserable, so often tearful and headachy, and tried to assure himself it wasn't because she was having an affair with her cousin Peter, that it couldn't be that — and failed, over and over again, to convince himself.

And meanwhile, she at the end of the table would dredge her mind for something to talk about, for jokes and chatter, for anything that would enable her to be the good wife Harry deserved. She was eaten with guilt about what had happened at Letty's party; had been convinced that Harry's abrupt departure had been due to the fact that he had seen her with Peter and had been bitterly hurt by it. To discover that the poor darling had actually had to go to look after a patient had so filled her with guilt that she had been beside herself. Indeed for the first time for over a year, the uppermost thought in her mind was not the child she didn't have, but the husband she did – and knew she wanted to keep.

Those few minutes with Peter had been tender and oddly exciting and comforting, but no more than that. Harry was, she knew, the centre of her life, and always would be, and somehow she had to make him realize that. So she would sit and chatter and watch him and worry about the distant look in his eyes, the perfect politeness he always displayed, and pray that she hadn't been too selfish for too long. It couldn't be too late to show Harry she could be the ideal wife, even without babies. It couldn't be –

And because of the way she was feeling, and because of her guilt, she couldn't say anything to Harry about the fact that it was almost two years since their visit to Professor Aaronson in Vienna. He had suggested she should come back – but how could she remind Harry of that the way she felt now? With her guilt about Peter to fill her mind, the need to go to Vienna again was somehow less imperative. At the present at least –

It didn't help her that Peter kept his distance so punctiliously. He had, the day after the party, sent her a stiff little note hoping she was well and apologizing carefully for 'any lack of care for your comfort that I might have displayed', a circumlocution she had found more embarrassing than a direct description of their impassioned kissing would have been, and that had been all. No further letters or calls came, and oddly, that had annoyed her. How dare he keep away from her, and thus deny her the privilege of avoiding him?

She couldn't know, of course, how unhappy Peter was over it all. It had been so mild and minor an episode, he would tell himself, lying awake thinking about it, night after night. A few kisses and caresses at a party; what was that to get excited about? In his own company of actors and actresses the bed-hopping that went on was bewildering in its energy. There must be people there who couldn't remember who they'd slept with a few weeks earlier, let alone who they'd kissed, yet here was he, an intelligent grown-up man, eating his heart out with guilt because of so insignificant an episode. He felt very old and very stupid as the year rolled on and autumn bit coldly and heralded winter and still he fretted over it all.

Not that his emotional state showed, or got in the way at all of his professional life. He was still busy preparing his tour and with it the other matters with which he was to deal while he took his actors and his skips full of costumes and scenery around Germany in the coming winter.

Every Tuesday evening he made his way to the house in Hampstead, not far from Jacob and Dora Landis' home, for the meetings of the committee, and added slowly and meticulously to the dossier of the work he was to do in Germany. Had anyone asked him why he went so often to the house he would have smiled and murmured something about ballet appreciation, since it was the house where Pavlova had lived for so long, and left it at that, though his affairs were actually far more important. But he never said a word to anyone outside the committee about them.

It was on a December Tuesday when the trees in the Hampstead gardens were frosted with ice, and the streets were hazardous with glassy slides made by the schoolchildren on their way home from school, that Jacob stopped him as he was about to leave after one of the meetings and asked him to come back to West Heath Drive.

'There's something I have to ask of you, Peter,' he said, with a slightly mysterious air. 'I can't talk about it here –' And he nodded as some of the other committee members passed him in the doorway on their way out and dropped his voice still further. 'Come, have a glass of brandy with me, and we'll see what we see –'

He'd gone willingly enough; the fact that he was so assiduously avoiding Lee didn't mean he had to avoid her father, and indeed it would have been difficult to do so now that he was involved with their shared work. Anyway, he saw no reason to suppose Lee would be at her father's home tonight. Never once in all the weeks the committee had been in action had her name ever come up; he and Jacob had behaved always in the most businesslike of ways when they were together.

So, when he followed Jacob into his drawing-room and saw not only Dora sitting there under the big standard lamp, but also Lee, curled up on the corner of the big sofa, his mouth had gone dry with surprise and apprehension.

'Hullo, Peter,' she'd said after a long pause, obviously as startled as he was, and got to her feet and stood there a little awkwardly, but as Dora was fussing about with drinks, and the offer of coffee and biscuits, if he'd rather, and cushions for his chair, the moment of embarrassment passed off and he was able to sit down in a relatively relaxed way and look at ease when Jacob started to speak to him.

'I'll tell you why I asked you here tonight, Peter,' Jacob began portentously. 'And you two, listen. Say nothing, just listen.' He looked ferociously at his wife and daughter and then turned back to Peter. 'Women!' he said expressively and spread his hands wide. 'Now, Peter, I've been thinking. We have ourselves a little problem. Nothing major, I'm sure, but a little problem.' He looked again at Lee and for the first time Peter realized he was uncomfortable too. 'Usually, we don't tell the world our affairs as a family, but with you working for the committee and all –' Peter saw Lee lift her head sharply; this was, clearly, news to her. 'I think we can share this matter with you, because to tell you the truth, we need a little help.'

Again he looked at Lee, and after a moment, 'Listen, Leah, you mustn't be annoyed with me. But I know you, I know how stubborn you are, and I'd not have a moment's peace if you went like you said you were going to. You understand me? Not a moment's peace. I know you'll go on your own if I don't do anything about it. You said Harry can't go with you –so what can I do? I have to do what a father has to do. It's because I love you, and I have to take care of you and –'

'Papa, don't you dare say a word!' Lee was now sitting very straight on the sofa, and staring at her father, her face white. 'You couldn't, you wouldn't –'

'If you say you won't go, I won't say another word,' Jacob said at once and she stared at him for a long moment, her face very still, and after a while he lifted his hands again and said, 'You see?'

'Look, sir, I don't want to be a nuisance,' Peter said, now acutely uncomfortable. Whatever all this was it was clearly going to be very embarrassing. 'I think perhaps I'd better be on my way and –'

'Peter, my daughter has to go to Vienna, she tells us – um – for *medical* reasons. I don't want to make things difficult, but I'd rather not tell you what the reasons are. Just say it's a medical matter and she has to see a doctor there. She insists she's going to go, and I can't get Harry to say she mustn't – even though he knows how things are there in Germany – so what can I do? I have to protect my child, don't I? I'm asking you, will you be her escort to Vienna when you take your tour? It won't – ah – it won't get in the way of any other business you may have –' And he gave him a look so eloquent of warning that it almost rang like a fire bell in the shadowy room. 'It'll give me some peace of mind. It might even help Leah,' and he looked at her with a glance of such compassion that Peter felt his throat tighten. 'And that's important to me, because it's important to her.'

'Vienna,' he said carefully, needing time to think and not knowing how to get it. 'You want me to take Lee – Leah to Vienna?'

'Yes,' Jacob said, and Dora looked up and said it too, firmly and unusually loudly. 'Yes.'

Peter looked at Lee then. She was now sitting with her head bent, staring down at her fingers interlaced in her lap. 'Do you want to come with me? Leah? Do you?'

She looked up then, directly at him, and her face was a little shadowed. She said nothing for a long time and then abruptly said, 'You used to call me Lee.'

He ignored that. 'Do you want me to take you there?'

She sighed, an odd little sound that seemed to indicate irritability more than anything else. 'Oh, I suppose so,' she said. 'I suppose so. I have to go, that's for certain, and Harry can't take me, and I was quite willing to go on my own. But like an idiot I told Mamma I was going and –' She shrugged. 'Now I've got Papa in a state,' and she looked at her father with a glance of exasperated affection that again made Peter's throat tighten. They wore their feelings high on their sleeves, this family, and had no shame about sharing them.

'Then I'll take you,' he said simply. 'If *you* want me to. Not for any other reason.' And he looked at Jacob and said as gently as he could, 'Really, sir, I don't want to sound disobliging, but Lee – your daughter is a grown-up person. She has to make her own decisions.'

'Grown up my left foot,' Jacob said vigorously. 'She's my girl, and I tell you she's not safe in Germany on her own. Even with you to look after her I won't know a moment's peace, but at least I'll know I've done the best I can.' He looked again at Lee, his eyes almost pleading with her. 'Is it so important you go? There must be someone here who can help you. It can't be the only place in the world you can get the care, Vienna. It's asking for trouble to go across Germany these days, a Jewish girl –'

'I'm having difficulties getting pregnant, Peter.' Lee said it in a clear voice, looking directly at him. 'I saw a man in Vienna the last time we went and he told me then if I hadn't conceived after a year, I could go back and he could do some special rather complicated tests for me. It's now over two years, and I've decided to go back. That's all there is to it. If you're taking me there, you've a right to know why.'

He'd put his hands up to stop her once the words were out, but of course it was too late and now he sat in exquisite embarrassment wanting to look anywhere but at her and unable to take his eyes off her face.

'You didn't have to tell me,' he said. 'I wouldn't have asked.'

'I know,' she said. 'That's why I had to tell you.'

'Then now we forget it.' Peter got to his feet. 'The tour starts in five weeks. I can take you direct to Vienna, and then leave you there while we do the first few weeks and come and get you as soon as I know you're ready to leave. There aren't any problems in Austria – you'll be safe enough once you're there. At least, there don't seem to be any problems there yet – and of course, once the tour's on its way I don't have to stay with it all the time. I'll be moving around quite a lot actually, setting up future venues, you understand, and leaving the day-to-day running with Gregory, the tour manager –' He'd have to find out how much she knew about the other work he'd be doing. It was going to be difficult enough to keep the two sides of his affairs apart as far as the actors were concerned; if he had to lie to her as well that would add to his problems.

'I'll see to it you have an exact itinerary of where I'll be, and then you can reach me any time you need me. Will that be all right, Jacob?'

Jacob too got to his feet. 'It'll have to be,' he said. 'If I had my way she'd go straight there, you'd stay with her all the time, bring her straight back—'

'If you had your way I wouldn't go at all,' Lee said and for the first time laughed and the atmosphere in the room seemed to lighten. 'But I have to try. If only to get the whole wretched business out of my system.' She looked again at Peter, briefly. 'I've let it get too important, I think,' she said. 'It's haunted me for – oh, ages. I wouldn't even tell my parents. I feel better now I have. And I even feel better now I've told you. But—' She hesitated. 'Don't tell Harry you know why I'm going, will you? I don't think he'd really understand. Not after I've always been so—' She shrugged. 'Well, just don't tell him.'

'I won't,' Peter said. 'I can be very discreet. It's one of my strengths.' And she went very pink and crossed the room to pour herself a drink, leaving him to look at her back.

'Poof!' said Jacob with relief. 'That's that settled then,' and he raised his glass towards Peter. 'Well, my boy, here's to successful journeyings. And happier returns.'

'Yes,' said Peter. 'Happier returns.' But he wasn't sure of what sort of returns he was actually wishing to have.

21

As soon as the train crossed the border between France and Germany, Lee realized how right Peter and her father had been in all they had said about their fears. When she'd made the same journey last time, with Harry, the formalities of passport-checking and customs had been brisk and official but fairly perfunctory, but this time that was all different. Despite the fact that it was two in the morning and the passengers had been asleep, the border police in their heavy noisy boots went stamping through the train shouting at the tops of their voices, demanding to see all passports at once, insisting that customs officers opened every single piece of luggage and taking an unconscionable time about scrutinizing everyone's documents. Lee, sitting on the edge of her bunk, gritty-eyed and yawning, was first irritated and then alarmed by it all and after a while went to the door and peered round it, just as Peter, wrapped in a thick woollen dressing-gown, came out of his sleeper next door.

'It's all right,' he murmured. 'I told you – this is how it is at all the border crossings into and out of Germany now. Just keep quiet – leave everything to me –' And she nodded and looked anxiously down the corridor to the knot of men standing and arguing with a small man in a very vivid green silk dressing-gown who was expostulating in rapid German over something the official had said about his passport. Through the steamed windows she could just see the straw-strewn platform of the little station outside and she shivered as she saw the number of uniformed men who were standing around there; it all seemed very menacing suddenly and she wished she hadn't been so stubborn. Once Peter had explained to her all about what he was doing and why he was doing it, telling her she had a right to know if she was travelling with him, she should have changed her mind, given up this obstinate search for a medical miracle –

But when Peter had explained it all at home in London, over afternoon tea at her comfortable St John's Wood house, she'd not been so alarmed as she was now, here at the border in the small hours of the morning. He'd told her of the boy in Cologne, and how haunted he had been by him ever since he'd had to refuse to help him, and how, when he'd heard about the committee that had been set up by her father and some of his influential Jewish friends to help refugees escape from Germany, he'd joined them.

'I just thought I'd raise funds and so on,' he'd said. 'I suppose I wanted to buy off my bad conscience. But then when they pointed out that I was ideally placed to go in and out of Germany and collect information, make sure the lines were laid properly for people trying to get out, because I'm not a Jew and they all are – well, it just grew from that. I'm a special courier for the committee now. While I've been setting up the tour I've also been organizing – well, the less you know the better. But people have been getting out through the systems I've set up and now I'm going to make them even more effective. Just you sit tight and you'll be all right with me. But expect things to be hard. They're getting very arrogant, these damned Nazis, the way they run things –'

And now she was seeing just how arrogant they were. The customs men had already been through the carriage and had searched her luggage with such diligence it would take her half an hour to repack it all properly, and now a man in a black uniform and highly polished boots was beside them, peering at them from beneath the glossy peak of his high-fronted cap, his glasses glinting in the dull glow thrown by the thin night-lights burning overhead.

He thrust out his hand and Peter took the two passports from his dressing-gown pocket and handed them over, smiling lazily.

'These what you want, old chap?' he said, drawling in a very loud Oxford accent, and Lee shot a sideways glance at him. Peter who was always so soft-voiced and gentle to sound as sneering as that? 'Hell of a way to wake a chap in the middle of the night. Couldn't you have waited till we got into Munich at breakfast time?'

'It is at the border the documents must be examined,' the man said, staring down at the passports in his hand, leafing through the pages and then looking sharply first at Peter and then at Lee to compare the photographs. 'This is the rule—'

'Bally stupid rule, if you ask me,' Peter said even more loudly, and with a more insulting drawl than ever, and Lee wanted to pull on his arm, tell him not to be so provocative, but the policeman seemed to be unperturbed.

'You are the leader of this group of actors further up the train, yes?'

'Yes,' Peter said mocking the man's flat delivery of the word, and yawned ostentatiously. 'And if you don't let me get back to sleep, then a pretty rotten show your people'll get at Munich tomorrow night, and pretty peeved your *Oberführer* or whoever your boss is will be—'

'And this is your *Frau*, yes, your wife?'

Peter's moment of hesitation seemed to Lee to be interminable, but the official seemed unaware of it and merely nodded as Peter actually put his arm across her shoulders and said loudly, 'Of course!'

They stood and watched him as he handed back the passports and went and knocked on the next door and then Peter said even more loudly, 'Back to sleep at last, ducky! Need your beauty shut-eye and all that—' And opened her door for her and the official turned his head then and frowned sharply.

'You have the separate sleepers?'

'Yes,' Peter lifted his brows at him. 'What's that to do with you?'

'She is your wife, you say, and you have the separate sleepers—'

'I suffer from insomnia.' Lee was amazed to hear the words coming out of her own mouth and with such aplomb, as though she lied every day of her life. 'My husband is very thoughtful in these matters. Darling, don't you dare wake me till we're into Munich! I'll be *useless* tomorrow if I don't get

193

some sleep –' And she shot a disdainful glance at the policeman and went into her compartment and slammed the door, to stand leaning against it, listening to her heart thumping as though it were itself a train going over a set of complicated points.

It seemed to take an eternity for the shouting and stamping to die away as the policemen and customs officials moved further on through the train and even longer for the doors to stop slamming, but then at last the train jerked and rattled and jerked again and slowly began to move, sluggishly gathering speed. At last she could take a deep breath and open her door again to peer out.

There was no one there apart from the guard. She could just see in the little cubby-hole at the end of the corridor his head nodding under the small light that burned overhead and she hesitated for a moment and then quietly stepped out and tapped on Peter's door.

It opened so fast it was clear he had been waiting for her, and he put his hand out and pulled her in and after a moment's resistance she let him. But she was very aware of the fact that she was wearing only a thin nightdress and wrapper and that he was also in his nightwear.

They had to stand very close in the small compartment and when the train rocked and threw them against each other he backed away and sat down on the bunk, and the movement made her more aware than ever of their enforced intimacy.

'I *had* to ask,' she said a little breathlessly. 'Why did you tell that lie? About – about me being your wife?'

'I don't know,' he said. 'It just seemed the right thing to do. We've got the same surname, and I thought – I'm supposed to be travelling for work, you see, so why should I bring my cousin with me? It wouldn't make sense to an official ass like that – better to make it logical, I thought. And it seemed so easy – same surname and so forth – if I'd thought about it in advance and we'd discussed it, I think we'd have agreed to do it anyway. Don't you?'

'I don't know,' she said. 'It just seemed to be so odd somehow. Like you being so sneering and well – rude – it really scared me –'

He shook his head, amused now. 'You don't understand the pusillanimous official mind, my dear. They're arrogant and overbearing and that's the sort of behaviour they understand and admire in others. And they think with very small brains, too. Everything has to be what they think it should be. Englishmen are drawling and stupid and rude and husbands and wives travel together but cousins don't and they share a sleeper and –' He laughed then. 'You lied superbly. I was most impressed. Perhaps I could find use for you in the company if I need an extra performer some time –'

'What else could I do?' she retorted. 'You'd started the thing off, so I had to –'

' "Ah, what a tangled web we weave when first we practise to deceive!" ' he said portentously and laughed again. 'Well, there it is. From now on we're the perfect example of wedded bliss. We bill and coo and sometimes you complain to me and nag the way Germans expect wives to complain and nag. It'll be easy for you, going by your performance so far –'

'Do we have to?' She was embarrassed again. 'It really seems unnecessary to me –'

'Does it? Did you see how thorough that damned fella was? And the customs people – they didn't miss a thing – look at my luggage.' And he jerked his head at the way his clothes were heaped untidily in his open suitcase.

'I suppose you could be right –' she said uneasily. 'And now you've started it, I suppose I'd better go along with it. But what about the others? The rest of the company? They know I'm not your wife. Won't they say something?'

'Leave them to me,' Peter said confidently. 'They'll do as they're told. Anyway they're so wrapped up in themselves, bless 'em, they won't even notice what the police say. Go back to sleep, Lee. It'll be Karlsruhe soon and another stop and then Munich in time for breakfast –'

'Munich –' she said and bit her lip. 'Peter, I was thinking – I know Papa and Mamma didn't say anything about them, but I've been wondering – Otto and Lise –'

'Who?' He sounded guarded, but she seemed not to notice.

'Otto and Lise Damont. They're cousins of ours. I – last time we came to Germany, Harry and I, we saw them –'

He was still sitting on the bunk as she stood there steadying herself against the door and he looked at her and after a moment moved sideways. 'Come and sit down,' he said sounding very casual and relaxed. 'You'll get exhausted standing there rocking like that–' And she hesitated and then obeyed, sitting in as small a space as she could, pressing herself against the wall at the head of the bunk, as he, in his turn, was punctilious about sitting as far away at the other end as he could. But they were both still very aware of their closeness.

'Now,' he said. 'What about Otto and Lise? And what about Munich?'

'They live there. When we came to Vienna last, we went to see them, to try to persuade them to leave, but they wouldn't. He's a Communist, I think – very political, anyway, and–' She swallowed. 'She was pregnant. Lise. I behaved rather badly about that. I got so jealous, you see–' She twisted her hands on her lap and looked down at them, not able to look at Peter, so close there beside her. 'I told Papa that – I said it wasn't worth making an effort for them. If they didn't want to come they were stupid, I said and – I really behaved very badly.'

'And now you want to make up for that?'

'Yes,' she said and glanced up at him, grateful for his ready understanding. 'Yes. Very much.'

'What do you want to do?'

'Can we leave the train at Munich? Go and see them, see how they are? And then go on to Vienna afterwards? Maybe you could find out a way to persuade them to leave, and use the – the systems you've organized and everything? I'd feel much better if we could, Peter. I really behaved dreadfully about them–'

He smiled and leaned forwards and allowed himself to touch her hand briefly. 'My dear, I know. Your father sees a lot more than you realize, you know. He didn't pay too much attention to what you said. He made up his own mind about what to do – and we've been planning to contact the Damonts in Munich right from the start. One of the first plans made for this trip was to see them, try again to get them out. If they're willing to go, that is, and God knows they ought to be by now. Bad as it was when you saw them all those months ago, it's a lot worse now –'

'Then I can see them myself? Apologize for the way I was when I saw them last time? I can't tell you how hateful I was –' And she bit her lip and looked at him with as honest a gaze as she could. 'Taking it all round I've been behaving abominably to a lot of people. You included.'

He went so red so suddenly that she wanted to touch him, but she didn't, pretending she hadn't noticed, and after a moment he shook his head.

'If anyone behaved badly it was me. At Letty's party – I really had no right to –'

'I was unhappy and you tried to comfort me. It was no more than that,' she said firmly. 'And you mustn't think of it again. You're the best cousin a woman could have, and I'm very grateful for you –'

'You don't have to be grateful –'

'Perhaps I don't. But I am all the same. Peter, can I come with you, in Munich? Instead of taking me right on to Vienna, now, let's go and see the Damonts at once, as soon as this train gets in. It's got to be better for you to stay with the tour for this first appearance, hasn't it? I know you said Gregory could cope with it all, but it'll look better to all those policemen, surely, if – anyway, I feel I want to. Please, Peter. I can't see Professor Aaronson until the end of the week anyway – they told me that when I wrote and said I was coming –'

He laughed then. 'Not so totally disinterested after all! If you've got to wait and see this doctor of yours you might as well see the Damonts now rather than on the way back, is that it?'

She blinked and then it was her turn to redden. 'Well, I suppose – well, yes, if I'm honest, I dare say if Professor Aaronson were waiting for me in Vienna I'd be in a rush to get there. As it is – well –' She lifted her chin. 'I did behave badly to the Damonts and I would like to put things right. Whether I'm trying to salve my conscience or just trying to behave well for a change doesn't really matter, does it? It's the final effect that counts. And I'm asking you if I can stop with you in Munich when we get there.'

He sat there swaying with the movement of the train, looking at her and considering. The behaviour of the border police had convinced him even more that there was a real risk for a Jewish girl travelling in Germany, even on a British passport. They could make problems if they wanted to, and if they did that could rebound on his own operation. What he was doing was, in German eyes, highly improper; finding ways for German citizens to leave the country of their birth, taking their own lawful possessions with them, would not be regarded as wrong by any other government, perhaps, but by this one it undoubtedly would, and anything that made it possible that the authorities would look closely at him and his troupe of actors was to be avoided. Lee alone in Vienna, which though it was Austria and technically had a separate government from Germany, could be such a risk –

He made up his mind quickly. 'All right,' he said. 'We'll leave the train at Munich instead of Vienna. Because of the tickets and the bookings we've got through to Vienna, I think we'd better say you're ill. Mmm, that'll do nicely. Tomorrow morning, look sick, and fuss a bit and I'll tell the guard and change the tickets so that we can pick up the journey again at the end of the week. And we'll go and find your cousins and see if you can make your peace with them, and while we're at it, we'll see if we can persuade them to get out of this damned country as soon as possible –'

22

Harry had never been a man to brood on his experiences. Essentially a sunny-tempered person, more interested in other people than in himself, introspection had always seemed to him a rather pointless occupation. But not now. Now he found that thoughts about Lee and what she was doing in Germany and why she had chosen to go there with Peter went round and round in his head like scampering little insects finding a way through a maze. Everything he heard, everything he saw seemed to remind him of his wife and what he was beginning to regard as her perfidy.

He became so aware of his changed thinking patterns that he actually became alarmed about them, and wondered if he was ill in some way, even toyed with the thought of consulting the Old Man's son, Max; he was an expert in these matters, an alienist or, as he preferred to call himself these days in the modern parlance, a psychiatrist; perhaps he could help with what was beginning to feel like paranoia. But his common sense came back, briefly, and pooh-poohed such a notion. He wasn't mad; he was jealous, and legitimately so.

His wife had insisted on going on a long journey with a man with whom she had once shared a secret and apparently passionate embrace; she had refused to wait a few months until he, her husband, had been free to take her where she wanted to go. Furthermore, she had refused to understand his reasons for that inability, had refused to realize his work problems. She had also, he felt, dismissed his medical knowledge and that had hurt most of all.

He had told her just that it was impossible to get away from Nellie's while Dr Hemmingway, his chief, was recovering from an attack of gout and had explained to her that Professor

Aaronson had already done as much as was possible for her. The extra tests he had suggested when he had seen her last in Vienna, Harry had said, had been little more than a sop, an attempt to leave her with a shred of hope to tide her over the disappointment she had been given. But she had ignored all that, had insisted on going to Vienna *now*, no matter what her husband told her, so wasn't he entitled to be distressed? Of course he was, he now told himself, whipping up his indignation. Any other man would have blown his top long since. Would have found solace elsewhere.

He had intended to keep well away from Katy after that disastrous night following Letty's party. He had avoided her with great assiduity, refusing her telephone calls and ignoring her letters, but three days after Lee had left for Vienna with Peter's troupe of actors, he had phoned her, his pulses thumping unpleasantly in his ears as he stood there in his empty drawing-room, waiting for the operator to connect him. Would she respond with anger at him, refusing to speak to him as he had refused to speak to her? He'd treated her very badly, after all, seducing her and then running away –

But once again his innate good sense came to reassure him. Of course he hadn't seduced her. The situation had been quite the opposite; she had wanted him for reasons entirely to do with her own needs and had set out to get him, and had been totally honest in her actions and words. She could hardly, he told himself as the bell rang repeatedly in his ear, bridle at him and behave as though she was an injured party.

And he was right. When she answered the phone sleepily, and he announced himself, the reaction was all any man could have wanted, especially a man as sore and sorry for himself as he had been for the past weeks, ever since Lee's journey had first been planned.

'Harry!' she crowed. 'Darling, how perfectly *divine* to hear your voice! Here was I thinking you were going to be all stuffy and dreary and spoil all our fun and here you are calling me! It's too, too lovely you've phoned, even at this ridiculous hour of the morning –'

'It's almost eleven!' he said, and could suddenly see her, that round face with its pointed chin and vivid green eyes, and smiled in spite of the shreds of uneasiness that still filled him.

'Eleven? The middle of the night, darling, positively the dark and dreary watches. I never get to bed before four or five, for heaven's sake – have to come down – all that adrenawhatsit stuff, remember?'

'I remember,' he said and then stood there staring out of the window, not certain what to say next.

'So!' she said after a long pause. 'You've phoned at last. Were you going to ask me to tea at the Ritz again? Do say you were.'

'Well, yes,' he said. 'That would be nice. Though I'm rather busy at the hospital. My chief of staff has gout and –'

'Gout!' She broke into a peal of laughter. 'Oh, really, Harry, darling, talking to you is like being in an H. G. Wells book. *The Time Machine* and all that – *do* tell me, does he sit with his foot all bandaged up and propped on a footstool and roar at you all and make you quake?'

'My dear girl, what do you think a doctor's life is? I'm not a schoolboy to be roared at! And gout isn't something to be laughed at, either. The poor man's virtually crippled with it and it's very painful, so mind your manners. And what it means to me isn't that I'm shouted at but that I'm hectically busy dealing with a great many ill patients who need my care, so mind your manners again!'

Again she laughed, clearly delighted to be talking to him after so long a time. 'I'll mind them very carefully, I promise. As long as you take me out to tea again and we can be friends just like we used to be. Can we?'

'As long as it is like it used to be,' he said carefully. 'Before – well, before. Just friends –'

'Oh, of course!' she said and again he heard that cascade of laughter. 'We'll be at the Ritz with hordes of people, won't we? Not here all alone in naughty Fulham!'

'Saturday, then?' It was easier to ignore the mockery in her voice.

'No, darling. I have a matinée on Saturdays. I'm in a play, remember? We opened just after Christmas – surely you saw the notices? I did frightfully well, didn't I?'

He hadn't read the notices for *Black Limelight*, having much less interest in the theatre than he would have cared to admit to her, but he knew better than to say so.

'Well, Sunday, then? You can't be working then.'

'Sunday –' she seemed to consider. 'Well, I think that should be possible – yes, make it Sunday. Four o'clock, as we used to?'

'Four o'clock. For cucumber sandwiches and cherry tarts –'

'Lovely darling, perfectly lovely,' she said and hung up and he stood there listening to the buzz in his ear and still staring unseeingly out of his drawing-room window. He was doing no harm, he told himself, none at all. Just finding a little company to fill the empty hours of the weekend; and why shouldn't he, when his wife had gone off so heartlessly and left him alone? There was no harm in it, none at all. As Katy had said, he wasn't going to Fulham – naughty Fulham, and as the operator clacked in his ear, 'Number please, number please,' and he hung up, he found himself blushing. Absurd to blush when there was nothing to blush about! All he was doing was finding some agreeable company to while away the lonely hours while Lee was on the Continent. That was all –

The Ritz was alive with the chatter of voices and the clatter of china and he sat there, as relaxed and cheerful as he'd been for a long time, watching the other people around him, and enjoying the overheard snatches of conversation. Such silly people, all so busy about such silly little affairs and such silly little intrigues! That pair in the corner, obviously flirting madly with each other; if they were any more affectionate they'd have to be put out, or have a bucket of water thrown at them, he told himself and then suddenly remembered Katy's voice on the telephone '– we'll be at the Ritz with hordes of people, not here all alone in naughty Fulham –' and found his lips curling into a smile. He'd have to tell Katy what he'd thought about that couple as soon as she arrived; it was something that would amuse her hugely, and he wanted to make her laugh.

Much of the joy of being with her was the way she found so much to enjoy in all that went on around her. An uncomplicated person, he'd thought as once again he shook his head at the waiter who was determined to bring his tea before his guest arrived. She enjoys life and takes all she can from it, and doesn't whine about what she can't have. The best company a man could have, and he pushed deeper into his mind the disloyalty towards Lee implicit in that thought, and returned his attention to other guests; people with elderly mothers they were trying to entertain, and people with unruly children they were trying to control, and women with lots of gossip they were trying to impart to companions who were determined to do all the talking themselves – they were all fascinating and more than enough to pass the half-hour he had to wait, for in his eagerness to see Katy he had arrived at the Ritz at half-past three.

By half-past four his fascination with the tea-drinkers had begun to wane. She had never been a good time-keeper, and until a quarter-past four he'd not been even slightly concerned, but now he was beginning to be irritated; this was verging on ill manners and he sat and glowered at the other guests now, trying to work up enough ire to march out and not come back. Let her arrive and find him gone, he told himself furiously, then she'll learn better behaviour. But he sat on until well past five, now adding anxiety to his irritation. Perhaps she was ill, had been involved in an accident on the way to meet him, had hurt herself in some way. And now he did get to his feet and go out to the hotel lobby to telephone.

But there was no answer from the Fulham flat and he stood in the kiosk and listened to the distant shrilling of the bell and felt his belly tighten with anxiety. Something must have happened to her, and he hung up the phone and went out into Piccadilly to stand there, undecided. He felt he wanted to go and look for her, but didn't know where to start a search and knew, really, that it was an absurd notion. To wander among eight million Londoners looking for one girl – ridiculous.

And then as he stood there in the dusk watching the traffic rushing past and the distant winking lights of Piccadilly Circus away to his right, the idea came into his mind. Letty. She didn't live with Letty any more but they had always been close. If anything had happened to her, surely Letty would know about it? And he turned on his heel and started to walk down Piccadilly past Fortnum and Mason's and Jackson's and Simpson's, his hands thrust deep in the pockets of his overcoat, trying not to let his anxiety for Katy completely fill his mind. He was being absurd; she was all right, of course she was, but all the same, Letty should know what had happened to her –

The entrance to Albany was of course locked and he stood hesitating for a moment, before ringing the bell. *Was* he being absurd? Would Letty look at him as though he was crazy? And above all would she wonder why on earth he was making appointments to meet Katy anyway? Wouldn't it all seem to her to be very peculiar if he were to go rushing into her flat jabbering about something happening to Katy – he shook his head and almost turned away and then stopped. After all, he'd lived here with Letty himself for a year; it would be the most normal thing in the world to be passing, to call and visit on a dull winter Sunday, and he turned back to the big doorway and rang the bell firmly.

The porter came shuffling to answer it at last, and, recognizing him, let him in. No need to send a message to see if Letty wanted this particular visitor, he assured Harry cheerfully, and saw him on his way along towards the Rope Walk and Letty's flat.

By the time he reached it, he had almost convinced himself that all he was doing was visiting a favourite aunt on an impulse. And if the conversation got round to her niece, well, so much the better. It would all be very simple and easy.

It was Mrs Alf who let him in and he looked a little surprised to see her standing there. She had often come to clean the flat for Letty when he had himself lived there, but never at weekends and seeing him she grinned that sharp little grimace of hers and said, 'Surprised to see me, are yer? Well, I'm surprised to be 'ere, an' no error, of a Sunday when I ought to be at 'ome with me feet up. But there, ever since Mr Theo's bin in London, everythin's as topsy-turvy as it knows 'ow to be. Miss Letty sends a message down my place Friday night, says as 'ow she's got Mr Theo comin' 'ere for 'is lunch an' that today an' would I come an' do the necessary, so wot c'n I do but come and do it? They're in there –' And she jerked her head towards Letty's sitting room. 'You go in and I'll get back to the kitchen an' that bleedin' washin' up or I'll be 'ere till gone midnight, and still due down the Gaff tomorrow mornin' crack o' dawn –'

He grinned. As long as he'd known Mrs Alf she'd been a groaner, always complaining about how much she had to do and all that Letty demanded of her, though he knew perfectly well – as did everyone else – that she adored Letty and would have been bitterly hurt and furiously angry if she hadn't been called on at every possible opportunity. Mrs Alf basked in Letty's reflected glory and the more she moaned about the work she had to do, the happier she was.

He was still grinning at the thought of her when he pushed open the living-room door, and at the sight that greeted him the grin froze on his face and slowly faded.

The curtains had been drawn against the dusk and made the room into a warm crimson cocoon in which the firelight gleamed on the polished furniture and made the ornate plaster of the ceiling shimmer, and in front of the fire, in a great armchair, Theo Caspar was sitting, his head thrown back against the cushions in a way that showed his very beautiful profile to great advantage. Opposite him, in the other armchair, Letty was sitting staring into the flames of the fire and between them, on a low pouffe, sat Katy, her head turned so that she could look adoringly up at Theo.

Letty had been talking when he opened the door and she turned to peer through the flickers of the firelight to see who it was and her face lifted with real pleasure as she recognized him.

'My dear Harry! What a pleasant surprise! What on earth are you doing here?'

'I came to – I thought I'd drop in to see you, Aunt Letty,' he said and coughed to clear the huskiness in his voice. And then not stopping to think added, 'I was supposed to be meeting someone at the Ritz for tea, but was let down. So, here I am, tealess. I thought perhaps –'

'Poor old Harry!' Letty said. 'Come and sit down and warm your obviously cold bones – you look as pale as Hamlet, I swear – and I'll ring for some tea for you. Ours seems to be past its best –' And she leaned forwards to feel the pot that stood on the tray before her, which was littered with empty plates and the remnants of hot muffins. 'Mrs Alf'll be delighted to make some more for you. She can have a splendid grumble then –' And she rang the bell beside the fireplace.

'Thank you, Aunt Letty,' Harry said, and came across to the hearth. Now he was angry, wonderfully icily angry, and after the very real anxiety of the past hour or so it was a good feeling. 'Hello, Theo. Are you well? Enjoying your visit?'

'Couldn't be better, dear boy,' Theo said without moving, though he opened one eye. 'Wonderfully sleepy and won't be disturbed for anyone. Wretched Letty's working me to death I swear, and this afternoon's the first time she's treated me like the fragile human being I am. I refuse to move or to utter another word.' And he closed the eye and settled himself even more comfortably in his armchair.

'Hello, Harry,' Katy said in a small voice from her pouffe and now he looked at her, one eyebrow up. She was looking at him with her brows raised in comical self-deprecation and her lower lip caught between her teeth. She was a picture of a naughty little girl caught out in a peccadillo and usually he would have melted at the sight of her. But not now.

'Oh, Katy! I didn't see you there. Last person I'd expected to see – and how are you? Well, I hope? No recent accidents or illnesses?'

'I'm very well,' she said, still sounding crestfallen. 'Though so madly busy, I seem to be in a whirl. Keep forgetting the most *frightfully* important things. You can't imagine – so stupid – only last week one of my dearest, most darling friends was madly annoyed with me because I'd arranged to meet him and then got in such a tangle I completely forgot, and left him waiting. But he's the sweetest person in all the world. He didn't fuss a bit and forgave me utterly.'

'Did he?' Harry said, and pulled over a chair to the fireside as Mrs Alf came in response to the bell. 'He must be a remarkable man. I doubt I'd be so stupid – I beg your pardon, so virtuous. To forgive people for unavoidable problems is one thing. Downright rudeness is quite another, of course –'

''Ere's yer tea then,' Mrs Alf said sourly, placing the tray she was carrying on his knees. ' 'Ere, 'old that while I gets rid o' all this mess –' And she rearranged the table so that his tray could be set invitingly in front of him and turned to take the wreckage of the others' collation away with her. 'People 'oo think other people's got nothin' better to do than run around making eternal cups o' tea for people's got another think comin'.'

'Isn't she wonderful, Harry?' Letty said and winked at him. 'Knowing what you needed without even being asked.'

'Wonderful my Aunt Fanny,' snorted Mrs Alf. 'Stood to reason, dinnit? Bloke'd want 'is tea, comin' in outa that there weather –' And she went out and snapped the door behind her, leaving Harry to pour his tea and eat his muffins.

Letty began to talk then, asking Harry how he was, and telling him how glad she was it had been possible to overlap Peter's tour with Lee's journey, '– because travelling isn't all it might be these days. I hear the border controls are getting very tiresome –' and he nodded as he chewed and listened, deliberately not looking at Katy even though he could feel her gaze fixed appealingly on him.

But as the tea warmed him and he relaxed in front of the great glowing fire and the pleasant laziness of the room filled him he began to be less angry. She was, after all, very young, and he had hauled her out of bed when he'd called her to make the arrangement. It would be quite reasonable for her to forget the appointment, and he set down his cup on the tray and turned to look at her. He'd forgive her with true magnanimity, he decided, and then felt a spurt of anger again; for she wasn't looking at him after all. She was sitting with her eyes fixed on the sleeping Theo's face, with a look on her own face that made his brows snap together. It was a chilling little look, and he remembered seeing it once before; that afternoon when they had shared tea at the Ritz and she had talked about her need for sophistication and her plans to obtain it for herself so that she'd give a better performance in her new play; she had worn it then. It was not exactly calculating, yet it was knowing and very aware and bright-eyed – she seemed to become aware of his glance then for she turned her head to look at him and at once smiled and the strange little expression was gone.

'Harry, dear,' she said very sweetly. 'I must go – I've so many things to do at home. Be a darling and take me back to Fulham, would you? I've all sorts of things I have to drag over there – things I left here when I moved and I really *can't* leave them in Aunt Letty's way any longer, can I Aunt Letty?'

'What things?' Letty said. She too seemed to have become sleepy and was leaning back in her armchair much as Theo was leaning back in his.

'I told you, darling,' Katy said easily, and scrambled to her feet. 'There's the suitcase and the box of bits of fabric – and if Harry has the time, it'd be so divine of him to help me take them all back to my place. You will, won't you Harry? Then we can chatter all the way in the taxi and it'll be madly cosy –'

'A splendid idea, Harry,' Letty said, without opening her eyes. 'If she stays here any longer she'll chatter our heads off, I'm sure, and I need some peace. So does Theo. Take her home and come and see me again – soon –' And she seemed to fall asleep as he sat there and looked at her.

'There,' Katy said softly. 'Now you'll have to be nice and forgive me! Come on, Harry. To Fulham – and we can have supper together, later, to make up for things, mm? Much later –' And she looked at him swiftly, her eyes glinting a little wickedly.

He should have refused. He certainly meant to refuse and opened his mouth to say so firmly, but all that came out was, 'All right –' and she held out her hand to him and pulled him to his feet.

'Bye, Aunt Letty!' she said softly, but Letty paid no attention at all, and Katy giggled softly.

'I'll come and see them both tomorrow,' she said to Harry as he held the door open for her. 'Dear Aunt Letty. So much to talk about –' But it was at Theo she looked back over her shoulder as she left.

23

It should have felt the same, for they all looked the same, the wide tree-shaded streets, the busy shops, the prosperous-looking passers-by, but it didn't. There was a sense of foreboding in the air, a sort of watchfulness, and it made her feel uneasy, and she said as much to Peter.

But he shook his head. 'You're imagining it, Lee, and you mustn't. It's because of what we're doing here, and what happened on the train at the border. It's made you nervous and that can be dangerous – because nervous people say and do silly things. Just relax, behave like an ordinary comfortable visitor, and everything'll be just fine. You'll see –'

But as matters turned out, her instinct had been right. They went first to the hotel where the company was to be accommodated during their stay in Munich, and Peter, with Gregory's help, busied himself about making sure that all was ready at the university theatre for their first performance, while Lee sat in her hotel room waiting for him. She would have preferred to sit in the hotel lounge where she could watch passers-by, but as Peter pointed out, that would seem odd, since she'd given such an excellent performance of being unwell when she left the train, and had maintained it right up to their arrival at the hotel.

'And you say there's nothing to worry about? And then make me go on putting on a show like this?' she'd protested and he'd smiled at her.

'Put it down to artistic attention to detail,' he'd said lightly. 'I like a fully rounded performance, you know? Just sit here and be patient. I'll be back as soon as I can, and then we'll go and find your cousins. It's really the best way.'

She had intended to do as he said; it was the sensible thing to do, after all, but as the morning drifted tediously away and she had her lunch in her room, as Peter had instructed, she became more and more restless. And when at two o'clock he telephoned and said there had been an unexpected hitch, that he wouldn't be able to get back to her until four o'clock, her usual cautious good sense abandoned her. She would not, she told herself firmly as she sat in front of the mirror and repaired her make-up, she would not sit here another moment being bored out of her mind. Peter said there was nothing really to worry about, that all his precautions were just artistic attention to detail? Fine. Then she'd be perfectly all right if she went out. She'd save time for them both by going to the gallery and talking to Otto. Later, Peter could come with her to the Damont home and meet Lise and the children and have supper with them.

She didn't admit to herself that there was an underlying reason for her impatience that had nothing to do with wanting to save time or relieve boredom. She had for a long time been uneasily guilty about her unkindness to Lise when she had last seen her. As soon as she had been told that Lise was pregnant she had become icy with resentment, and her coldness had shown in every word she had said, every glance she had given her. Lise had been first bewildered and then hurt; Lee had known that and at the time hadn't cared. She had left the Damont home with the most sketchy of farewells and no word of thanks for the hospitality she had been shown, and ever since the guilt had grown and spread inside her. To face Lise wasn't going to be easy – but it would be a lot less painful if she saw Otto first, and had his company when she met his wife again.

So, she hurried down to the lobby and asked the head porter to call a taxi for her and stood on the steps outside waiting for it as she pulled on her gloves, looking round her with a lively interest. It was cold and the wind was whipping her ankles sharply, but it was better than sitting alone in a stuffy dull bedroom, and she felt her spirits lift. Perhaps it wouldn't be so bad to see Lise again, she thought optimistically; she was a nice woman, she'd have forgotten Lee's rudeness by now surely, and as the taxi arrived and she ran down the steps to get into it, she was smiling a little, hopefully. And didn't notice the man who detached himself from the conversation he'd ostensibly been having with the hall porter and who immediately followed her.

At first she thought the taxi-driver had made a mistake, and she repeated the address to him in loud slow English, but he just nodded vigorously and pointed at the place and then held out his hand for his money, and she got out of the cab and paid him, her mind in a whirl. This wasn't the gallery she and Harry had come to; where were the iron grilles that had covered the windows, and the glimpses beyond of cool white walls and cubist paintings and large if rather odd sculptures? She turned again to the taxi-driver to protest, but he was already letting in his clutch and ignored her as he drove away with a squeal of tyres on the road and again she turned and stared at the shop front.

It was the right place after all, she realized. There next door was the chocolate shop where Otto had stopped to buy a treat for the children before taking them out to his suburban home, and there on the other side was the very expensive-looking dress shop Lee could remember noticing. But the gallery was far from the same. In the centre of the big window was one painting on an easel and she looked at it and frowned. It showed a pair of lusciously plump girls in country dress with blonde plaits drooping over their shoulders, their arms entwined and their faces smiling vapidly out of a framework of sheaves of corn and wreaths of poppies and she tried to imagine it among the vivid colours and shapes that had been Otto's display of paintings; and failed totally. This was dull and boring stuff, compared with that, and she marvelled, at the edge of her mind, at how much her taste had developed. When she'd come to Munich before she'd thought Otto's paintings odd, even disgusting; now she found this chocolate-box insipidity a good deal more disagreeable, and she shook her head at herself and marched across the pavement and into the gallery. To stand outside in the biting February cold thinking about art was perfectly absurd. She would go in, find out if this was still Otto's gallery, and if not where he had gone, and that was that—

Inside the gallery was completely unrecognizable. The white walls had been replaced with a heavy figured wallpaper and there was a great deal of gold about, on the frieze above the wallpaper and most especially on the frames of the paintings.

The paintings. She blinked as she looked round at them. If the one in the window had made her think of chocolate boxes, these made her think of jigsaw puzzles. Idealized bright-eyed, yellow-haired people jostled cheek by jowl with fairy-tale castles perched on ridiculously soaring crags and characters from Wagner operas set in painfully heroic poses, while dotted about the floor were sculptures of yearning maidens in white marble and stern heroes in grey marble. It was all very oppressive and heavy and she shook her head as she stared round.

'*Guten Tag*,' a voice said softly and she whirled to look at the tall man in a pin-striped suit and a singularly high collar who was standing looking at her.

'Er – good afternoon,' she said. 'I mean – *Guten Tag*–'

'You are American?' the man said and smiled widely. 'How good of you to visit my gallery, madam–'

'English,' Lee said and managed a smile. 'Ah – this is your gallery, you say?'

He sketched a small bow. 'Indeed, madam. I am owner, organizer, salesman, all functions in one.'

'I see – um – have you been here long?'

He was beginning to look suspicious and she felt her own nervousness increase.

'Long, madam? It depends on what you mean by long.'

'Oh, I was just wondering,' she said as airily as she could. 'It's just that last time I was in Munich I remember visiting this gallery and it looked different then–'

'No doubt,' he said. 'Now, what may I show you? Are you interested in purchasing a painting? Or perhaps a sculpture? I am happy to make all necessary arrangements for shipping items to your home. It is a service I am glad to provide and charges are moderate. You will not find a more realistic set of prices anywhere in München than you will here–'

'I – er – was looking for something for my bedroom,' Lee

said, trying to visualize one of the heavy paintings that surrounded her in the cool blue and white delicacy of her St John's Wood home. 'Something pretty, you know, and small and – well, suitable for a bedroom –'

He nodded, all businessman again, the watchfulness quite gone. 'I have, I think, the very items. You are – ah – it is correct to address you as *Frau*, rather than *Fräulein*? You seem very young, if I may be permitted to say so, and one wonders –'

'I am married,' Lee said shortly. 'Though what has that to do with the matter I don't –'

The man smirked. 'But, madam, there is all the difference in the world! A bedroom for a maiden lady needs flowers, prettiness, delicacy; but a bedroom for a married lady – ah, there is a difference! I must find something that will please not just yourself, but your husband also, must I not? Come this way, if you please – I will demonstrate –'

She followed him for want of any idea of what else to do. To stand there and say bluntly, 'Where is Otto Damont? This is his gallery. Why isn't he here? What are you doing here? Where is my cousin?' would be impossible, yet how was she to find Otto if she didn't say it?

He led her to the back of the gallery where Lee could remember Otto showing her and Harry the vivid Kandinsky painting. What had it been called? She could see it clearly in her memory, the purple wash of paint, the toughness of the sand the artist had added to his canvas, and she blinked. If it were here now, it would look as shocking as a naked woman in the middle of a busy shopping street – and even as the idea came into her head she blinked again, for the paintings the man was showing her were all of naked women. They stood in mock coy poses leaning against pillars draped in fabric, staring artlessly at birds in cages and all showing great spreads of pink and white dimpled flesh that looked as cold and uninviting as the marble of the statues that stood around, and yet had a leering quality about it that made her feel uncomfortable.

'Your husband will enjoy these, I am sure,' the man said softly, standing a few steps behind her. 'And if he enjoys them I am sure you will – shall we say – benefit from his pleasure – yes?' He was so close she could feel the warmth of him as she stared at the paintings and she felt a sudden and very powerful sense of revulsion.

'He would loathe them,' she said sharply. 'They're exceedingly nasty,' and she stepped aside and at the same time turned so that she could get away from his physical proximity and also look at him.

'Where is the man who used to own this gallery?' she said, as steadily as she could. 'I preferred the sort of paintings he had. I would like to go and see them again.'

The man looked consideringly at her. The suspicion that he had seemed to show before had quite gone; now he was very self-contained, very much in control and he lifted his brows at her after a moment and said, 'The previous owner, madam? Who was he?'

'You must know,' she retorted. 'You must have bought this place from him. Where is he?'

'I'm afraid I cannot say, madam,' he said with an air of regret, but it was as spurious as the flesh in the paintings behind her and she knew he was sneering at her. 'I dealt solely through lawyers when I obtained this property. However—' He followed her, for she had moved again, walking purposefully towards the front of the gallery. If he won't tell me, she was thinking, we'll just have to go out to Otto's house. He's horrible, this man. He's slimy and horrible and I want to go—

'However,' the man said again, as she reached the door. 'I am happy to be of what help I can. Please to wait, madam, and I'll telephone to the office of the lawyer who arranged the transaction. I am sure he will be able to tell us in a matter of moments where your friend—where the previous owner is to be found. If you will wait, madam—' And again he sketched the servile little bow with which he'd first greeted her and went away to the little office at the back of the gallery where she and Harry had drunk schnapps with Otto and talked about the girl who had been working for him while she spied on him, and why he had employed her—

She stood at the door, uncertainly. To find Otto now, before Peter and she went to the house later today, would be good; she could then still hide behind him a little when the time came to meet Lise again. It could be worth waiting for that and she lifted her chin as she heard the soft murmur of the voice on the telephone, wishing not for the first time that her German was good enough to make it possible to understand.

Why she suddenly became so frightened, she didn't know. All she was aware of was standing in the thickly carpeted gallery with its oppressive reds and golds hanging over her, and then, a moment later, being out in the street with her heart pounding and her legs shaky beneath her as she took deep gulps of the icy air. There was something in that shop that had terrified her and she didn't know what it was, but she knew how to deal with the terror; she ran pelting along the street like a child just out of school, so that people turned and stared at the spectacle of a well-dressed woman behaving like a street arab, but she didn't care. She just wanted to get as far away from the gallery and that horrible man with the smile and the soft voice as she possibly could.

How she got back to the hotel she didn't really remember. She walked for a long time, after her shaking legs and her shortness of breath refused to allow her to run any more, walking as purposefully as she could in what seemed to be the right direction, and for once she felt there was a guardian angel looking after her, for the roads she chose eventually led to the centre of the city. And at just after four she almost stumbled up the steps of the hotel and went to the desk to ask for her key.

But she didn't have a chance to get the word out, for there was a grip on her arm so tight that she almost squealed and she turned to see Peter, his face white and very set, looking down at her.

'Oh, Peter!' she said, her voice shrill with relief. 'I'm so glad to see you! I went to –'

'My dear, I told you not to go out while you weren't feeling well!' he said and his voice was uncharacteristically loud too. 'It is better for you to rest! Now, you must come and lie down immediately –' And he tucked his hand more firmly into her elbow and pulled her very strongly indeed towards the lift, and she was too glad to see him, to feel his strength beside her, to protest.

He chattered all the way up in the lift, scolding her for being headstrong and going out as she had, telling her she looked tired, had made herself more ill, on and on until at last they were in her bedroom and she could sit on the bed and Peter could stand there with his hands in his pockets, looking down at her.

'You put the fear of God into me, Lee,' he said, and his voice was tight and thin. 'Don't you dare to do such a thing again. For two pins I'd throw up the whole expedition and take you straight back to London on the next express. Are you mad? Where did you go? And didn't you realize you'd be followed, wherever it was?'

'Followed?' she said and stared at him, her eyes widening with fear. 'Why followed? I wasn't doing anything I shouldn't –'

'Not in your own opinion, perhaps, but these damned Nazis – they run a secret police, for heaven's sake! You surely know that! They're keeping up surveillance on damned near every foreigner that comes into the country. We've got two of 'em following the actors – spotted them as soon as we got to the theatre – and I saw one this morning I was suspicious about – and he came into the hotel right after you, just now. You must be more careful, Lee!'

She was pale now, too, and she bit her lip miserably as she looked up at him. 'I'm sorry, Peter. I meant no harm – I just thought if I could go to the gallery, see Otto first, it'd make it easier this evening when we go to their house –'

He sat down on the bed beside her and took her hand in both of his. She was cold and he felt warm and comforting and she held on to his grip tightly.

'Well? Did you see him?'

'No. He's not there. There's a horrible place now, all great gallumphing nudes – really horrid. They made me feel all – I don't know. Grubby. The man in the place did too. He – I asked where Otto was. He was so creepy, you see, made me feel so uncomfortable, I just blurted it out. He said he'd never met him, that he'd bought the gallery through a lawyer and then he said he'd phone the lawyer and ask him for me and I – well, I don't know what happened. I was waiting while he phoned and I got too scared – I just ran –'

He sat there in silence for a moment and then got to his feet.

'I've been doing a bit of work on my own account, Lee. That's why I didn't get back as soon as I promised –'

She frowned. 'But you said there was a hitch at the theatre.'

'So I was lying. I went with one of my contacts to the house. The Damont house. I had the address from your father, and I thought – let's just say I preferred to go there without you as the first step. It was odd –'

'Odd?'

He was standing now beside the window, peering out from behind the curtain to the street three floors below. 'Mm. Very. How long did you say your cousins had lived there?'

'I don't know – always, I think. I mean, all the time they'd been married. And that must be – well, Wilhelm their oldest boy, he must be –' She worked it out in her head, remembering the tall leggy boy she had met on her last visit. 'He's around fifteen, I suppose. So –'

'A long time,' Peter said. 'Well, they don't live there now. We said we were from an insurance firm, sent to see them about a claim, and the people at the house said it was all wrong, must be the wrong address completely. No one of that name there, never had been –'

She sat and gazed at him, feeling fear filling her belly like water running into a tank. Her face felt stiff and her lips moved sluggishly when she spoke. 'Why, Peter? What does it mean? What's happened to them?'

'I don't know.' Peter turned from the window. 'And that damned fellow I saw follow you into the hotel is outside now, in the street. On the other side. It's all – you've got to leave here, Lee. Now you've actually gone and asked someone about Otto and his whereabouts. I'm probably fussing like a mother hen, but your father'll kill me if I don't take good care of you. You'll go to Vienna first thing tomorrow. I'll take you there myself and –'

'But we've got to find Otto and Lise and the children –' she began, but he shook his head and came and sat down beside her.

'No, my dear,' he said gently. 'Not you. I'll look for them. You can't. I've got a couple of people making some very careful enquiries for me. No, don't look like that – it's safe. You don't think I've set up this refugee thing of ours single-handed, do you? Of course there are other people involved. And the local chap who went with me to the Damonts' will tell me what there is to be told. You go to Vienna, spend your time there seeing your doctor, and then we'll see where we go from there. If Otto and Lise are still here in Munich then we'll see them on our way back to London. If not –'

'Well?'

He took a sharp little breath. 'If not, we go straight home. No, there's no sense in arguing. If not, we go straight home. Now, go and have a bath and go to bed. You've had a bad day, and it won't do you any harm. I'll order some dinner to be brought up to you and the maid'll see you're in bed, and that's all to the good. They'll believe, perhaps, you're just a sick girl who went out when she shouldn't and tired herself. As long as that man in the gallery doesn't know who you are, and you got away before the people he was phoning arrived, no harm done. Apart from that chap downstairs, of course, who saw you.'

He got to his feet and looked down at her. 'Well, I dare say we can carry it all off, whatever happens. Goodnight, Lee. I won't be in again till the morning. But remember I'm in the next room if you need me. Just bang on the wall, all right?'

He grinned then a little crookedly. 'They're still trying to work out downstairs why a man with a wife like you should ever consider having a separate room. Remember you're ill, won't you? Or they'll all think I'm a complete – well, never mind. Goodnight, Lee. We'll sort it all out somehow. Don't worry.'

And he was gone, leaving her staring at the door which had closed behind him and wishing, quite violently, that they had been sharing a room after all.

24

By the end of her first day in Professor Aaronson's clinic, Lee had forgotten all about how she had felt in Munich. Her fears for Otto and his family, her embarrassment at the thought of meeting Lise again, her frightening experience at the gallery, all melted away as her obsession with her own need for a pregnancy came back. The long session of history-taking with one of Professor Aaronson's assistants, the reiteration of her long and almost frantic yearning to conceive made her mind narrow back into the concentrated beam of self-concern that it had been almost from the start of her marriage. Her thinking dwindled into its tired old grooves again and she felt the tension inside her increase while she talked only about her health, her habits, and the normal workings of her body. It was as though she and her baby hunger were all that mattered in the world.

But it was a bit different this time. As the second and third days passed and she went through the tests for which she had come to the clinic, the eternal collection of specimens of her blood and the checking of her temperature, her pulse, her blood pressure, she slowly found herself becoming more irritated than distressed. She had longed for the chance to come back here, to be put through the series of assays of her hormone levels of which Professor Aaronson had spoken when he had last seen her, and had been sure she would find comfort in having them done, but now, sitting in the high white bed in the little white and chrome cell that was her clinic room she found herself sometimes wondering if, after all, it was worth it. To think of nothing but her own body, her own needs, all the time – it was getting more than a little wearing. Perhaps the time had come to face the fact that, maybe –

But that was not to be thought of. She had come all these hundreds of miles for one purpose only; to find out if it would be possible one day to have the babies she so yearned to have. To consider, even for a moment, the possibility that it wasn't all that important, that there were other things to be done, other life to be lived, other matters to be thought about, was out of the question. So, she narrowed the beam of her mind even more and concentrated on all that the Professor and his assistants did, and refused to let herself think about anything else.

Until the Professor came to see her on the fourth day of her stay in the clinic, arriving late in the evening when she had eaten her supper and was sitting up in bed, propped upon pillows and leafing through an Austrian magazine. Since she could read very little of its colloquial German and it was therefore extremely boring, she greeted him with great warmth as he came in and sat down on the edge of her bed.

'Professor, how good of you to come to talk to me! Have you good news for me? Have you discovered that –'

He raised one hand in protest at her excitement and she subsided and sat with her hands folded in front of her, looking at him hopefully.

'We have discovered only the state of your cycle at the moment, my dear Frau Lackland. The blood and urine tests, the checks on your blood pressure and so forth are all as they should be, and reveal a healthy young woman. Whether you are also a fully functioning young woman – to discover this we must be patient. In two weeks' time, we repeat the tests, with special reference to the blood hormone assays and –'

'Two weeks!' she said. 'But I'd thought – just this few days and then –'

He shook his head. 'Come, *gnädige Frau*, you are the wife of a doctor! You should know better than this! The hormone pattern of the female is based on a monthly structure. The time of ovulation is midway in the cycle. To assess your ability to conceive we must see what the hormones are doing at the time of ovulation, whether you actually do produce this vital component for a pregnancy –' And he permitted himself a wintry little smile. 'And for this, you must wait here another two weeks. However –'

He hesitated, and she looked at him eagerly. 'However?'

'It is difficult, this matter I must discuss with you –' He took off his glasses, rimless spectacles with gold ear-pieces, and rubbed the ridge they had left on the bridge of his nose and she thought – he's younger than I thought – tired, and worried, but not so old. Not so much as forty, perhaps. And I thought he was past fifty –

'Well?' she said. 'If it's bad news I had rather have it now than wait for it.' She swallowed then, realizing what she had said. 'I mean, if you've got to tell me that even if you do the tests in a fortnight's time it won't be of any use –'

He waved away all she said, shaking his head almost irritably. 'It is not about your prognosis I wish to speak, *gnädige Frau*,' he said. 'It is a more difficult matter. You are a foreigner, you do not perhaps understand the way politics affects our lives in Austria today –'

'I know what's happening in Germany, if that's what you mean,' she said, and then on an impulse added, 'I – my parents are Jewish, Professor. My husband is not, but that does not alter the fact that I have a concern – an understanding – of the problems –'

He seemed to relax for the first time, his shoulders slumping a little. 'This is a great help,' he said. 'A great help. Now, listen to me, please. It is important. There are rumours that in the next few days there will be a proclamation of *Anschluss* –'

'Of what?'

'*Anschluss*. Union with Germany. Our Government will cease to be a truly Austrian one – if it has been for some time, but I will not speak of that. The matter is as follows. I am, as you so shrewdly guessed, a Jew. That my family has lived in Vienna for more generations that we can count, that we have served this country in all the ways of which we are capable, that we have endowed and run this clinic which is, as you know, one that is famed everywhere in Europe, is beside the point. Here we are Jews first, Austrians second. And if *Anschluss* is proclaimed then we are in trouble. The Germans – we – my family and I, you understand – we are not yet certain of what we intend to do. We are talking – we are talking so much that I am exhausted with it! We are talking of leaving quietly, going to Italy, and from there, who knows? Whoever will have us, wherever I can find a place to continue my researches. It is a difficult decision to make. I am thinking all the time of my clinic, my patients, the projects in hand – and I am thinking also of my wife, and my children and my aged mother, who is a very nervous person and – well, it is all very painful.'

He looked at her owlishly and she wanted to reach out and hug him, to make that tired anxious look on the old-young face smooth away. But she sat still with her hands folded on the counterpane of her bed and said nothing, just looking at him.

'I am telling you all this, my dear lady, because it is only right you should know. If we go, my family and I, we go quickly. No ceremony, hmm? No gold watches or present-ations of silver salvers –' again he managed that cold little smile. 'And I do not wish you to suffer from our decision. I have left in your notes full and detailed accounts of the tests that are to be repeated in two weeks' time. Of the various dosages of injected hormones from my own development of these materials that you must be given should the readings be so-and-so and such-and-such – you understand me? I have tried to foresee every possibility. I have told them also that if I am not able to continue your treatment personally, your notes are to be given to you to take home to your doctor husband. He perhaps can find another expert in these matters to take care of you –'

His voice died away and he sat and looked at her, and then, slowly, put his glasses on again; and seemed to vanish behind them. He was as he had been from the first day she had met him; a serious and quiet scientist. There was nothing of the tired frightened man who had been sitting there a moment ago and she felt a small chill as she lifted one hand to reach out to him and then dropped it, unable to make the contact.

'My advice to you is to wait and see what your tests reveal in two weeks' time, *gnädige Frau*,' he said formally, and got to his feet. 'Then on your return to London, when you and your husband are – ah – once again together, you understand, and sharing your marital experiences, the hormone treatment may be commenced, as advised in the notes. My staff will give you the supplies. You must guard them very carefully –'

'You're sure they'll be all right, your staff?'

'I must trust them' he said. 'I have no one else I *can* trust. They will see to it you are given your correct ampoules. You need have no fears on that score.'

'I wasn't worrying about that,' she said almost sharply. 'I was worrying about you. If you're making these plans – to go away, and you've told them, couldn't they – isn't there a risk that someone among them will tell the authorities, and so prevent you? Wouldn't it be better for you and your family to say nothing, just to go and –'

He shook his head. 'I could not treat my patients so,' he said. 'They are as important to me as my family. I cannot abandon either. That is my dilemma.'

He went to the door and stood there looking at her for a moment. 'I hope you have your babies, my dear. They give a family such joy, these little ones. I know that my babies are to me of such delight. But let me tell you – your life is still good if you have no babies of your own. There are many who will need you, other people's children who will be crying for love and care and –' He shook his head. 'I am only afraid that one day that may be the need of my own two. They are so young – seven and nine. Such happy little boys – you see why it is so difficult? *Gute Nacht, gnädige Frau Lackland.* I wish you all success and happiness. And –' He paused as he opened the door and looked back at her. '*Shalom aleichem.* Peace go with you –' And then he was gone.

She managed to wait another week, as February blew itself out in the wildness of March, but it became more and more difficult. She had nothing to think about but what might be happening to Peter, in Munich, and about what might be happening to Professor Aaronson, who was, she was told by one of the nurses when she enquired as casually as she could, 'at home today with a cold –' and about the tension that seemed to be spreading itself through the clinic. She tried listening to the radio, but however hard she struggled she wasn't able to muster enough of her schoolgirl German to understand what was being said, and for the same reason could get no sense from newspapers. When she asked the nurses who brought her her meals about the news they were bright and antiseptic and soothing, as nurses always are, telling her brightly she must rest, not worry about such matters as the news, there was no news of significance anyway – and they would hurry away on their clacking heels with their starched skirts rustling importantly, leaving her alone and edgy and more and more frightened.

And then at last, on the eleventh day of her stay in the clinic, Peter came back. When he had delivered her there he had told her he would be keeping in touch with the clinic by telephone and would collect her as soon as they said she might leave, and also told her very firmly that on no account was she to set foot outside the place until he came for her, and she had been alarmed enough by her Munich experience to be totally obedient. So, when he arrived in her room one morning soon after breakfast, while she was setting out the day's first patience game, the only occupation she had to fill the interminable hours, she shrieked with delight and leapt to her feet, sending the playing cards flying in a shower.

'Oh, Peter, how marvellous to see you! I've been so lonely and so bored here –'

He came in and closed the door behind him carefully and sat on her bed and she sat beside him with her face so stretched with smiles that it almost made her cheeks ache.

Until she could look at him more carefully and could see how tired and upset he was.

'Peter! What is it?'

'It's going to be bad, Lee. The Germans are marching in here to Austria, and I've got to get you out. Never mind how I know, I just do. You've got to leave today – I know your treatment isn't finished, they told me downstairs you're supposed to be having more tests next week but–'

She bent her head, not wanting to look at him. 'It doesn't matter, Peter,' she said. 'I've been thinking a lot about it all – I've had plenty of time for that.' Now she did lift her head and looked at him with her eyes as candid as she could make them.

'I've been dreadfully selfish and not a little stupid, I think. I let myself get hysterical, drive poor Harry nearly mad, and you – well, I'm embarrassed to even think about it, let alone talk about it.'

'You don't have to worry about me,' he said swiftly. 'It's you I'm concerned about. If you leave now, will you be able to get the treatment you need in London? They said downstairs that you shouldn't go yet – that Professor Aaronson had said when he went off sick that you were to be given your notes after the tests were done, to take back to London, but they couldn't let you have them now, not until he came back and –'

'I don't think he will be back,' she said and he raised his brows at her, puzzled. 'He's gone, I think; he tried to tell me – he's Jewish, you see. It was – it's all dreadful. He said there'd be *Anschluss* and that if that happened he'd have to go –'

'If he's already gone, then he's a wise man,' Peter said vigorously. 'I certainly hope he has. The Nazis are giving Jews a worse and worse time in Germany. God knows what they'll do after they come here to Austria. Look, I've got to get you away, and I'll try to get the notes out of these people here, so that you can get the treatment you need at home and then –'

She shook her head. 'If you try to do that, then they'll start to think you know more than they do, and that the Professor's gone, won't they? And they might try to make it hard for him, go after him or something – I don't know – I think we ought just to leave. If that's what you think is best. I don't want to make things harder for the Professor – and as for myself –' She hesitated. 'As for myself, I'll just have to live with it, won't I? I can't have everything I want –'

He sat and thought for a while, staring at the bright window with his eyes wide and then he nodded. 'I'd like to say it was all right, that you could stay, but all my instincts tell me to get us out now. Not just you, either. I'm worried about the company. Things haven't been all they might be in Munich. I want to get us on our way. Can you get your things together, Lee? I'll go down, pay the bill, tell them you've got to go home because there's illness in the family – something of that sort –'

'Yes,' she said at once and got to her feet and then, as he reached the door called after him. 'Peter, what about Otto and

Lise? Did you find out what was happening? Where are they?'

He stood at the door for a long moment and then turned and looked at her. 'It's not good, I'm afraid. All my people could find out was that yes, there was a family who used to live there in that house. Parents, big boy, two girls, a baby, but they'd gone away. That was all they'd say. I think we'll have to accept it, Lee. They've left. All we can do is hope one day they'll get in touch again, that they got away without any difficulty –'

'If they didn't, where could they be?'

He was silent again for a long time and then came back and sat on the bed. 'I'm not sure I should tell you this. But – damn it, you aren't a baby. And the more people know what's happening the better the chance of stopping it. Lee, they're sending Jews to labour camps. Resettlement camps, they say they are. Some in Bavaria, some in Eastern Germany, Celle, places like that –'

'And do you think they're there? But what can children do in a labour camp? They aren't able to work –'

'The name doesn't say anything about what really happens there. I've got reports back, awful reports –' Again he hesitated but she put her hand on his arm and after a moment he went on. 'It seems they have a high death rate in these places. What happens there to cause it, no one'll say, but there are rumours. Awful rumours.'

'Oh, God,' she said in a soft voice and then more loudly, 'Oh, God.'

'I know. I didn't believe it either,' he said and she held on to his arm tightly, grateful for his ability to read the thoughts in her mind. 'But the stories are so many, and so consistent –'

'Peter, we've got to find Otto and Lise, if they're still in Munich. Is it possible they are? Did your – those people you said who were finding out for you, are they sure they've gone?' She was shaking his arm now as she spoke, pleading with him to reassure her, but all he could do was shake his head.

'I don't know,' he said. 'I just don't know. The only source of information they've got is a woman who used to clean the house for the family. She lives in a village outside the city, and used to work in the Damont house all week, go home weekends. She's the one who told Else – my contact – that they'd lived there once–'

'Can we go and see her, Peter? This cleaner woman? After we leave here? Just so that we can be sure that–'

'I'd really rather you didn't, Lee,' Peter said. 'I know how you feel, but I promised your father. I've got to get you back home safely, and I won't breathe properly again till I do. I swear. I wish I'd never agreed to this crazy scheme in the first place.'

She flashed a grin at him. 'Thank you!'

'You know perfectly well what I mean! Look, Lee, you've got to go home. Don't argue, please–'

But she knew she'd won. There was a note in his voice that told her he was as anxious about the Damont family as she was and she smiled at him now and said softly, 'We have to go, Peter. You know we do. I'll get dressed, you sort things out downstairs and we'll go to the station. The first train out of here to Munich, that's what we want. And then to that village and then–' She swallowed. 'Then, after that, I promise you that we'll go straight home. But I must find out first.'

He went without another word, and she dressed as fast as she could and put her things in her suitcase and then stood waiting for him and looking round the little room. The bed was crumpled but otherwise everything looked as it had the day she had arrived; blank and clinically clean and anonymous, and she tried to remember her feelings as they had been the first time she had come here, almost three years ago, and again how she had felt when she had arrived here a fortnight ago.

Obsessive, that was how she had been. Totally wrapped up in herself and her own hunger and disappointment. There had been no room in her mind for anything else but the functioning of her own body, and standing here now looking at that high narrow bed she marvelled a little. How could she have been so narrow? How could she have been so selfish? And she contemplated the self she had been and the person she now was and thought – I'm like a creature that crept into a chrysalis and changed without knowing it. Whatever I was when I went in, now I'm different. I've got other things to think about, other people to concern myself with. I'm better. I was sick with myself, and now I'm free and it's good—

When Peter came back to fetch her, she left without a backwards glance. What she was leaving behind was not, as she would have thought only as recently as a fortnight ago, her last hope of ever being happy. She was leaving a self she no longer knew or wanted to know. She felt renewed and eager and hopeful as she followed Peter into the echoing ticket hall of the main railway station of Vienna and he booked their first-class seats for Munich. Maybe, after all, they'd find where Otto and Lise were, once they'd talked to this woman they were going to see. Then she could really feel good about herself again, ready to go home to Harry and make up to him for the dreadful way she had treated him for so long.

Her lips curved as she thought of Harry, at home in London, lonely probably and oblivious of the change that had come over her. He would be so happy when she got back, she told herself fondly. I'll make it all up to him, every bit, for all the bad times I've given him. Dear Harry. It will be lovely to see him again—

25

How Harry was able to work at all he wasn't sure. He would go through the afternoon clinics, talking to patients politely, taking their histories, nodding sympathetically as they told him of their woes, but hardly hearing a word they said. He would sit and write up notes at the end of each out-patients' session and find himself staring at the blank page ten minutes after he should have finished, and not a word written. He would stand beside the students and the other doctors on ward rounds, apparently listening as carefully as any of them and then find that a perfectly ordinary question had to be repeated twice before he heard it and even then he hadn't the remotest idea what they were talking about. And the more he worried about how he was behaving, the worse the behaviour became.

Even his chief, newly recovered from his own recent illness, noticed it, telling him gruffly one afternoon that he seemed to need a holiday, and he seized the opportunity and agreed.

'Not being quite as well looked after as I'm used to, I suppose,' he said. 'My wife's away, you see, and—'

'Well, you coped so well for me while I was off sick, that I dare say it's your turn,' Dr Hemmingway said. 'Take a week off, m'boy, get some rest. It's clearly what you need.'

Is it? he asked himself in the deeper recesses of his mind even as he eagerly accepted the offer. Is it? Couldn't it make things worse? Give me too much time to see her? Certainly he'd been seeing a great deal of her ever since that night when he'd taken her home from Letty's, and the results had been miserably confusing, to say the least.

He'd intended, that evening, to be very firm with her. He would tell her precisely what he thought of ill-mannered people who made appointments and then forgot them, he'd promised himself — but somehow it just didn't work out the way he meant it to. She had collected her boxes of odds and ends from her old bedroom at Letty's — and it was perfectly obvious that she wasn't at all in need of them, but had made them an excuse to ensure he would take her home — and then had sat beside him in the taxi, chattering nineteen to the dozen, so that he couldn't tell her how angry he was. Anyway, by the time they reached Sloane Square and were on their way down the King's Road towards Fulham, he'd forgotten all his ire. She was as she had been since he had first met her; funny and easy to be with, as confiding as a child, yet exciting in a way no child could ever be — and it seemed the most natural thing in the world to stay and go on listening to her chatter after he had carried her boxes to the flat.

And having done that, there was no return. Making love was something she wanted to do, and when Katy wanted to do something, somehow it seemed to happen. And he had to be honest and admit that he wasn't averse to it happening either. He loved his Lee dearly, for all the strain she put on him and for all her captious ways, and still wanted her above all other women, but he was a healthy young man with the same physical needs as any other, and Katy, with her uncomplicated attitude to sex, seeing it as something that was healthy for her much as bracing walks in the fresh air and good food were healthy for her, was hard to resist. She didn't wait to be coaxed, didn't expect to be asked; she just threw herself at him, twining her arms and legs round his like an affectionate snake, and it would have taken a much less responsive — and much less unhappy — young man to resist her.

For he was unhappy; the longer Lee was away the worse it got. He would imagine her with Peter, see her drifting closer to him and therefore further from himself and he would ache with the misery of it — and there was Katy to comfort him, and so he let her. And then felt worse than ever as guilt about his own behaviour was added to suspicion about his wife's. It was no wonder that as the days passed that he became more and more anxious and distrait.

He tried to talk to Katy about how he was feeling, seeing her as the only person in whom he could confide, but somehow it was never possible. If he suggested taking her out to dine she would agree with radiant delight, and arrange to meet him as soon as the curtain came down on her play, and then, when he collected her at the stage door, would tell him sunnily that she knew he wouldn't mind because he was such a darling, but she'd booked a table at the Ivy so that divine Bunty and Dan and dear old Binkie could join them, and the evening would become a noisy frolicsome affair with much squealing of laughter and exchange of outrageous theatrical gossip that made it totally impossible for there to be any conversation between the two of them. And even when they were at her flat it wasn't possible to talk properly. She would chatter away as she flitted about the room arranging her curtains and her lighting and her little dishes of smoky incense and then curl up on the cushions and give him that wicked inviting little glance of hers – and after that talking, really serious talking, just wasn't possible.

So, when the chief gave him that week off he decided that he would have to use some of it to think properly. He couldn't go on as he was, getting more and more tangled in his own guilt and doubts, and on the first of his days off, acting totally on impulse, he took himself to Jermyn Street to the Turkish baths there. To sit in steam and to be massaged and pummelled would do him good, he decided, and might help him sort out his thinking a little.

The place was rather busy, but it was quiet. There were a few pallid men with sagging faces and paunches clearly there to work off the previous night's debauchery, carrying with them even in their nakedness an odour of brandy and cigars, and a couple of twisted elderly men with the misshapen joints of advanced arthritis, and as he tied his towel round his hips he shivered a little. Seeing old and sick people at the hospital was just part of his job; he never looked at the damaged bodies he saw at Nellie's and thought, one day, that could be me – patients were patients, materials to be worked on, to be looked after, to be patched up and comforted as best he could; they weren't examples to him that he could use in his own life. But here it was different. In these steamy surroundings where the pale scrubbed wooden boards of the seats and the dripping tiles of the showers and the walls of the steam rooms gleamed dully in the misted light they were all just men, naked men, and his own young firm muscles and flat belly bore the threat of becoming like the old men he saw; one day his skin would sag and droop like old parchment, and his bones would sharpen and make knife-like ridges down his shins, and his eyes would become sticky and red-rimmed and – he shivered again and, wishing he'd not come here after all, took himself to the bar that had been set across one corner and began to do some lifts, holding on with tightly clenched fists and lifting his body so that his chin touched his knuckles. He'd show them that he was young and vigorous, that his joints were strong and supple and his muscles unknotted – but no one looked at him and he knew he was really trying to show himself.

He had reached the seventeenth lift and was beginning to doubt he'd make the target of twenty he'd set himself when a voice behind him made him falter and lose the smoothness of his rhythm and he dropped to the floor and turned irritably to see who had spoiled his attempt; and his face cleared as he saw Theo standing behind him.

'Dear me, such energy,' Theo said, and grinned lazily. 'As soon as I saw you I thought – that guy has to be a visiting American, a Californian at least. No Englishman would be caught displaying himself to such advantage at eleven in the morning.'

'Well, I am an American!' Harry said. 'Virginian, though. What I wouldn't be caught dead doing is being a Californian. What are you doing here?'

'Oh, getting a few creaks out of my bones,' Theo said lazily. 'And perhaps seeing who I might run into–' And again he grinned lazily but this time there was an edge to his glance that puzzled Harry for a moment. And then he saw, over Theo's shoulder, that one of the men he had categorized in his mind as being there at the baths to work off a night of too much brandy was looking at Theo with a decidedly lascivious look in his eye. Theo was completely naked; he had tossed his towel over one shoulder and was standing with his legs braced apart and his hands set on his hips in a way which displayed his body very well, and suddenly Harry felt his face redden. He hadn't given much thought to the sort of private life Theo might lead; he was a friend of Letty's, a famous film star who was noted for his beauty, and that had been all the knowledge he had or wanted of him. To see him now standing in that deliberately provocative pose in a milieu that was totally masculine made him for the first time give some thought to what sort of man Theo might be. And that embarrassed him.

Theo laughed then, as amused as if he had been able to read every word of the thought that had come into Harry's mind.

'My dear chap,' he said and now his drawl was even more pronounced. 'Don't look like that! It's not the end of the world, you know! We all have to find our satisfactions where we can. I must say, it's a pity you're so ferociously what you are. You've a most charming way with you and you're nicely built, aren't you?' And he let his gaze slide over Harry's chest and shoulders in a way that increased Harry's discomfiture. He was, suddenly, very glad indeed they were in a Turkish bath for that gave him a perfectly valid reason for being red in the face and sweating rather more than was usual.

'My wife has no complaints,' he said shortly and turned away to go to the steam room and Theo followed him.

'Nor has Miss Katy, I gather,' he said and laughed.

At once Harry whirled. 'What did you say?'

Theo put his hands up in mock alarm. 'My dear boy, you do jump down a man's throat so!' he murmured. 'I'm just telling you what Katy told me!'

'And what did she tell you?' They had reached the steam room now and it was empty but for themselves, and Harry pulled the door closed very firmly to keep out any other bathers. '*What* did she tell you?' Harry said again, more urgently this time.

'Why, that she was having a delightfully torrid affair with you, that you were very sweet if a little intense, and that soon she'd have to do something to send you off home to your wife again. She has, I must tell you, other plans –' and he chuckled then. 'Not that the little minx'll be able to carry 'em out. She's been trying to ogle me in the most blatant fashion ever since I got here! I told her I'm not at all interested in silly little girls, but that makes not an atom of difference to her. She's certain she can cure me. Would you believe it? These people who will persist in thinking men like me are sick when we feel perfectly marvellous. It's too stupid. But there it is, she's determined she can make me into a boring straight. She tells me of her affair with you as, I gather, a way of showing me what a tremendously experienced person she is, and how much delight she'll be able to bring to my poor impoverished sex life. Actresses – they really are too much!' And he settled himself more comfortably on the bench and smiled again at Harry. 'So you see? There's no need to get into a lather. It's only me she's said it to –'

Harry had listened to all that Theo had said with a sense of increasing horror, and now seized on that last sentence. He was so anxious that he actually sat down next to Theo and took hold of his arm.

'Only you she's told? But how can you know that? If she's told you that I – that we – I mean, oh, my God!' and he let go of Theo's arm and leaned back against the wall. The sweat was running down his face in good earnest now, and it felt like tears on his cheeks. 'Who else has she chattered to? I wish I'd never set eyes on her –'

'You won't be the first to think that, and I doubt you'll be the last,' Theo said equably. He too was leaning back against the wall, letting his shoulders relax, clearly greatly enjoying the steam. 'I know the Katies of this world, my boy. They're delicious fun, they're probably a glorious armful – I wouldn't know of course, but there are boys like that too, and God knows I've suffered enough at *their* hands in my time – and they're out always and for ever for themselves. They *mean* no harm, not a scrap of it, but oh, boy, can they hand it out! They just go from person to person taking what they want and then going on their merry way and not caring what havoc they leave behind. Lethal types, positively lethal –'

'What on earth am I to do?' Harry was staring at the opposite wall now with his face set in lines of the most abject misery. 'Lee – my wife'll be back soon and I – Goddam it, I want Lee! No one else! And now this!'

Theo cocked an eyebrow at him. 'Did she give you a bad time, old boy? Your wife?' he said sympathetically, and without thinking Harry nodded and said, 'Yes. Oh, yes, she did. I meant no harm, of course I didn't, but she'd been so miserable and then –'

How it was he did it he was never to know. He had been repelled by Theo at first, had been, in a rather prim way, shocked by the realization that he was the sort of man he was, but sitting there in that empty steam room, each as naked as the other, he found at last the confidant and friend he needed. He poured it all out, every bit; the way Lee had been because of her childlessness, his own sense of failure because he'd been unable to help her, the embrace about which Katy had told him on the night of Letty's party, and now, her absence with Peter in Europe, and Theo listened and in his silence was eloquent, offering precisely the sort of sympathy Harry needed.

At last he stopped, the cascade of words trickling away to a silence, and Theo sat up and stretched and said thoughtfully, 'That child – she really ought to be removed from the scene, oughtn't she? From all you've said, it's clear that there's no real harm done. No, don't look like that, you foolish boy. There isn't. I've met your rival, this Peter. He's no threat to you! He's not the sort of man to go poaching other men's wives. He's so upright he gives one a crick in the neck. Too virtuous to be true. Anyway, he's madly involved in his job. He's the crusading sort, you know? I've met many like him. They're the salt of the earth, and from where I stand, deadly boring. But no threat. No, what you need is Katy removed from the scene and time to sort out your problems with your wife. She *is* a silly woman, your wife, isn't she?'

'She is not!' Harry flared. 'She's very intelligent and –'

'Oh, intelligent!' Theo said and waved that away. 'That's very likely. But silly as well. Some of the silliest people I know are the most intellectual. But I dare say she could learn, as long as you were free to concentrate on her. Look, I'll get rid of Katy for you.'

'Get rid –' Harry said, and tried to see Katy in his mind's eye, and there she was, the round face and the pointed chin, the wickedly laughing green eyes and that look she got sometimes when she was thinking, and he knew suddenly, and at last, what the look was.

'Get rid of her?' he said again slowly. 'She's so calculating that you'll never get her to do anything that she doesn't want to – that isn't good for her–'

'Aha!' Theo said and looked at him again with that comically raised eyebrow. 'You've realized at last! That's precisely it! Katy does what Katy wants. She's so ambitious she'll swallow herself one of these days. It's sad, but there it is. She's a user and always will be. Well, I'll let her get her own way without actually letting her climb into bed with me.'

He leaned back and laughed again. 'That'll fox her,' he said. 'She wanted to get me to take her to Hollywood when I go back, you see. She thought the best way to get there was in my bed. And I'll take her anyway and she won't know why. That'll be good for her–' And he laughed again. 'Not knowing why. So do stop fretting, my dear boy. You'll sort things out with your wife when she gets back from wherever she is, and you'll discover that Peter's no problem and it'll all be fine. Now for heaven's sake get out of here before I forget myself and make a pass at you, because you really are too good-looking for your own good.'

26

I do wish Harry was here, Lee thought and had to blink to hold back the tears that rose to her eyes and then pulled her shoulders back, controlling herself firmly. This is no time to get stupid about Harry, she told herself. We'll have to manage on our own somehow. But all the same if he were here, he'd get the woman to talk. He'd treat her like a patient, and coax it all out of her and she'd trust him. She obviously doesn't trust us –

Peter looked at her and lifted his brows in a sort of resigned anxiety, and then started again. '*Frau Weber*,' he said. '*Bitte – die Familie Damont – wo ist die Familie Damont? Ich bin ein Freund. Die Dame hier ist eine Kusine – bitte, gnädige Frau Weber – können Sie helfen? Verstehen Sie?*'

'I don't think she understands your German, Peter.' Lee couldn't help it. When they'd arrived outside the small and rather shabby house at the end of the village street, after what seemed like hours of looking for it, she'd promised him she'd say nothing, would leave all the talking to him, but they'd been standing on the doorstep now for what seemed like ages, and still the woman just stood there staring at them with uncomprehending eyes, her arms folded inside the apron which she had pulled up to reveal a heavy black dress over thick legs and clog-clad feet.

Peter took a sharp little breath, clearly both furious with her and alarmed; to speak English when he was trying so hard not to draw attention to themselves – and Lee looked at him with her face stricken with guilt. It had just come out; she hadn't meant to forget his warning and she opened her mouth to speak again but, just in time, closed it as an obviously curious neighbour went shuffling past on the roadway, staring at them as she went.

But at last the woman on the doorstep had reacted, for now she made an odd sound in her throat and as Lee looked at her jerked her chin in a beckoning movement and stood aside to let them into the house; and after one swift glance at Peter, Lee went in, and he followed her.

The door opened directly into the living-room of the house. It was small and very dark, for the window was a narrow one and the sill so loaded with leafy plants that what little winter light there was couldn't struggle in, but there was a fire glowing in the broad and highly polished kitchen range which gave some illumination and after a moment or two Lee's eyes accustomed themselves to the light level and she could look around.

Everywhere it was as clean as a room could be. The furniture though made of dull heavy wood was layered with polish, and the floor, covered with a vividly coloured rug made of rags, looked as though it had never seen dust in its life. Everywhere there were shelves laden with carvings and toys and knickknacks of all sorts, cheap and jovial but none at first glance worth more than a penny or two, and the overall effect was of cosiness and warmth. Lee, with a tremulous smile, looked at the woman who had closed the door behind them and had now come to stand before them.

'Nice,' she ventured. 'Very nice. It's – *sehr gemütlich*. Nice –' And extraordinarily the woman smiled too.

'I make for you the *Kaffee*,' she announced and her voice was thick, as though she had a cold in her throat, and the hoarseness grated on Lee's ears. 'I make for you *Kuchen*. You should sit, eat –' and she took Lee's arm and led her to a chair beside the fire and after a moment Lee sat down, and Peter came and stood behind the chair, one hand protectively on her shoulder. It felt good to Lee to have it there, and briefly she put up her own hand and touched his.

'You speak English, Frau Weber,' Peter said, keeping his voice low. 'I did not expect –'

'In my youth I work at the Gasthof Amerika – in Munich. I learn good English there. I do not forget.'

She was busying herself at her kitchen range, pulling a

coffee-pot forward to stand over the coals, and then went to a cupboard in the corner and brought out a red tin box and thick white cups and saucers, setting it all on her table with a certain flourish. It was as though, Lee thought, she wasn't in her own kitchen at all, but on view in a restaurant and for a moment she wanted to smile. This woman, who couldn't be less than sixty-five, was feeling young again; that was it. The mention of her youth in the hotel in Munich –

'Please, Frau Weber,' she said and leaned forwards. 'Can you help us? We were told that you – we understood that your last job was with a family in Munich. The Damont family –'

'I do not work any more,' she said, and her voice was stronger now, though still very hoarse. 'I am a widow. I am old. I have my –' She lifted her chin and looked over Lee's shoulder for a moment and then let her eyes slide away. 'I have my responsibilities.' And Lee too looked over her shoulder but all she could see was a heavy door, firmly closed. 'Yes,' Frau Weber said again. 'My responsibilities. I cannot work longer for the families in Munich.'

'It must have been hard work for you when you did,' Peter cut in smoothly as Lee was about to speak again, and his hand tightened on her shoulder in warning. 'Such a journey – it took us two hours in the train. To do that every day, it must have been hard for you –'

'Hard!' Frau Weber went to the range again to peer into the coffee pot. 'Yes, it is hard. I must go every Sunday night, I come back every Friday night, after I light the fire, cook the food. It is hard. I do not do this any more.'

'I'm sure you're wise,' Peter said sympathetically. 'Very wise. The people you worked for – I hope they treated you well?'

At once she looked guarded. 'People? What people?'

'Your employers.'

She shrugged. 'In forty years I worked for many people.'

'The ones you worked for last, though. They were good to you?'

'Why do you ask this? I make you *Kaffee* and *Kuchen* because I think you are tourists, you have missed your way, so I make you some refreshments, then you go on your journey. That is why I ask you in, *ja*? So why do you ask me these questions?'

'Because we are tourists who have lost our way,' Peter said promptly. 'We are like all tourists, very inquisitive. It is to pass the time, you understand. Nothing more. We travel, we pass the time hearing about the people of the places we visit.'

Again she looked at him with those hard blank eyes and then, slowly, nodded. 'You do not make enquiries for any official purpose. You are just what I think you are. Visitors—'

'Yes,' Peter said and leaned forwards and looked at her, very closely. 'Look at me, Frau Weber. Am I an official person? Can't you see I can be trusted to be just a visitor? Can't you?'

It was as though he were sending out some sort of invisible energy, he stared at her so fixedly, and she stood there staring back at him for a long time; and then the lid of the coffee-pot began to chatter as steam lifted it and she took a sharp little breath and turned and seized the pot from the stove and bore it to the table.

She poured the coffee and gave it to them solemnly, handing them the thick white cups as though they were the most delicate of bone china, and then loaded a plate with biscuits from her tin and handed that as well and Lee after a moment took one. She wasn't hungry but she knew better than to insult Frau Weber by refusing.

The biscuit was thick and heavy in her hand. It was golden-brown, sugar-covered and glistening and as she bit into it and the sweetness crumbled on her tongue she felt, suddenly, as though she were once again sitting in Otto and Lise's sitting-room. Lise had given her a biscuit like this and without thinking, she exclaimed, 'Oh, this is lovely! Cousin Lise gave me these, with just this taste!'

Frau Weber bridled then, her face becoming mottled with colour. 'I teach her the way—' And Lee looked up at her, standing there with her plate of biscuits in her hand and saw tears, round and oily, forming in the corners of her eyes and sliding down her heavy jowls.

'You taught her well, Frau Weber,' she said gently. 'Very well. I ate them just like this at her house two years ago. When I visited my cousin Otto and his wife and his children. I tasted them and these are the very same. You taught her well—'

Frau Weber nodded and went back to her table and poured coffee for herself and they all sipped the bitter blackness of it in silence, Lee and Peter watching the old woman over the rims of their cups, and she standing there beside her table with her head bent as she sipped steadily.

The coffee seemed to strengthen her resolve, suddenly, for she put the cup down on the table with a little clatter and came to sit on the chair facing Lee and stared at her.

'So. You are the cousin of the Damonts? From England?'

Lee nodded.

'Yes, I remember your visit. She told me. This is your husband?' And she looked briefly at Peter.

'No,' Lee said. 'My husband is a doctor at home in England. He could not come with me this time. This is my cousin. He wants to help me. Help us. He wants to help the family to be – to be safe –' She hesitated, not sure what to say next but Frau Weber nodded.

'*Juden raus*,' she said unexpectedly. 'Hey? That's what they say, these men in boots. *Juden raus*. What do they know? All those years with the family, and always the kindest of people. When my Ernst died, God rest his sweet soul in everlasting heaven, they look after me. They give me more money, offer me a permanent home with them – did the Nazis make such help for a widow woman? They just say *Juden raus* –' And she turned her head and spat with extraordinary accuracy into her fire and the sharp hiss of the coals sounded loud in the small dark room.

'Where are they, the Damonts?' Peter said and she looked up at him and again the tears were in her eyes.

'Gone. Where do I know? They've gone. One morning, Willi comes –' And now the tears were running freely. 'Willi, so tall and good, that boy. I cooked for his barmitzvah. Such things I cooked and he loved them so much! Ever since he was a baby, Willi was my special one. And Willi comes and brings – he comes and says they must go. His Poppa has already been taken, and the little girls have been put on a train, they are trying to go to Vienna, where Frau Damont has her sister's family, and he must try to go separately. His Poppa, his Momma, gone to a camp–' And she shook her head as her thick voice rasped to a silence and she took a large red bandanna from her apron pocket and blew her nose loudly.

'What did Willi bring, Frau Weber?' Peter said and the old woman shook her head and wouldn't look at him, but he said it again, louder this time. 'Frau Weber, what did he bring? You said he came to bring – and then you stopped. What did he bring?' The insistence in his voice increased as again he repeated the question and Lee reached up to hold on to his arm to stop him, wanting to protest, for Frau Weber was crying bitterly now and shaking her head, trying to deny the pressure of Peter's questions. But he wouldn't stop. He shook off Lee's hand and said it again, more loudly. 'What did he bring to you? You must tell me – I must know. What did he–'

And then stopped as they heard it, and he turned his head and stared at the door behind them as Lee did the same. It came again, unmistakable and louder still, and now Frau Weber got clumsily to her feet, and still wiping her eyes with her red handkerchief went across the room, pushing them aside to reach the door.

When she opened it the sound got louder and as Frau Weber went up the stairs that the door had revealed Lee turned and looked at Peter and said breathlessly, 'Peter! Could it be–'

'Hush,' he said and turned back to the door and watched. They stood there in silence, listening. Behind them the fire hissed a little and above their heads floorboards creaked as Frau Weber moved about and they could hear her voice murmuring, and the sound that had so startled them stopped, and then the footsteps became heavier, more purposeful, and Frau Weber reappeared on the staircase, making her way down to them, looking over the burden she carried, making sure she moved carefully. She came into the room and stood there looking at them and then said heavily, 'You see? What else can I do but take him? What else can I do?' And the child in her arms turned his head and looked at Lee, and his small face puckered and his mouth opened as he saw the strangers there, and he turned back and buried his head in Frau Weber's neck.

By the time they had eaten supper the child had become less shy. He still sat only on Frau Weber's lap, refusing to go to

Lee, however much she tried to coax him, but he was at least willing to look at her now, watching her from behind the bulwark of Frau Weber's large freckled arm, and when, after she'd sung a few words of 'Peter Piper Picked a Peck of Pickled Peppers' at him and he laughed, opening his mouth to reveal very white small teeth, she felt as though she had achieved something very remarkable indeed.

But it wasn't enough. She felt fear rising in her as she contemplated what was to come and looked again at the boy; but he wasn't interested in her any more. He had turned to rest his head against Frau Weber's broad front and was tugging on the wisps of greying hair that were lying on her shoulders.

'Frau Weber,' she said then. 'It's all very well to *say* we can do it – but will he let me? He loves you so much. You've only got to look at him to know that he loves you –'

The old woman looked down at the child and her heavy face lifted into a smile of great tenderness and the child laughed and pushed both hands up and tried to pull her mouth open and she laughed too, and Lee sat and watched them and wanted to pull the child away, to hold him in her own arms, make him crow with delight at her like that –

'We'll have to make it work, Lee,' Peter said. 'We've got to. You heard what Frau Weber said. She can't –'

The old woman lifted her head then and looked at Peter and after a moment got to her feet and brought from a dark corner of the room a high chair which she set against the table, and sat the child in it. She tied a piece of clean rag round his neck and put one of her biscuits into his hand and he set to work contentedly chewing it, rubbing the crumbs over his face and into his dark hair and clearly greatly enjoying himself.

'If I could keep him, do you think I would let him go?' she said with a sort of ferocity in her voice, that hoarse heavy voice that had so grated in Lee's ears when she had first heard it. 'Do you think if I thought I could be here long enough to look after him I'd let you have him? Never, never. But I know. Three months I have known and worry, worry, and now you are here and I can see the way out. A bad way out for me, a good way out for Meyer –' And again she took the red bandanna from her pocket and blew her nose, but there was more of

243

anger in her movements now than sadness, and Lee could feel the rage that was boiling in her. Yet she was helpless; they all were, and she leaned forwards now and said impulsively, 'Frau Weber, isn't an operation possible? They do such operations for such illnesses – my husband, I know, tells me – if it is that, I can pay –'

'Money?' Frau Weber said and looked at her with such venom that Lee shrank back. 'If it was so easy, would I let him go? I get the money if I need it, I would have the operation. I have neighbours, someone would have him for me till I was well. But – I will not be well. The doctor tells me, it is months, perhaps weeks. Soon I do not talk at all, soon I do not eat. All the throat is cancer, not just the voice – all the throat. And you offer me money!'

'She spoke from kindness, Frau Weber,' Peter said softly. 'Nothing more. Just kindness.' And after a moment the old woman took a breath and turned and looked at Lee again.

'Yes,' she said. 'Yes. Kindness. But it is too late for kindness.'

'So you will let us take him to England, to his people there?' Peter said. 'You'll let him go with us?'

'What else can I do?' The thick hoarse sounds hung in the air, filling it with the anguish that was in that heavy old body and they sat there frozen for a while, until the baby wailed and held out his hands to Frau Weber and said, '*Mutti – Mutti –*'

Lee went white then. 'Peter!' she said. 'He can talk!'

'Of course he talks,' Frau Weber snapped. 'He is two years old now. Of course he can talk. He says many words –'

'German,' Lee said and stared at Peter and he looked back and said nothing, his upper lip caught between his teeth.

'Yes,' he said, after a while. 'Yes, I see what you mean. I think, you know, we'll have to –' He got to his feet. 'Frau Weber, the doctor here. He's a good man? Not a Nazi?'

'Dr Kleber, a Nazi? His son wanted to be a policeman and they said – *Berufsverbot* – the law says he is politically unsuitable. So the boy runs away from home and Dr Kleber says it is the fault of the *Schweinhund* Nazis – Dr Kleber a Nazi?' And again she spat into her fireplace, disgust clear in every movement.

'Good,' Peter said crisply. 'Then he'll help. We'll have to tell him what we're doing. And that Meyer must sleep as much as possible on the journey. He'll understand why we must take the baby away?'

'He will understand,' Frau Weber said. 'He it was warned me I must never let the boy use the public lavatories, gave me a certificate to say he had to have the operation for his health –'

'Operation?' Lee said and Frau Weber flicked a scornful glance at her.

'Meyer is circumcized,' she said. 'They take children away for this,' and Lee closed her eyes, chilled by the calmness of the thick voice and the images her words conjured up.

'Where do I find him?' Peter was at the door. 'I must see him now. The sooner we get away the better. Where is Dr Kleber's house, Frau Weber?'

For a brief moment it looked as though she wasn't going to tell him. She was standing beside Meyer, her hand on his head and staring down at him and he was laughing again, pushing the remnants of his biscuit into his smeared mouth and she looked at him and then at last up at Peter.

'Beside the biergarten. At the other end of the village, next to the biergarten,' she said, and now her voice was so thick the words were only just comprehensible. 'Tell him I sent you, he will do what you need. And please be soon back. If he's going, I want him gone. Soon. I want him gone.'

27

The baby was getting heavier and heavier, and Lee wanted to transfer him to her other arm, thinking that would ease the ache in her shoulder muscles, but she was afraid that it would disturb him; it had taken so long to get him to sleep in the first place that any risk of waking him now was not to be contemplated.

At first, they had thought the medicine that Dr Kleber had given Peter for Meyer would work perfectly. The doctor had come to the small house himself, had given her the green ribbed bottle and explained in very slow, pedantic English exactly how she must use it. Five drops, no more, on a lump of sugar, every four hours. No more, and the baby would sleep. After they had passed the border of course, there would be no more need.

'Then he will wake and be lively,' the doctor had said rather ominously, and had put one bony finger under Meyer's chin and looked at him with his face expressionless. 'After the border he can be just a baby. A baby who cries and talks and is lively. Not a Jew, not a refugee. A baby. So until the border he must sleep. Five drops on a sugar lump. No more, just five drops.'

So they had given him the first dose as Frau Weber had sat with him on her lap, and he had chattered and laughed at her, and then, fifteen minutes after chewing up his sugar lump, his eyes had glazed and swum and he had mumbled a little and fallen asleep; and Frau Weber had thrust him on to Lee's lap while she went upstairs and packed a small bag with clothes for him. He had gone on sleeping, all through the parting from the old woman – who had not wept, but stood in frozen silence in the middle of her clean cluttered little living-room watching them – and while Dr Kleber accompanied them to the station, talking all the time. He assured them that he would explain to any who asked that the child had been taken ill, that he had arranged for him to go to hospital in Stuttgart, that no one would be suspicious of the child's disappearance.

'I will say Stuttgart and not München, so they will not be surprised Frau Weber does not visit him,' he had said as they stood on the platform of the small railway station, waiting for the local train that would take them back to Munich, where they would be able to pick up the Orient Express on its way back to Paris. 'In Stuttgart is a specialist in the diseases of children who taught me when I was a student. I will say I have sent the boy there. I will also say –' He had hesitated. 'I will also say he was so ill he could not get better. The heart disease, I will tell the people who ask. And eventually I will say sadly he has died. Then there can be no trouble with police. They notice such things, these Nazi police. They notice too much. We do not want problems for Frau Weber.'

'About Frau Weber,' Lee said awkwardly, but determined to do what she felt was right. 'She got angry with me when I offered – when I asked if it would help to pay for an operation.'

The doctor had shaken his head, his face as blank as ever, but there was regret there all the same. 'Too late,' he had said briefly. 'Too late.'

'Then let me provide some – a little comfort –' Lee had said. 'I mean, if I send you money, when – later, when she needs good food, wine, nurses –'

Dr Kleber had thought for a moment. 'Money for food and wine, no. She will not be able to eat. Money for nurses – well, she will be cared for by nuns. But if you wish to send money to them – if it will help you –'

'It will,' Lee had said, grateful that he understood so well her need to give something to the old woman left so bereft in her small house. 'It will. As soon as I reach London, I'll send it.'

And Dr Kleber had nodded and for the first time smiled at her. And still Meyer had slept on.

But then, when at last the train arrived and they had settled themselves on it, and Dr Kleber had lifted his hat to them and gone, the baby had woken. They had sat in the middle of the

crowded compartment as the small train fussed its interminable way through country station after country station, as
he cried and fought in Lee's arms, staring up at her with eyes
filled with fear and confusion as the strangeness of his
company and the befuddlement caused by Dr Kleber's
medicine battled inside his small head, and the other
passengers looked on curiously and, often, somewhat censor-
iously, as Lee did her best to soothe him, praying her
inexperience in handling him wouldn't show.

She was unable to do more than rock the child, croon at
him, which added to her tension. She could not speak to him,
dare not make any sounds but formless ones, Not only was
Peter convinced it was risky to speak English; the baby
wouldn't understand it anyway. To hear foreign words might
make him more agitated rather than less, and Lee knew it. So
she bounced him and crooned nonsense syllables at him and
Peter sat beside her, tense and watchful, as other passengers
came and went and sat and stared at the obvious foreigners
with naked and unashamed curiosity.

But then, at last, just before they reached Munich, he had
fallen asleep again, his struggles to overcome the medicine
defeated, and they had breathed again, and got off the local
train as fast as they decently could, Lee carrying Meyer and
Peter close behind her with the small bag Frau Weber had
packed.

'It's chloral,' Peter murmured in her ear as they went along
the platform towards the exit that led them to the taxi rank
where they could get transport to the main-line station for the
next stage of their journey. 'The doctor warned me it could
happen, but hoped it wouldn't.'

'What?' Lee was getting breathless now. The child was
heavy; he seemed to be a dead weight in her arms and she was
beginning to tremble with the effort.

'The drug he gave him. It's called chloral. It makes some
people agitated, apparently. He thought Meyer'd take it all
right, but he warned me. If it happens, he said, don't give him
any more. It'll make him worse rather than better. It's going to
be a tough journey, Lee. Hold on hard, and do as I say. All the
time—'

The express was due to leave at ten minutes past ten, and they got to the station with an hour to spare. Peter settled Lee in the buffet, finding a corner table where she could lean her back against the wall, and told her to feign sleep if anyone came near her.

'It's the best way to be left in peace,' he said. 'I'll get tickets, pick up the bags from the left-luggage office and phone the company. Gregory'll have to manage alone from now on. We'll get on the train as soon as I've done all that. It should be in – it's due here from Salzburg just before nine – so we should be all right. Just sit tight and wait–'

The next half-hour was the worst, she decided, that she had ever spent. The child, lying against her shoulder and breathing deeply, snoring a little, dribbled against her neck and that made her skin itch, but she didn't dare move to relieve it, and the longer she sat still, the worse the itching became. And then her arm, the one which was bearing the most of Meyer's weight, developed pins and needles and she could have cried with the discomfort; but she sat doggedly on, watching the people in the marble walled room, smelling coffee and beer and *Würst* and garlic and trying to look relaxed and comfortable; just an ordinary young mother travelling with her baby –

At last Peter came back, and at the sight of his tall body pushing its way in through the revolving doors of the buffet she felt her eyes fill with tears of relief and when he reached her side and looked down at them he smiled reassuringly and murmured, 'It's all right, Lee. We'll be all right. The station's just its normal self. No police around that I can see, no reason to think anyone will pay us any attention at all.'

'You'd think we'd committed a crime,' she said, and felt a spurt of anger, and that helped get rid of the moment of tearfulness. 'I'm doing nothing wrong – I shouldn't have to skulk like this. He's my baby, my family. Why shouldn't I travel with him? It's wicked that we have to be so scared.'

'I know,' he said. 'I know. And it could be I'm fussing too much, imagining villains where there aren't any. Maybe no one will care in the least what we do, and who we take out of the country with us. But I've learned enough in the past few months about what's going on here in Germany these days to

249

make me very jumpy. I'd rather be safe than sorry. So keep up the care, Lee, my dear. Keep it up. Just be calm and do what I say.'

And he put one hand under her elbow to lift her to her feet, and as she rose, Meyer stirred in her arms and began to whimper and she went white.

'I'll take him,' Peter said. 'I can easily. The luggage is already on the train – I couldn't get us first-class compartments, but I've got us on the train and that's what matters – so I'll take him. Give him to me –' And he took Meyer from her arms as he whimpered more loudly and began to struggle. But Peter was a match for him, and wrapped the blanket which was round him more firmly across the child's shoulders and arms so that his movements were hampered, and held on tightly.

By the time they reached the train he had subsided into sleep again, and Lee whispered to Peter as they settled themselves into the carriage, 'Shall we give him some more of that stuff when he wakes again? It's so much better when he sleeps –'

But Peter shook his head, and leaned back and settled Meyer more comfortably against his shoulder. 'Won't risk it,' he murmured, looking across at the only other inhabitant of their compartment, a large old man wrapped in a heavy shawl who was fussing with a hot-water bottle which he kept arranging and rearranging against his legs. 'Dr Kleber said don't, if he gets restless. It's a paradoxical reaction, apparently. Can't risk it. He'll just get out of hand altogether, he said. So, no – just sit tight and hope for the best –'

And for a while it seemed all would be well. The train started on time, and after fussing even more with his hot-water bottle, demanding that the guard who came round to check tickets refill it, the old man on the other side of the compartment settled down to sleep after glowering at them malevolently and, as Meyer too slept heavily on, Lee could slide into a restless slumber herself.

The movement of the train, the exhaustion that filled her – for it had been an extraordinarily emotional as well as physical day – combined with her hunger (for they had eaten nothing since lunch, except for Frau Weber's *Kuchen*) made her dream heavily. She was running, trying to catch a train, knew that if she didn't someone would come and throw her into prison and she'd be there for ever, would never see her Harry again, and in her dream she wept, frantic with fear, yet knowing she was only dreaming; and that somehow made it worse rather than better and she cried out, opening her dreaming mouth in a desperate attempt to make enough noise to waken her real self – and did wake to find Peter holding her shoulder and saying urgently, 'Lee. It's all right. Lee! Be quiet – it's all right.'

But the harm had been done, for even as Peter spoke and she sat and stared at him with sleep-filled frantic eyes the train slowed and rattled and at last stopped, and the old man in the corner and Meyer woke at the same time.

The next fifteen minutes were dreadful. Meyer cried and cried and could not be comforted, holding himself rigid in Peter's arms, arching his back and clenching his fist as he bawled, his face red and his eyes tightly closed, against tears which edged their way out to streak his cheeks, and the old man in the corner first glanced at them and then began to swear, in loud guttural German that Lee couldn't understand, but knew was full of fury.

And then, even above the din that Meyer was making they heard the voices and the slamming doors further down the train. They had reached the border.

It was Peter who saved the day. Suddenly he stopped trying to hold on to Meyer, but sat him down on the seat next to Lee, as she sat staring anxiously out of the window at the station platform outside, which could just be seen in the pools of light thrown by the high lamps strung above the railway line, and reached for the bag Frau Weber had given them.

'We're idiots,' he muttered at her, as the old man across the compartment went on with his monotonous swearing and Meyer wept on, though less noisily now, as fatigue seemed to take over his small body. 'Idiots – the poor little scrap must be starving! God knows I'm hungry – here, has she put any – oh, God bless Frau Weber, here it is –' And he thrust into Lee's hands a bottle of milk with a screw top and then went diving into the bag again to find a mug.

'Here we are – give him some of that. Then maybe there's a

biscuit here – he liked the other one she gave him –'

The slamming doors outside were louder now, as were the voices, as the police came nearer to their compartment, and with her fingers trembling with anxiety, Lee fumbled with the bottle. But she managed to put the milk into the mug and as Peter took the bottle back, offered the drink to Meyer.

For a dreadful moment it seemed it wouldn't work, as still he sat with his eyes screwed up, weeping, and then he opened his eyes and saw the mug and lunged for it, and began to drink noisily as Lee held it to his lips as carefully as she could. He seemed to go on drinking until Lee became alarmed; if he drank so fast he might be sick and then what a drama with the angry old man across the compartment –

But Meyer wasn't sick and when he lifted his face from the empty mug, Peter held out the biscuit and Meyer looked at her and then, as the door of the compartment opened, took the biscuit from Peter's hand.

The guard came in, followed by the policeman, and Lee looked up at him, a quick scared little look, and then looked down at Meyer. He was sitting beside her, staring owlishly at Peter, who was now sitting on the facing seat, leaning over to murmur to him, and she thought – clever Peter. You've done it. You've done it, and she felt tears in her eyes again, just as she had in the buffet at Munich station and thought confusedly – be careful – must be careful – and took a deep tremulous breath.

The policeman had held out his hand to Peter, demanding passports, and Peter had given them to him and the policeman studied them, looking from Peter to Lee and back again and then at the baby, and he frowned sharply and opened his mouth to speak, and Lee felt her eyes widen with sudden terror as the realization of what the man was about to say washed over her like a cold sea-water wave. They'd overlooked it. She and Peter, they'd overlooked the most important thing of all.

Meyer had no passport.

She threw a frantic look at Peter and it was as though she'd given a warning shout, for he, catching her glance, suddenly went white, just as the old man in the corner lumbered to his feet, and pushed his way across the compartment towards the door shouting something unintelligible.

The guard and policeman together put up their hands to stop him but the old man paid them no attention at all; he just pushed them aside with his bulk, which, now he was standing up, was revealed as being even more impressive than it had seemed when he was sitting down, and went out into the corridor still shouting at the top of his voice, and at once the guard and policeman followed him and they were sitting alone and staring at each other. What was more, Peter had the passports in his hand, for the policeman had dropped them on the seat beside him as he turned to follow the old man out.

'What's going on?' Lee whispered after a while as the shouting outside went on, but Peter lifted his brows and shook his head.

'Quiet. Let me listen,' he murmured. 'Just be natural. Behave as though nothing has happened –' And again he leaned forwards to look at Meyer who was now sitting leaning against Lee and looking sleepy again. He seemed to have been made drowsy both by his crying bout and the slaking of his thirst, and he blinked back at Peter and suddenly smiled, and Lee, looking down at him, saw his cheeks become round and without thinking put her hand on his and made a crooning little noise in her throat.

The baby turned and looked up at her and for a moment his face seemed about to crumple, as though he were disappointed in what he saw, and she touched his head, the way she had seen Frau Weber do, and made the little noise again; and this time Meyer smiled at her too, if rather doubtfully, and she felt her chest tighten with a sudden mix of emotions she couldn't sort out at all. She was relieved that he wasn't crying, and touched by his bravery as he seemed, in the middle of all the confusion that had seized his small life, to have a resilience to smile at a total stranger, and angry that he should have to be put through such an experience; and there was something else in the mix too which she couldn't identify, and she touched his head again and smiled at him as he turned back to look at Peter.

There was a noise outside the train now, and she leaned forwards to look out of the window. There, further up the platform, she could just see the guard and the policeman, and then a couple more policemen came hurrying up too, and there was a little crush of them there, their heads together, all talking loudly. The group moved then, seeming to split apart, and as she watched, her face pressed against the window in an effort to lengthen the range of vision, two of the policemen emerged from it, holding firmly by the elbows their erstwhile companion. He was still shouting at the top of his voice and trying to struggle against the police grip, but it made no difference; despite his bulk the two policemen led him off, and they disappeared through a door at the far side of the platform.

'Peter,' she said breathlessly. 'That old man who was so upset – they've taken him off the train –' And then there was a whistle down the platform, the train jerked and the platform began to move past the windows. 'Peter! Is it – are we through? And what's to happen to the old man? And –'

The train gathered speed, rattled over the points by the signals and the string of lamps overhead outside lost definition and blurred into a single streak of light as the speed increased and settled down to a steady rocking. The door opened and the guard came in and began methodically to remove the luggage that had been piled on the rack above the old man's head.

Lee stared at him and then at Peter, and he made a face at her, to warn her to be quiet, and then said in German as casually as he could, 'Anything wrong?'

'Nothing is wrong,' the guard said, not looking at him as he took the bags out into the corridor. 'There is no problem. All is normal – soon we reach Strasbourg. At 4.10 am Strasbourg.'

'Where's our fellow passenger gone?'

'He changed his mind,' the guard said repressively. 'He leaves the train –'

'Without his luggage?' Peter persisted.

'This is not a matter to discuss!' the guard said, now clearly flustered. 'It is an internal matter. Not for tourists. An internal matter. It is completed. All is normal.' And he went, closing the compartment door behind him with a loud snap.

'I – Peter!' Lee said and looked at him with her eyes wide with hope. 'What do you think? Is that it?'

'It has to be,' Peter said slowly. 'That was the border police – and any moment now we'll be out of Germany and into France – I think we've got away with it.' And he looked down at the two passports still in his hand. 'Even without a passport for Meyer. It's incredible, but I think we've managed it. And we'd no right to, overlooking something as basic as that–'

Lee laughed, then, a shaky little sound. 'Maybe if we'd thought about it we wouldn't have dared. As it is, we did, and here we are almost in France, on our way home and–' And she leaned down and picked up Meyer and sat him on her lap. 'And he's safe. He's safe and he's coming home with me!'

'Yes,' Peter said, and looked at her face, radiant over Meyer's head, as she hugged the child close. 'Yes. I don't know what the old man had done, or why they took him off, but I'm bloody glad they did, poor devil. If they hadn't, they'd not have forgotten us–'

And Lee nodded at him, too excited and relieved to be able to say a word, but as she looked down at Meyer, who stared back at her in drowsy puzzlement, she saw the old man's face glowering at her. A bad-tempered old man who'd fussed over hot-water bottles and sworn at them. She'd found him threatening and disagreeable when she'd first seen him, but now she was filled with a vast brimming gratitude. And at that moment she knew she was never to forget him, ever, for the rest of her life.

28

'But you can't pick a baby up and take him out of the country, just like that!' Harry said, staring down at the grimy child in Lee's arms, his face blank with amazement.

'But, darling, we *did*,' Lee said very reasonably, and smiled at him and then down at Meyer. 'As you see – and, oh, Harry, it's been an incredible journey. Trying to manage a baby's nappy when you're not very good at it anyway, on a train that's rocking like – like a roller coaster and then on a ship that's bucketting the way that steamer was, is the most awful business, especially when he wriggles as much as this little creature does. And then, the poor darling was seasick, and I didn't feel too marvellous, but Peter was simply splendid and looked after both of us, and here we are. I'm so relieved you got the message – when we phoned from Boulogne it was a dreadful line and I could hardly hear what they said at Nellie's, but I told them it was frightfully important that you be here to meet me –'

'I got it,' he said a little grimly. 'They had the impression that you were desperately ill and that it was a life and death matter that I be here –'

'Oh, the silly creatures!' Lee said and hugged Meyer again as he began to whimper. 'I told them it was important, of course, but I didn't say anything about life and death. If it'd been anything really awful Peter would have phoned, wouldn't he? Not me –'

The baby was crying now in good earnest, and she began to rock him, crooning at him softly, and Harry flicked a glance at Peter standing beside her, still silently, for he hadn't said a word other than 'Good afternoon,' since they had arrived. 'I suppose I must thank you,' he said a little stiffly. 'It was good of you to look after her. What is all this about this baby? Who is he?'

'I think I must leave it to Lee to explain everything,' Peter said. 'She'll want to anyway –' and he rubbed his face with both hands. 'I really am exhausted. I've had no sleep for forty-eight hours and it's beginning to tell.' And indeed he looked grey, with deep violet shadows under his eyes.

But Harry could feel no spark of sympathy for him. It was all he could do to control his anger enough to stop himself hitting the man, let alone anything else.

'Peter's been so marvellous, Harry darling,' Lee said as the child at last stopped crying and they began to walk up the platform towards Victoria's main concourse. 'He looked after Meyer so that I could sleep, and managed to get milk for him when Frau Weber's supply ran out, and even washed the nappies in the train washroom – though I told him there was no point because we couldn't dry the wretched things, but he found the guard had a little brazier and he let us dry them over that so we could keep Meyer comfortable – and oh, he's been marvellous –'

'But who *is* the child?' Harry was determined not to pay any further attention at all to Peter. 'I'm in a complete fog –'

'He's Meyer Damont,' Lee said, and she stopped walking, so that the two men had to stop too, and the crowds of other hurrying passengers eddied round them as water eddies round a rock as the tide comes up the beach. 'I'm sorry, darling, to be so confused, but it's really been the most incredible journey. The thing is –' She took a sharp little breath through her nose, and even in the big echoing station with the hiss of steam and the clatter of luggage trolleys and the cry of porters all round them, it was clearly heard. 'They've had to leave Munich, Harry. We – we think – we're afraid that they've been sent to one of the camps. Not the girls – apparently they got away to Vienna, and Peter says we can put out some enquiries about them from here, though now the Germans have taken over in Austria it's going to be pretty awful – and we don't know where Wilhelm is at all. But we managed to find Meyer – he's the baby, you see, Otto and Lise's baby. And Frau Weber who was looking after him is ill and – oh, darling, there's so much to explain. Please, let's go home, and get Meyer settled and then I'll tell you everything. But we have to stop at the chemists' at Victoria first, because there are things I need – more nappies and powder and things like that, and then I'm going to need some clothes and a cot and so forth for him, though maybe we can leave that till tomorrow – we'll manage for tonight – oh, there's so much to do!'

Harry stared at her, at her face radiant with excitement, at the smear of soot on one cheek, at her rumpled hair and her clothes which looked as though she'd slept in them for a week and not just a couple of nights, and blinked. She hadn't looked as beautiful as this since the day they had married, he thought confusedly. There was an incandescence about her as though a lamp had been lit behind her eyes that sent a glow all around her.

He wanted to say so, to tell her how marvellous it was to see her looking so happy, to let her know how grateful he was just to have her back, to say how miserable he'd been without her, how eaten with jealousy and remorse and rage and shame, but all he could do was say stupidly, 'Then he's staying with us tonight?'

'He's staying for always, Harry,' Lee said gently. 'He hasn't anyone but us, now, you see. We're his English family, aren't we? He only has you and me to be his parents and Mamma and Papa to be his grandparents – that's all he's got till we can find Otto and Lise again. If we ever find them – I've made up my mind, you see, he's got to be ours – you aren't going to say no, are you? You couldn't – you couldn't possibly say no!'

Peter moved then, taking a few steps further along the platform, setting down the bags he was carrying beside the luggage van and beckoning a porter to collect the rest of their cases as they were unloaded. Tired as he was, with a tiredness that made him feel oddly detached and floating, as though he were not really there but walking through a dream, he felt Harry's animosity towards him and found himself as angry with him as Harry clearly was with himself. He could no longer trust himself to bite his tongue and knew that unless he kept his physical distance there was a real risk that his anger would blaze up. And though that would be personally gratifying, it would upset Lee. So it couldn't be allowed to happen.

Why he should be so sulky Peter had no idea; all he knew was that he'd brought the blasted man's wife back to him safe and sound after an adventure that could have been a disastrous one, and he had uttered only the most perfunctory and grudging of thanks. What was more his response to Lee had been less than welcoming. Any other man would have hugged her, kissed her, taken the baby from her arms to relieve her of her burden, but all Harry Lackland had done was glower and ask questions in a staccato little bark. For two pins, Peter thought furiously, I'd knock the bounder out of his socks, but it would upset Lee if I did, and anyway, what was the point? The man's Lee's husband and she loves him.

There could be no doubt of that in Peter's mind; all through the long journey when there had been time to talk in a soft whisper above the sleeping Meyer's head she had prattled on and on about Harry; about how happy she thought he would be when she told him of her decision to take Meyer to be their own baby; about how good a doctor he was, and what a good father he'd be to Meyer; how patient he had been with her all through those awful months when she'd been so stupidly obsessed with getting pregnant, and how determined she was to make it all up to him. And Peter had listened to it all and felt his own heart die a little. He couldn't deny that there had been a brief moment, there behind those screens at Letty's party, when he had held her so close and she had clung to him, when hope had wriggled its way through him. Perhaps the marriage was a dead one, perhaps she was going to leave Harry, perhaps she would be available to be patiently courted and wooed by someone else? By him. But after this journey he knew for certain that that had been a vain and stupid hope. She was as much in love with this graceless sulky husband of hers as she had ever been, and there wasn't a thing Peter could do about it.

So he stood out of earshot, able to hear only the murmur of their voices as Lee and Harry stood in the middle of the platform and she talked and talked, her chin tilted upwards so that she could look earnestly at Harry while he stood in silence and listened to her, as he stared at the baby in her arms.

But then he spoke, as somewhere along the platform an engine released its excess steam in a great wash of sound and Peter could see Harry's lips moving, though he couldn't hear even the blurred murmuring of Lee's voice now and saw Lee's face change, become puzzled and then blank with amazement. She shook her head and turned and looked along the platform to where Peter was standing and then she looked up at Harry and smiled. It was a smile of pure incredulity, and Peter looked at her, trying to imagine what it was Harry had said about him that had created that reaction. That he himself was the subject under discussion Peter was quite certain, and he actually took a small step towards them, to go and ask them, but then the total exhaustion that was hovering very close now made his legs actually tremble and he turned away. He needed home and a bath, and his bed, several days of bed, before he could even think of anything else. Even Lee. And he lifted his chin and called as loudly as he could, 'I'm going! Your bags are here – the porter'll take them for you. I can manage on my own –' And he began to walk towards the barrier, following the last of the boat train's passengers from the now almost empty platform.

There was a little rush of footsteps behind him and then Lee's hand was on his arm.

'Peter!' she said breathlessly. 'Wait a moment – I haven't said a proper thank you. And I must, though I don't know how to. You were marvellous, absolutely marvellous and I'll never stop being grateful to you. Not ever –' She looked back over her shoulder and he looked too and saw Harry standing where she had left him, awkwardly holding Meyer in his arms as the baby leaned back a little against his restraining hand to stare into his face with a puzzled air. 'Harry's grateful too,' she said. 'I know he is. He's being a bit silly, I think, but it's all a lot for him to take in – I have to talk to him and – well, anyway, thank you Peter – thank you so much –' And she lifted herself on her tiptoes and for a moment he thought she was going to kiss his cheek; and then she bit her lip and subsided and stepped back.

'You do understand how grateful we both are, Peter?' she said appealingly. 'You do understand?'

And he looked over her shoulder at Harry and then nodded, very wearily. 'I understand. Goodbye, Lee. Take good care of young Meyer. But then, I know you will –' And he turned and went, almost unable to lift his feet, towards the taxi rank and home and sleep. It was, at this moment, the only thing in all the world he cared about.

She had taken the top drawer out of the big old Victorian tallboy from the spare bedroom, and padded it with a folded blanket and a linen sheet from their own bed. She had bathed Meyer, talking to him softly all the time as she splashed the warm scented water over his plump little legs and he had, after a while, begun to play, taking the lid of Harry's celluloid soap dish which she had given him and making it float and laughing as it filled with water and sank. She had wrapped him in a thick towel and sat down with him beside the kitchen range as Ellen, their little maid of all work, bustled about excitedly making bread and milk for him, sugaring and buttering it with a lavish hand, and then had spoon fed him as he sat there leaning against her sleepily. And then she had pinned a nappy round him and put him to sleep in the drawer and sat there on the edge of her bed, singing to him until at last he fell asleep, his arms thrown up above his head and his hands closed into small fists, looking, for the first time since Harry had seen him, as comfortable and contented as a baby of his age should look.

All the time Harry had watched her, silently, following her from bathroom to kitchen and back to the bedroom, and now they sat together in the quiet room, she on the bed, he on the armchair near it, lit only by one lamp burning in the corner, and listened to Meyer's soft snuffling breathing, and looked at each other.

'We are going to keep him, aren't we, Harry?' Lee said, after a while.

'There'll be legal problems, won't there?' Harry was temporizing and he knew it. 'You can't just snatch up a baby and keep him –'

'I talked to Peter about that – I thought of it, you see. I'm not completely stupid – and there are ways. The committee, Papa's committee, you know. They're bringing in refugees more and more. That's why Peter was going to Germany at all, really. It wasn't just the tour. The actors are still there, with Gregory in charge – Peter was just using the tour as a cover for the other things he wanted to do. He'd gone to get people out, and he says that when they get children out, without their families, they can be adopted legally here. Talk to Papa tomorrow, Harry. He'll tell you.' She stopped then and her face changed. She had been looking at him pleadingly but now she lifted her chin and her expression became firmer. She looked very certain of what she was saying.

'I can't let him go,' she said. 'He needs me – he needs both of us. But even more than that, I need him.' She turned her head to look down at the drawer beside her on the floor. 'I need him,' she repeated softly. 'And I hope that will make you need him too. Because I love you, I want what you want. I'd thought you were the same about me. That what I wanted to make me happy was the same that you wanted –'

'It is,' he said at once. 'Oh, it is. But Lee –'

'No buts about Meyer,' she said, and then made it into a question. 'No buts about Meyer?'

He paused then and turned his own head to look at the child, and as he did, he snuffled again and wriggled in his sleep and turned over so that he pulled his covers off, and without stopping to think Harry leaned down and very gently rearranged the blanket so that Meyer was warmly covered again.

'No,' he said after a long pause. 'No. Not if we can make it all legal. If you're sure you want him and it can be arranged –'

'I'm sure,' she said and her face was as radiant as it had been at Victoria that afternoon. 'Oh, Harry, I do love you, and I'm sorry about being so hateful to you for so long, and I'm going to make it all up to you. I promise, I'm not going to fuss any more about getting pregnant, not ever again. I was mad for a while, I think – quite mad –'

She had slipped from her place on the bed to come and kneel before his armchair with her hands on his knees as she looked up at him, and at the sight of her face, so alight with happiness, he felt the sickness of his own guilt fill him and he shook his head and swallowed and put both his own hands over his face.

'Lee, my darling, please don't – Lee, there's something I have to tell you – I must tell you, now, and I don't know how to –'

She didn't move, still crouching there in front of him with her hands on his lap, but he felt the moment of chill in her almost as though she had touched him with cold fingers.

'What is it?' she said after a long moment. 'Are you – am I too late to make it up to you, Harry? Are you too angry with me for all the bad times I gave you to be happy with me now I'm happy with Meyer? Is that it?'

'Oh, no, never,' he said, and took his hands away from his face to set them over hers, and look at her, staring into her eyes. 'I can never be happy with anyone but you. All I want is for you to be content and – and – as you are now. All glowing. You've not looked as you do now since we – I can't remember when. To have you like this for always and always – that's the only thing I want. But – things happened while you were away. I –' Again he swallowed. 'I have to tell you and I can't. It's all such a tangle. I meant no harm but I was lonely and you were so upset and I thought you'd gone off with Peter because you cared for him –'

'I told you at Victoria when you said that that it was crazy! Peter? He's – well, he's just Peter. A marvellous friend, the best friend anyone could have. But go off with him – as anything else but a friend? It's crazy! I can't imagine why you should get such an idea. It was a baby I wanted, not another husband! I have you, and I want you and I'll never want anyone else –'

'I thought I was the same,' he said wretchedly. 'That I'd never want anyone else and I don't – but it just sort of happened. She's that sort of girl. She doesn't care, you see. She's only interested in herself and what she wants – she doesn't *care*. And neither do I. I was just – oh, I don't know. Dazzled, I think – just dazzled –'

Still she hadn't changed position, but now the moment of withdrawal he'd felt in her was over. The chill had gone and he felt her closeness as though it were a thick blanket, covering him.

'Harry, don't say any more.'

'But I have to tell you – explain – so that you can understand and I hope forgive me and –'

'I don't want to know,' she said firmly. 'Do you hear me? I want no details about any – about anything that happened to you while I was away, or who you saw, or what you did – or anything at all. I've been away, and now I'm back. That's all. There's nothing to say, nothing to do, nothing to forgive.'

She turned her head and looked at Meyer asleep in the drawer beside them. 'You see? There's only us three now. Just us three and nothing and no one else matters.'

She lifted herself on her knees so that their faces were close. 'Kiss me, Harry,' she said. 'Kiss me and then take me to bed. I've a lot of loving to do –'

EPILOGUE

Cecily had bidden everyone to be at her party at nine o'clock but by half-past ten only half the guests had arrived. It was clear that although the family had agreed to bow to Cecily's demand that they all see in the New Year at her house in Russell Square, just as in the dear old days they had always gone to darling Grandmamma Phoebe's house for the occasion, they had no intention of being there any longer than they had to.

'Bad enough we have to go at all,' as David Henriques complained to his brother Samuel when they closed the office in Poultry that afternoon, having totted up as best they could the amount of money their chain of chemists' shops had made that year (and it was considerable). 'Can't leave till half-past twelve at the earliest, not on New Year's Eve, so you can be quite sure I'm not going there a moment before eleven.'

And Samuel had agreed and launched himself into a diatribe about Cecily's airs and graces and ridiculous attempts to be the great autocrat her mother had been, and her total inability to be anything but exceedingly boring.

But by eleven most of them had arrived, and the big hot rooms were buzzing with talk and the clink of glasses and the clatter of knives and forks. One thing about Cecily; she was much more lavish in her hospitality than Phoebe had been, and kept an excellent table. The food was good and there was a great deal of it, and everyone was eating it in large quantities.

Almost everyone. Gertrude Croxley was not. She wasn't going to risk putting on as much as an ounce, even on New Year's Eve, for the dress she was wearing, in the most clinging of oyster satins which showed very clearly every vertebra on her long back, would not hide any bumps at all. And to be successful this winter one had to be thin, thin, thin; what was it the Duchess of Windsor, the ex Mrs Simpson, was supposed to have said? 'One can't be too thin or too rich –' Well, there was no risk of Gertrude ever being too rich, she told herself gloomily, but she could manage to be thin. Her figure was one of the vital assets in her still continuing search for a husband and she looked round the big room full of well-dressed and well-fed people and scowled. There was no chance she'd find any hopefuls here, among her horrible family; it really was ridiculous to have agreed to come at all. She'd have been far better off spending New Year's Eve at one of the screamingly funny little clubs in Mayfair which her crowd frequented.

Across the room Lily Tollemache was sitting close to her sister Ethel, her jaws never stopping as she went without a break from chewing to talking and back again, and as Gertrude caught her malicious gaze she turned away. She'd have to find someone else to talk to at once; to be at risk of having one of that awful pair coming and wittering in her ear was dreadful, and she looked round quickly, and then made purposefully for Harry Lackland, who was standing leaning against the fireplace talking to Emilia and Max.

'– never been so busy in all my professional life,' Max was saying as she came up. 'At last some of the physicians are beginning to realize it's no failure in them to admit a patient may have emotional or psychological problems with which they can't deal. They send me more and more cases these days –'

'I wish someone'd send my brother to you,' Emilia said tartly. She was staring across the room at Johanna who was sitting beside her mother in the far corner and not talking at all; just sitting staring down at her hands on her lap and looking the picture of misery. 'Or at least to someone like you. The way he's behaving makes me think he really must be mad rather than bad –'

She stopped short as Gertrude joined their little group and smiled at her, but Max wasn't deterred; he nodded agreeably at her and said to his wife, 'He's not mad, my love, just thoroughly spoiled. And since your mother died he's really got the bit between his teeth, though she was as bad as he was, truth to tell. I can see those two divorcing soon. This could be a rough new year for Jo, poor girl. Not that she's entirely blameless. If only she'd stand up to him more instead of drooping about all the time – I tell her, but she doesn't listen to me. Or to Mother or Dad.' He sighed. 'We'll just have to stand by and pick up the pieces, I'm afraid. Not much else we can do. But mark my words – this time next year, there'll be the first real scandal the Lackland family's ever known–'

'Then it's been lucky,' Gertrude said sharply. 'I dare say there are plenty of skeletons lurking in any number of closets if the truth were known. Just look around at them all – self-satisfied and smug and–'

'Self-satisfied?' Emilia said and frowned. 'My dear girl, hardly everybody! Look at my father-in-law there. You can hardly call him self-satisfied, or Cousin Jacob, either.' The two men were sitting side by side in a window seat, their heads together, talking earnestly and seriously and Gertrude looked at them and made a grimace.

'Well, not them perhaps,' she allowed. 'But there are plenty of this family who ought to be smacked, they're so awful and complacent and full of themselves. What about Letty, so – so puffed up because she's such a famous person and all the rest of it, and that precious Theo who never has a word for anyone? You can't imagine they've no secrets to hide – and why aren't they here, anyway? Aren't we good enough for them?'

'I wouldn't know,' Max said, and he put his hand on his wife's arm to stop her, for she had opened her mouth wrathfully and he knew she was about to say something very scalding. 'I try not to meddle in their affairs, you know. I don't feel it becoming in me–'

'Letty isn't here,' Harry said, and he too looked ruffled by the spitefulness that had been in Gertrude's tone, 'because she's in America, making arrangements about the new film she's made with Theo. They seem to think it could do very well there. She told me, you know, Max, that she expects to sell it right across the whole country, which in America could mean a great deal of money for her. Lots of things happen locally, of course, but when it's federal then it's very big business indeed. Letty was telling me before she went that

267

she's really very hopeful about it –'

But Gertrude was not to be deflected from her course. She was in a bad temper and didn't care who knew it. 'Well, I dare say she could have waited to see the New Year in with her family if she'd had a mind to. And Theo – and that niece of hers who always used to show off so much – every time I've been at a family party this last year she's made it impossible by her antics –'

Harry was very pink now and he tightened his mouth, clearly biting back a very acid retort, but Gertrude prattled on. 'I can't see why she thought so well of herself. Very ordinary creature, actually. Not any sort of a beauty. Merely childish and bouncy, and rather common, if you ask me –'

'Well, it's clear they don't agree with you in Hollywood,' Emilia said, and turned to smile at Harry. 'That little lady is going to be an enormous success, isn't she? I understand she's making a film with Theo. I don't know what else the New Year will bring the rest of the Lacklands, Harry, but it's obvious it'll be world-wide fame for young Katy at least. Does she keep in touch with you and Leah?'

'Not really,' Harry said and his voice was clipped. 'Too busy, I imagine. As indeed, we are too. Not much time for correspondence these days.'

'I'm sure not,' Emilia said warmly, and continued to turn her shoulder so that Gertrude was excluded from their group. '*Do* tell me about the baby. I saw him with Leah just a couple of weeks ago – he really is the most delicious little thing! Reminded me of our David at the same age, except of course that the clever little creature speaks two languages!'

'Not for much longer,' Harry said as, following Emilia's lead, he too turned to show a cool shoulder to Gertrude. 'He's learning so fast it's incredible – and the more he speaks of English the less he seems to remember of his German. It's just as well, I think. We don't want him to feel odd man out later on. Especially as –' He hesitated and looked over his shoulder to see if Gertrude were listening, but to his relief, she had taken the hint and gone sulkily away, and he relaxed. 'Well, I'll tell you two, but don't spread it around for a while. Lee's pregnant. That's why she isn't here tonight.'

'There, I knew it!' Emilia said triumphantly and reached out and patted Harry's shoulder with great affection. 'When I last saw her I thought – now, you look interesting! How wonderful. I couldn't be happier for you.'

'I couldn't be happier for myself,' Harry said and grinned suddenly. 'I must tell you, Max, old man, it's an interesting phenomenon. We'd been having problems, you see. Lee's had all the tests and so forth, actually went to Vienna to see Aaronson – you know, the hormone man? There was nothing anyone could do, it seemed. She just wasn't ever going to have her own babies and that was that. But ever since she's had Michael to look after she's been a new woman. Relaxed, happy – and here she is, pregnant! There's some interesting research to be done on this, don't you think? The links between mind and body functions and how they act and react on each other –'

'Indeed yes!' Max said eagerly and launched himself into a discussion of the hormonal influences on behaviour and Emilia laughed and turned to leave them to it.

'I'm going to talk to Mother Miriam,' she announced. 'Tell Leah how thrilled I am, Harry, and if she needs anything just to let me know. And my love to small Michael – and I do think you're wise to rear him to be as English as possible. Changing his name will be much better for his peace of mind –'

Max laughed as she went away. 'You see, Harry? She thinks she's as much a psychiatrist as I am! Well, she could be right – now about the effects of oestrogen levels on mood swings in women of reproductive age –'

'Hello, Peter,' Emilia said, and squeezed his arm and he turned and looked down at her and grinned with real pleasure. He was very fond of this sister-in-law of his, and he set an arm round her shoulders and hugged her.

'How lovely to see you!' he said. 'How are things with you?'

'Never mind me,' she said in the direct way that was so much a part of her and which was one of the qualities she had that he most liked. Her clever ugly face looked up at his and her eyes were alight with intelligence and concern. 'What's this I hear about your leaving Letty? Giving up the stage?'

He hesitated, standing looking at her with his face as expressionless as he could make it. 'Who's been gossiping about me?' he asked lightly.

'Oh, Peter, you know better than to ask that. This entire family never does anything *but* gossip! If I could remember, I'd tell you, truly I would. *Is* it true, though?'

He thought for a little while, standing staring down into his glass, and then he lifted his head and looked at her. 'It's true. That I'm leaving Gaff Productions and working for Letty, that is. But not giving up the stage. I'm going to work abroad. That's all.'

'Abroad? Where?'

'Germany.'

'Germany? Is that wise? I mean, I know Chamberlain said all that about peace in our time in September, but you surely didn't believe that, did you?'

'Of course I didn't. That's why I'm going.'

'Why you're –' She looked closer at him, her forehead lined with anxiety. 'Peter, what are you up to? This all sounds very odd.'

'It isn't odd, Emilia,' he said and smiled at her, his face creasing pleasantly. 'I'm just doing what I think has to be done. There are things that are happening in Germany that shouldn't be. To Jews, you know, and not only to them. I hear that people like – people like Theo are having a bad time too. And the sick and – well, never mind. I could be wrong. I hope I am. But I'm going to work there for a while and find out and see what I can do. Wish me luck, Emilia, and for heaven's sake don't tell Ma what I'm doing. She frets herself silly, bless her, and I don't want her bothered. Warn Max too, will you? I'll talk to him myself before I go next week, but all the same – don't forget, will you?'

'I won't,' she said and stood there with her hand tucked into his arm, saying nothing but very aware of the bond there was between them. And feeling a small spiral of fear for him starting to curl inside her.

Across the room Philip Lewis, the eldest of Cecily's brood of grandchildren and great-grandchildren, coughed loudly and clapped his hands and they all turned to look at him.

Outside in the street they could hear the klaxons blaring and above that, the slow clanging of the clock on St Thomas's church round the corner.

'Silence, everyone, silence!' Philip cried and beamed around at them all. 'Just another second or two to go – there! The first stroke! Happy New Year, everyone! Happy 1939 to all of us! May it be joyous and prosperous and healthy – but above all may it be peaceful!'

And the Lackland family drank the toast, and kissed each other and laughed and shouted their way into the last year of the decade as Peter slipped away and left them to it.

He had a lot to organize for the coming year and there was no time to waste on celebrating its arrival. He had other things to do.

A Selection of Arrow Bestsellers

Bestselling Fiction

☐ Dancing Bear	Chaim Bermant	£2.95
☐ Hiroshima Joe	Martin Booth	£2.95
☐ 1985	Anthony Burgess	£1.95
☐ The Other Woman	Colette	£1.95
☐ The Manchurian Candidate	Richard Condon	£2.25
☐ Letter to a Child Never Born	Oriana Fallaci	£1.25
☐ Duncton Wood	William Horwood	£3.50
☐ Aztec	Gary Jennings	£3.95
☐ The Journeyer	Gary Jennings	£3.50
☐ The Executioner's Song	Norman Mailer	£3.50
☐ Strumpet City	James Plunkett	£3.50
☐ Admiral	Dudley Pope	£1.95
☐ The Second Lady	Irving Wallace	£2.50
☐ An Unkindness of Ravens	Ruth Rendell	£1.95
☐ The History Man	Malcolm Bradbury	£2.95

ARROW BOOKS, BOOKSERVICE BY POST, PO BOX 29, DOUGLAS, ISLE OF MAN, BRITISH ISLES

NAME ....

ADDRESS ....

....

....

Please enclose a cheque or postal order made out to Arrow Books Ltd. for the amount due and allow the following for postage and packing.

U.K. CUSTOMERS: Please allow 22p per book to a maximum of £3.00.

B.F.P.O. & EIRE: Please allow 22p per book to a maximum of £3.00.

OVERSEAS CUSTOMERS: Please allow 22p per book.

Whilst every effort is made to keep prices low it is sometimes necessary to increase cover prices at short notice. Arrow Books reserve the right to show new retail prices on covers which may differ from those previously advertised in the text or elsewhere.

A Selection of Arrow Bestsellers

ARROW BOOKS, BOOKSERVICE BY POST, PO BOX 29, DOUGLAS, ISLE OF MAN, BRITISH ISLES

NAME ....

ADDRESS ....

....

....

Please enclose a cheque or postal order made out to Arrow Books Ltd. for the amount due and allow the following for postage and packing.

U.K. CUSTOMERS: Please allow 22p per book to a maximum of £3.00.

B.F.P.O. & EIRE: Please allow 22p per book to a maximum of £3.00.

OVERSEAS CUSTOMERS: Please allow 22p per book.

Whilst every effort is made to keep prices low it is sometimes necessary to increase cover prices at short notice. Arrow Books reserve the right to show new retail prices on covers which may differ from those previously advertised in the text or elsewhere.

Bestselling Women's Fiction

☐	Destinies	Charlotte Vale Allen	£2.95
☐	Hester Dark	Emma Blair	£1.95
☐	Nellie Wildchild	Emma Blair	£2.50
☐	Playing the Jack	Mary Brown	£3.50
☐	Twin of Fire	Jude Deveraux	£2.50
☐	Counterfeit Lady	Jude Deveraux	£2.50
☐	Miss Gathercole's Girls	Judy Gardiner	£2.50
☐	Lisa Logan	Marie Joseph	£1.95
☐	Maggie Craig	Marie Joseph	£1.95
☐	A Long Way From Heaven	Sheelagh Kelly	£2.95
☐	The Gooding Girl	Pamela Oldfield	£2.75
☐	The Running Years	Claire Rayner	£2.75
☐	The Pride	Judith Saxton	£2.50

ARROW BOOKS, BOOKSERVICE BY POST, PO BOX 29, DOUGLAS, ISLE OF MAN, BRITISH ISLES

NAME ....

ADDRESS ....

....

....

Please enclose a cheque or postal order made out to Arrow Books Ltd. for the amount due and allow the following for postage and packing.

U.K. CUSTOMERS: Please allow 22p per book to a maximum of £3.00.

B.F.P.O. & EIRE: Please allow 22p per book to a maximum of £3.00.

OVERSEAS CUSTOMERS: Please allow 22p per book.

Whilst every effort is made to keep prices low it is sometimes necessary to increase cover prices at short notice. Arrow Books reserve the right to show new retail prices on covers which may differ from those previously advertised in the text or elsewhere.

Arena

☐ The Lives of the Indian Princes	Charles Allen	£4.95
☐ Confessions of an Irish Rebel	Brendan Behan	£2.95
☐ Dancing Bear	Chaim Bermant	£2.95
☐ Let It Come Down	Paul Bowles	£2.95
☐ The After Dinner Game	Malcolm Bradbury	£1.95
☐ Eating People is Wrong	Malcolm Bradbury	£2.95
☐ Rates of Exchange	Malcolm Bradbury	£2.95
☐ So the Wind Won't Blow It All Away	Richard Brautigan	£2.95
☐ Ten Years in an Open Necked Shirt	John Cooper Clarke	£3.50
☐ The Wit and Wisdom of Quentin Crisp	Quentin Crisp	£2.50
☐ Thy Tears Might Cease	Michael Farrell	£2.95
☐ Boys on the Rock	John Fox	£2.50
☐ Selected Letters of E. M. Forster	Ed. Mary Lago & P. N. Furbank	£4.50
☐ Pudding and Pie (Nancy Mitford Omnibus)	Nancy Mitford	£3.95
☐ Mourners Below	James Purdy	£2.95

ARROW BOOKS, BOOKSERVICE BY POST, PO BOX 29, DOUGLAS, ISLE OF MAN, BRITISH ISLES

NAME ....

ADDRESS ....

....

....

Please enclose a cheque or postal order made out to Arrow Books Ltd. for the amount due and allow the following for postage and packing.

U.K. CUSTOMERS: Please allow 22p per book to a maximum of £3.00.

B.F.P.O. & EIRE: Please allow 22p per book to a maximum of £3.00.

OVERSEAS CUSTOMERS: Please allow 22p per book.

Whilst every effort is made to keep prices low it is sometimes necessary to increase cover prices at short notice. Arrow Books reserve the right to show new retail prices on covers which may differ from those previously advertised in the text or elsewhere.